PETER

*False Disciple and Apostate
according to Saint Matthew*

PETER

False Disciple and Apostate according to Saint Matthew

*Second Edition
with
Responses to Reviews*

Robert H. Gundry

WIPF & STOCK · Eugene, Oregon

Wipf and Stock Publishers
199 W 8th Ave, Suite 3
Eugene, OR 97401

Peter
False Disciple and Apostate According to Saint Matthew
By Gundry, Robert H.
Copyright©2015 by Gundry, Robert H.
ISBN 13: 978-1-5326-6348-2

Publication date 10/2/2018
Previously published by Wm. B. Eerdmans, 2015

Contents

Foreword	vii
Abbreviations	ix
Bibliography of Secondary Literature Consulted	xii
1. Introduction	1
2. Peter in Matthew Prior to Matthew 16:13-23	6
3. Peter in Matthew 16:13-23	15
4. Peter from the Mount of Transfiguration through the Garden of Gethsemane	31
5. Peter's Denials of Jesus along with the Suicide of Judas Iscariot	43
6. Matthew's Omissions of Peter	63
7. False Discipleship in Matthew	70
8. Persecution in Matthew	90
9. A Recapitulation and Some Possible Implications	98
Afterword	107
Index of Modern Authors	109
Index of Ancient Texts	112
Addendum: *Responses to Reviews*	120

Foreword

In this book I argue that, differently from the rest of the New Testament, the Gospel according to Saint Matthew portrays Peter as a false disciple who publicly apostatized and who, like all false disciples whether or not they have publicly apostatized, is destined for eternal damnation. The argument arises solely out of exegetical considerations, not at all out of anti–Roman Catholic bias, though traditional Roman Catholics will doubtless be disturbed by the argument and its conclusion. Given the popularity of Peter as a supposedly reassuring example of imperfect but genuine discipleship, many Protestant and Orthodox believers will likewise be disturbed. Others may not care. For me as a conservative evangelical Christian, what matters is the understanding that makes best sense of Matthew's text when it comes to Peter.

Naturally, a portrayal of Peter as false, apostate, and damned raises the theological issue of the saints' perseverance or, as it is called in some quarters, eternal security. But this issue gets no discussion here, except to say that in the following pages my references to loss of salvation have to do with the loss of a salvation that might have been had in the end, not with the loss of a salvation that was truly had in the first place. Non-Calvinistic readers will attach a different understanding, of course.

The contentiousness of understanding Matthew's Peter as a false disciple who apostatized combines with the enormous volume of secondary literature on Peter to require unusually heavy documentation in the following argument, especially in its first and longest parts. Despite that enormous volume of secondary literature, a failure therein to relate to the portrayal of Peter the major, intertwined Matthean themes of false disci-

Foreword

pleship in general and persecution in particular — or even to treat these themes in and of themselves — has left a big hole that, in the last parts of this book, I have tried to fill.

Following an initial inclusion of full bibliographical information, footnoted references to commentaries on Matthew will contain, after an indication of authorship, only the designation *Matthew, Matthieu, Matthäus,* or *Matthäusevangelium,* as the case may be. Since discussions will not involve the Hebrew of Old Testament texts, chapter-and-verse numbering will follow that in standard English versions. Translations of ancient texts are my own. For readers' convenience, parallels in other Gospels to Matthean passages are indicated even when a discussion ignores those parallels as irrelevant to the points at issue.

Finally, my thanks to Jon Pott for accepting this monograph for publication by William B. Eerdmans Publishing Company, to Jennifer Hoffman for shepherding the monograph through its editorial process, and to the rest of Eerdmans' staff for the excellence of their work.

ROBERT H. GUNDRY

Abbreviations

AB	Anchor Bible
ABRL	Anchor Bible Reference Library
Acts Pet. 12 Apos.	*Acts of Peter and the Twelve Apostles*
AnBib	Analecta biblica
2 Apoc. Bar.	*2 Apocalypse of Baruch*
Aristotle *Poet.*	Aristotle *Poetics*
b. Yoma	*Babylonian Talmud, Tractate Yoma*
BBR	*Bulletin for Biblical Research*
BECNT	Baker Exegetical Commentary on the New Testament
BETL	Bibliotheca ephemeridum theologicarum lovaniensium
BibInt	*Biblical Interpretation*
BJRL	*Bulletin of the John Rylands University Library of Manchester*
BSac	*Bibliotheca sacra*
BTB	*Biblical Theology Bulletin*
BTZ	*Berliner Theologische Zeitschrift*
BZ	*Biblische Zeitschrift*
BZNW	Beihefte zur Zeitschrift für die neutestamentliche Wissenschaft
cf.	*confer*, compare
ch./chs.	chapter/chapters
1 Chron	1 Chronicles
1 Clem.	*1 Clement*
2 Clem.	*2 Clement*
CNT	Commentaire du Nouveau Testament
ConBNT	Coniectanea neotestamentica or Coniectanea biblica: New Testament Series
1 Cor	1 Corinthians
Deut	Deuteronomy
EBib	Etudes bibliques
ed.	edited by

Abbreviations

e.g.	*exempli gratia*, for example
enl.	enlarged
esp.	especially
et al.	*et alii*, and others
ETL	*Ephemerides theologicae lovanienses*
Eus. *Hist. eccl.*	Eusebius *Historia Ecclesiastica*
Exod	Exodus
f./ff.	following page/following pages
Gal	Galatians
Gen	Genesis
GNS	Good News Studies
Heb	Hebrews
Hos	Hosea
HTKNT	Herders theologischer Kommentar zum Neuen Testament
ICC	International Critical Commentary
i.e.	*id est*, that is
Isa	Isaiah
Jas	James
JBL	*Journal of Biblical Literature*
Jer	Jeremiah
Josephus *Ant.*	Josephus *Antiquities of the Jews*
Josh	Joshua
JSNT	*Journal for the Study of the New Testament*
JSNTSup	Journal for the Study of the New Testament: Supplement Series
Jub.	*Jubilees*
KEKNT	Kritisch-exegetischer Kommentar über das Neue Testament (Meyer-Kommentar)
2 Kgdms	2 Kingdoms (in the Septuagint)
1 Kgs	1 Kings
Lk.	Luke
LXX	the Septuagint
m. Sanh.	*Mishnah, Tractate Sanhedrin*
m. Yoma	*Mishnah, Tractate Yoma*
Matt/Matth./Mt.	Matthew
n./nn.	note/notes
N.B.	*nota bene*, note well
NCBC	New Cambridge Bible Commentary
nf	Neue Folge, new series
NICNT	New International Commentary on the New Testament
NIGTC	New International Greek Testament Commentary
NovTSup	Novum Testamentum Supplements
NT	New Testament
NTS	*New Testament Studies*
Num	Numbers
op. cit.	*opere citato*, in the work cited
OT	Old Testament

Abbreviations

p./pp.	page/pages
par.	parallel
Plutarch *Mor.*	Plutarch *Moralia*
Ps/Pss	Psalm/Psalms
QD	Quaestiones disputatae
QL	Qumran literature
4QpPs	*Pesher on the Psalms* among the Dead Sea Scrolls from Cave 4
1QSa	*Rule of the Community* among the Dead Sea Scrolls from Cave 1
repr.	reprinted in
Rev	Revelation
rev. ed.	revised edition
RTP	*Revue de théologie et de philosophie*
1 Sam	1 Samuel
2 Sam	2 Samuel
SBT	Studies in Biblical Theology
Sib. Or.	*Sibylline Oracles*
SNTSMS	Society for New Testament Studies Monograph Series
SNTSU	Studien zum Neuen Testament und seiner Umwelt
T. Job	*Testament of Job*
T. Sol.	*Testament of Solomon*
THKNT	Theologischer Handkommentar zum Neuen Testament
2 Tim	2 Timothy
trans.	translated by
TS	*Theological Studies*
v./vv.	verse/verses
viz.	*videlicet*, namely
vol./vols.	volume/volumes
WBC	Word Biblical Commentary
WUNT	Wissenschaftliche Untersuchungen zum Alten und Neuen Testament
Xenophon *Mem.*	Xenophon *Memorabilia*
Zech	Zechariah
ZECNT	Zondervan Exegetical Commentary on the New Testament
ZNW	*Zeitschrift für die neutestamentliche Wissenschaft und die Kunde der älteren Kirche*

Bibliography of Secondary Literature Consulted

Albright, W. F., and C. S. Mann. *Matthew: Introduction, Translation, and Notes.* Anchor Bible. Garden City, N.Y.: Doubleday, 1971.
Allen, Willoughby C. *A Critical and Exegetical Commentary on the Gospel According to S. Matthew.* International Critical Commentary. Edinburgh: T. & T. Clark, 1907.
Barber, Michael Patrick. "Jesus as the Davidic Temple Builder and Peter's Priestly Role in Matthew 16:16-19." *Journal of Biblical Literature* 132 (2013): 935-53.
Barton, Stephen C. *Discipleship and Family Ties in Mark and Matthew.* Society of New Testament Studies Monograph Series 80. Cambridge: Cambridge University Press, 1994.
Bauckham, Richard. *Jesus and the Eyewitnesses: The Gospels as Eyewitness Testimony.* Grand Rapids: Eerdmans, 2006.
Beare, Francis Wright. *The Gospel according to Matthew: Translation, Introduction and Commentary.* New York: Harper & Row, 1981.
Becker, Jürgen. *Simon Petrus im Urchristentum.* Biblisch-Theologische Studien 105. Neukirchen-Vluyn: Neukirchener Verlag, 2009.
Bigane, John E., III. *Faith, Christ or Peter: Matthew 16:18 in Sixteenth Century Roman Catholic Exegesis.* Washington, D.C.: University Press of America, 1981.
Bird, Michael F. *The Gospel of the Lord: How the Early Church Wrote the Story of Jesus.* Grand Rapids: Eerdmans, 2014.
Biven, David. "Matthew 16:18 — The Petros-Petra Wordplay: Greek, Aramaic, or Hebrew?" *Jerusalem Perspective* 46-47 (1994): 32-36, 38.
Black, David Alan, ed. *Perspectives on the Ending of Mark: Four Views.* Nashville: Broadman & Holman, 2008.
Blomberg, Craig L. *Matthew.* New American Commentary 22. Nashville: Broadman & Holman, 1992.
Bockmuehl, Markus. *The Remembered Peter: In Ancient Reception and Modern Debate.* Wissenschaftliche Untersuchungen zum Neuen Testament 262. Tübingen: Mohr Siebeck, 210.

Bibliography of Secondary Literature Consulted

———. *Simon Peter in Scripture and Memory: The New Testament Apostle in the Early Church.* Grand Rapids: Baker Academic, 2012.
Bond, Helen K. *Caiaphas: Friend of Rome and Judge of Jesus.* Louisville: Westminster John Knox, 2004.
Bonnard, Pierre. *L'Évangile selon Saint Matthieu.* 2nd ed. Commentaire du Nouveau Testament. Paris: Delachaux & Niestlé, 1970.
Bornkamm, Günther. *Jesus of Nazareth.* Translated by Irene McLuskey and Fraser McLuskey with James M. Robinson. New York: Harper & Brothers, 1960.
———. *Tradition and Interpretation in Matthew.* Philadelphia: Westminster, 1963.
Böttrich, Christfried. *Petrus: Fischer, Fels und Funktionäre.* Biblische Gestalten 2. Leipzig: Evangelische Verlagsanstalt, 2001.
Boxall, Ian. *Discovering Matthew: Content, Interpretation, Reception.* London: SPCK, 2014.
Broadus, John A. *Commentary on the Gospel of Matthew.* An American Commentary on the New Testament. Philadelphia: American Baptist Publication Society, 1886.
Brown, Jeannine K. *The Disciples in Narrative Perspective: The Portrayal and Function of the Matthean Disciples.* SBL Academia Biblica 9. Boston: Brill, 2002.
Brown, Raymond E. *The Death of the Messiah: From Gethsemane to the Grave: A Commentary on the Passion Narratives in the Four Gospels.* Anchor Bible Reference Library. 2 vols. New York: Doubleday, 1994.
Brown, Raymond E., et al., eds. *Peter in the New Testament: A Collaborative Assessment by Protestant and Roman Catholic Scholars.* Minneapolis: Augsburg; New York: Paulist, 1973.
Bubar, Wallace W. "Killing Two Birds with One Stone: The Utter De(con)struction of Matthew and His Church." *Biblical Interpretation* 3 (1995): 144-57.
Bultmann, Rudolf. *The History of the Synoptic Tradition.* Translated by John Marsh. Revised edition. Peabody, Mass.: Hendrickson, 1963.
Burgess, Joseph A. *A History of the Exegesis of Matthew 16:17-19 from 1781 to 1965.* Ann Arbor: Edwards Brothers, 1976.
Burnett, Fred W. "Characterization and Reader Construction of Characters in the Gospels." *Semeia* 63 (1993): 3-28.
———. "Characterization in Matthew: Reader Construction of the Disciple Peter." *McKendree Pastoral Review* 4 (1987): 13-44.
Byrskog, Samuel. *Jesus the Only Teacher: Didactic Authority and Transmission in Ancient Israel, Ancient Judaism and the Matthean Community.* Coniectanea biblica: New Testament Series 24. Stockholm: Almqvist & Wiksell International, 1994.
———. "A New Quest for the *Sitz im Leben*: Social Memory, the Jesus Tradition and the Gospel of Matthew." *New Testament Studies* 52 (2006): 319-36.
Calvin, John. *Commentary on a Harmony of the Evangelists: Matthew, Mark, and Luke.* Translated by William Pringle. 2 vols. Grand Rapids: Eerdmans, 1949.
Caragounis, Chrys C. *Peter and the Rock.* Beihefte zur Zeitschrift für die neutestamentliche Wissenschaft 58. Berlin: de Gruyter, 1989.
Carson, D. A. "Matthew." Pages 23-670 in vol. 9 of *The Expositor's Bible Commentary.* Edited by Tremper Longman III and David E. Garland. Rev. ed. Grand Rapids: Zondervan, 2010.

Bibliography of Secondary Literature Consulted

Carter, Warren. *Matthew and the Margins: A Sociopolitical and Religious Reading.* The Bible and Liberation Series. Maryknoll, N.Y.: Orbis, 2000.
Cassidy, Richard J. *Four Times Peter: Portrayals of Peter in the Four Gospels and at Philippi.* Interfaces. Collegeville, Minn.: Liturgical Press, 2006.
Claudel, Gérard. *La Confession de Pierre: Trajectoire d'une Péricope Évangélique.* Etudes bibliques. New Series 10. Paris: Gabalda, 1988.
Conard, Audrey. "The Fate of Judas: Matthew 27:3-10." *Toronto Journal of Theology* 7 (1991): 158-68.
Cousland, J. R. C. *The Crowds in the Gospel of Matthew.* Novum Testamentum Supplements 102. Leiden: Brill, 2002.
Croy, N. Clayton. *The Mutilation of Mark's Gospel.* Nashville: Abingdon, 2003.
Cullmann, Oscar. *Peter: Disciple, Apostle, Martyr: A Historical and Theological Study.* Translated by Floyd V. Filson. 2nd ed. Library of History and Doctrine. Philadelphia: Westminster, 1962.
Davies, W. D., and Dale C. Allison Jr. *A Critical and Exegetical Commentary on the Gospel according to Saint Matthew.* 3 vols. International Critical Commentary. Edinburgh: T. & T. Clark, 1988-1997.
Deines, Roland. *Die Gerechtigkeit der Tora im Reich des Messias: Mt 5,13-20 als Schlüsseltext der matthäischen Theologie.* Wissenschaftliche Untersuchungen zum Neuen Testament 177. Tübingen: Mohr Siebeck, 2004.
Demacopoulos, George E. *The Invention of Peter: Apostolic Discourse and Papal Authority in Late Antiquity.* Philadelphia: University of Pennsylvania Press, 2013.
Doering, Lutz. "Schwerpunkte und Tendenzen der neueren Petrus-Forschung." *Berliner Theologische Zeitschrift* 19 (2002): 203-23.
Dschulnigg, Peter. "Gestalt und Funktion des Petrus im Matthäusevangelium." Studien zum Neuen Testament und seiner Umwelt: Serie A 14 (1989): 161-83.
———. *Petrus im Neuen Testament.* Stuttgart: Katholisches Bibelwerk, 1996.
Ehrman, Bart D. *Peter, Paul, and Mary Magdalene: The Followers of Jesus in History and Legend.* New York: Oxford University Press, 2006.
Elliott, Mark Adam. *The Survivors of Israel: A Reconsideration of the Theology of Pre-Christian Judaism.* Grand Rapids: Eerdmans, 2000.
Evans, Craig A. *Matthew.* New Cambridge Bible Commentary. New York: Cambridge University Press, 2012.
Finley, Thomas. "'Upon This Rock': Matthew 16:18 and the Aramaic Evidence." *Aramaic Studies* 4 (2006): 133-51.
Fitzmyer, Joseph A. "The Meaning of the Aramaic Noun כפא/כיפא in the First Century and Its Significance for the Interpretation of Gospel Passages." Pages 35-43 in *"Il Verbo di Dio Vivo": Studi sul Nuovo Testamento in onore del Cardinale Albert Vanoye, S.I.* Edited by José Enrique Aguilar Chiu et al. Analecta biblica 165. Rome: Pontifical Biblical Institute, 2007.
———. *To Advance the Gospel: New Testament Studies.* New York: Crossroad, 1981.
Fornberg, Tord. "The Figure of Peter in Matthew and 2 Peter." *Indian Theological Studies* 32 (1995): 237-49.
France, R. T. *The Gospel of Matthew.* New International Commentary on the New Testament. Grand Rapids: Eerdmans, 2007.
Frankemölle, Hubert. *Matthäus.* 2 vols. Düsseldorf: Patmos Verlag, 1994-1997.

Bibliography of Secondary Literature Consulted

Gaechter, Paul. *Das Matthäus Evangelium.* Innsbruck: Tyrolia Verlag, 1963.
Garland, David E. *Reading Matthew: A Literary and Theological Commentary on the First Gospel.* Reading the New Testament Series. New York: Crossroad, 1995.
Gerhardsson, Birger. "Confession and Denial before Men: Observations on Matt. 26:57–27:2." *Journal for the Study of the New Testament* 13 (1981): 46-66.
Gibbs, Jeffrey A. *Matthew 11:2–20:34. Concordia Commentary.* Saint Louis: Concordia, 2010.
Gibson, Jack J. *Between Jerusalem and Antioch: Peter, James and the Gentiles.* Wissenschaftliche Untersuchungen zum Neuen Testament. Second Series 345. Tübingen: Mohr Siebeck, 2013.
Gnilka, Joachim. *Das Matthäusevangelium.* 2 vols. Herders theologischer Kommentar zum Neuen Testament. Freiburg: Herder, 1986-1988.
Goodacre, Mark. "The Rock on Rocky Ground: Matthew, Mark and Peter as *Skandalon.*" Pages 61-73 in *What Is It That the Scripture Says? Essays in Biblical Interpretation, Translation and Reception in Honour of Henry Wansbrough OSB.* Edited by Philip McCosker. New York: T&T Clark, 2006.
Goulder, Michael. *St. Paul versus St. Peter: A Tale of Two Missions.* Louisville: Westminster John Knox, 1994.
Grappe, Christian. *Images de Pierre aux deux premiers siècles.* Études d'histoire et de philosophie religieuses 75. Paris: Presses Universitaires de France, 1995.
Grundmann, Walter. *Das Evangelium nach Matthäus.* 2nd ed. Theologischer Handkommentar zum Neuen Testament. Berlin: Evangelische Verlagsanstalt, 1971.
Gundry, Robert H. *Commentary on the New Testament.* Grand Rapids: Baker Academic, 2010.
———. "In Defense of the Church in Matthew as a *Corpus Mixtum.*" *Zeitschrift für die neutestamentliche Wissenschaft und die Kunde der älteren Kirche* 91 (2000): 153-65.
———. *Mark: A Commentary on His Apology for the Cross.* Grand Rapids: Eerdmans, 1993.
———. "Matthean Foreign Bodies in Agreements of Luke with Matthew Against Mark: Evidence That Luke Used Matthew." Pages 1467-95 in *The Four Gospels 1992: Festschrift Frans Neirynck.* Edited by F. Van Segbroeck et al. Bibliotheca Ephemeridum Theologicarum Lovaniensium 100. Leuven: Leuven University Press/Peeters, 1992.
———. *Matthew: A Commentary on His Handbook for a Mixed Church under Persecution.* 2nd enl. ed. Grand Rapids: Eerdmans, 1994.
———. "On True and False Disciples in Matthew 8.18-22." *New Testament Studies* 40 (1993): 433-41.
———. "The Refusal of Matthean Foreign Bodies to Be Exorcised from Luke 9,22; 10,25-28." *Ephemerides Theologicae Lovanienses* 75 (1999): 104-22.
Hagner, Donald A. *Matthew 1–13.* Word Biblical Commentary 33A. Dallas: Word, 1993.
———. *Matthew 14–28.* Word Biblical Commentary 33B. Dallas: Word, 1995.
———. *The New Testament: A Historical and Theological Introduction.* Grand Rapids: Baker Academic, 2012.
———. "Righteousness in Matthew's Theology." Pages 101-20 in *Worship, Theology and Ministry in the Early Church: Essays in Honor of Ralph P. Martin.* Edited by

Bibliography of Secondary Literature Consulted

Michael J. Wilkins and Terence Paige. Journal for the Study of the New Testament: Supplement Series 87. Sheffield: JSOT Press, 1992.

Hare, Douglas R. A. *The Theme of Jewish Persecution of Christians in the Gospel according to St Matthew*. Society of New Testament Studies Monograph Series 6. Cambridge: Cambridge University Press, 1967.

Heil, John Paul. *The Death and Resurrection of Jesus: A Narrative-Critical Reading of Matthew 26–28*. Minneapolis: Fortress, 1991.

———. *Jesus Walking on the Sea: Meaning and Gospel Functions in Matt 14:22-33, Mark 6:45-52, and John 6:15b-21*. Analecta biblica 87. Rome: Biblical Institute Press, 1981.

Helyer, Larry R. *The Life and Witness of Peter*. Downers Grove, Ill.: InterVarsity Press, 2012.

Hengel, Martin. *Saint Peter: The Underestimated Apostle*. Translated by Thomas M. Trapp. Grand Rapids: Eerdmans, 2010.

Herron, Robert W., Jr. *Mark's Account of Peter's Denial of Jesus*. Lanham, Md.: University Press of America, 1991.

Hoffmann, P. "Der Petrus-Primat im Matthäusevangelium." Pages 94-114 in *Neues Testament und Kirche*. Edited by J. Gnilka. Freiburg: Herder, 1974.

Holtzmann, H. J. *Die Synoptiker — Die Apostelgeschichte*. 2nd ed. Hand-Commentar zum Neuen Testament. Freiburg im Bresgau: J. C. B. Mohr (Paul Siebeck), 1892.

Kähler, Christoph. "Zur Form- und Traditionsgeschichte von Matth. xvi. 17-19." *New Testament Studies* 23 (1976/1977): 36-58.

Keener, Craig S. *Acts: An Exegetical Commentary*. Vol. 1: *Introduction and 1:1–2:47*. Grand Rapids: Baker Academic, 2012.

———. *A Commentary on the Gospel of Matthew*. Grand Rapids: Eerdmans, 1999.

Kessler, William Thomas. *Peter as the First Witness of the Risen Lord: An Historical and Theological Investigation*. Tesi Gregoriana, Serie Teologia 37. Rome: Gregorian University Press, 1998.

Kingsbury, Jack Dean. "The Figure of Peter in Matthew's Gospel as a Theological Problem." *Journal of Biblical Literature* 98 (1979): 67-83.

———. *Matthew as Story*. 2nd ed. Philadelphia: Fortress, 1988.

Klein, Günter. *Rekonstruktion und Interpretation: Gesammelte Aufsätze zum Neuen Testament*. Beiträge zur evangelischen Theologie 50. Munich: Kaiser, 1969.

Kraus, Wolfgang. "Zur Ekklesiologie des Matthäusevangeliums." Pages 195-239 in *The Gospel of Matthew at the Crossroads of Early Christianity*. Edited by Donald Senior. Bibliotheca ephemeridum theologicarum lovaniensium 243. Leuven: Peeters, 2011.

Krentz, Edgar. "Peter: Confessor, Denier, Proclaimer, Validator of Proclamation — A Study in Diversity." *Currents in Theology and Mission* 37 (2010): 320-33.

Kvalbein, Hans. "The Authorization of Peter in Matthew 16:17-19: A Reconsideration of the Power to Bind and Loose." Pages 145-74 in *The Formation of the Early Church*. Edited by Justein Ådna. Wissenschaftliche Untersuchungen zum Neuen Testament 183. Tübingen: Mohr Siebeck, 2005.

Lagrange, M.-J. *Évangile selon Saint Matthieu*. 7th ed. Etudes bibliques. Paris: Gabalda, 1948.

Lampe, G. W. H. "Church Discipline and the Interpretation of the Epistles to the Corinthians." Pages 337-61 in *Christian History and Interpretation: Studies Presented* to *John Knox*. Edited by W. R. Farmer et al. Cambridge: Cambridge University Press, 1967.

———. "St. Peter's Denial." *Bulletin of the John Rylands University Library of Manchester* 55 (1972/1973): 346-68.

Lampe, Peter. "Peter (the Disciple)." Pages 1-4 in vol. 10 of *Religion Past and Present: Encyclopedia of Theology and Religion*. Edited by Hans Dieter Betz et al. 14 vols. Leiden: Brill, 2011.

———. "Das Spiel mit dem Petrusnamen — Matt: XVI. 18." *New Testament Studies* 25 (1978/1979): 227-45.

Lapham, F. *Peter: The Myth, the Man and the Writings: A Study of Early Petrine Text and Tradition*. Journal for the Study of the New Testament: Supplement Series 239. Sheffield: Sheffield Academic Press, 2003.

Laurentin, René. *Petite vie de saint Pierre*. Paris: Desclée de Brouwer, 1992.

Lohmeyer, Ernst. *Das Evangelium des Matthäus*. Edited by Werner Schmauch. 3rd ed. Kritisch-exegetischer Kommentar (Meyer-Kommentar). Göttingen: Vandenhoeck & Ruprecht, 1962.

Luomanen, Petri. "*Corpus Mixtum* — An Appropriate Description of Matthew's Community?" *Journal of Biblical Literature* 117 (1998): 469-80.

Luz, Ulrich. *Matthew 1–7: A Commentary*. Translated by Wilhelm C. Linss. Minneapolis: Augsburg, 1989.

———. *Matthew 8–20*. Edited by Helmut Koester. Translated by James E. Crouch. Hermeneia. Minneapolis: Fortress, 2001.

———. *Matthew 21–28*. Edited by Helmut Koester. Translated by James E. Crouch. Hermeneia. Minneapolis: Fortress, 2005.

———. *Studies in Matthew*. Translated by Rosemary Selle. Grand Rapids: Eerdmans, 2005.

Maier, Gerhard. "The Church in the Gospel of Matthew: Hermeneutical Analysis of the Current Debate." Pages 45-63 in *Biblical Interpretation and the Church: Text and Context*. Edited by D. A. Carson. Exeter: Paternoster, 1984.

Marguerat, Daniel. "L'église et le monde en Matthieu 13,36-43." *Revue de théologie et de philosophie* 110 (1978): 111-29.

Markley, John R. *Peter — Apocalyptic Seer: The Influence of the Apocalypse Genre on Matthew's Portrayal of Peter*. Wissenschaftliche Untersuchungen zum Neuen Testament. Second Series 348. Tübingen: Mohr Siebeck, 2013.

McIver, R. K. "The Parable of the Weeds among the Wheat (Matt 13:24-30, 36-43) and the Relation between the Kingdom and the Church as Portrayed in the Gospel of Matthew." *Journal of Biblical Literature* 114 (1995): 643-59.

McNeile, Alan Hugh. *The Gospel According to St. Matthew*. New York: St. Martin's, 1965.

Meier, John P. *A Marginal Jew: Rethinking the Historical Jesus*, vol. 2: *Mentor, Message, and Miracles*. Anchor Bible Reference Library. New York: Doubleday, 1994.

———. *A Marginal Jew: Rethinking the Historical Jesus*, vol. 3: *Companions and Competitors*. Anchor Bible Reference Library. New York: Doubleday, 2001.

———. *Matthew*. New Testament Message 3. Wilmington, Del.: Michael Glazier, 1980.

Merkel, Helmut. "Peter's Curse." Pages 66-71 in *The Trial of Jesus: Cambridge Studies in Honour of C. F. D. Moule*. Edited by Ernst Bammel. Studies in Biblical Theology. Second Series 13. London: SCM, 1970.

Bibliography of Secondary Literature Consulted

Merkle, Benjamin L. "The Meaning of Ἐκκλησία in Matthew 16:18 and 18:17." *Bibliotheca sacra* 167 (2010): 281-91.
Migbisiegbe, Guillaume. "Entering into the Joy of the Master or Being Cast Out into the Outer Darkness: Re-Imagining the Eschatological Judgement in Matthew 25,30." Pages 607-19 in *The Gospel of Matthew at the Crossroads of Early Christianity*. Edited by Donald Senior. Bibliotheca ephemeridum theologicarum lovaniensium 243. Leuven: Peeters, 2011.
Mitchell, Margaret M. "Peter's 'Hypocrisy' and Paul's: Two 'Hypocrites' at the Foundation of Earliest Christianity." *New Testament Studies* 58 (2012): 213-34.
Nau, Arlo J. *Peter in Matthew: Discipleship, Diplomacy, and Dispraise*. Good News Studies 36. Collegeville, Minn.: Liturgical Press, 1992.
Neirynck, Frans. *Evangelica II: 1982-1991, Collected Essays*. Edited by F. Van Segbroeck. Bibliotheca ephemeridum theologicarum lovaniensium 99. Leuven: Leuven University Press, 1991.
Nicholls, Rachel. *Walking on the Water: Reading Mt. 14:22-33 in the Light of Its Wirkungsgeschichte*. Biblical Interpretation Series 90. Leiden: Brill, 2008.
Nolland, John. *The Gospel of Matthew: A Commentary on the Greek Text*. New International Greek Testament Commentary. Grand Rapids: Eerdmans, 2005.
O'Collins, Gerald. "Peter as Easter Witness." *Theological Studies* 73 (2012): 251-74.
Oropeza, B. J. *In the Footsteps of Judas and Other Defectors: The Gospels, Acts, and Johannine Letters*. Apostasy in the New Testament Communities 1. Eugene, Ore.: Wipf & Stock, 2011.
Osborne, Grant R. *Matthew*. Zondervan Exegetical Commentary on the New Testament. Grand Rapids: Zondervan, 2010.
Overman, J. Andrew. *Church and Community in Crisis: The Gospel according to Matthew*. The New Testament Context. Valley Forge, Pa.: Trinity Press International, 1996.
Patte, Daniel. *The Gospel According to Matthew: A Structural Commentary on Matthew's Faith*. Philadelphia: Fortress, 1987.
Perkins, Pheme. *Peter: Apostle for the Whole Church*. Columbia: University of South Carolina Press, 1994.
Pesch, Rudolf. *Die biblischen Grundlagen des Primats*. Quaestiones disputatae 187. Freiburg: Herder, 2001.
———. *Simon-Petrus: Geschichte und geschichtliche Bedeutung des ersten Jüngers Jesu Christi*. Päpste und Päpsttum 15. Stuttgart: Hiersemann, 1980.
Plummer, Alfred. *An Exegetical Commentary on the Gospel According to St. Matthew*. 1915. Repr., Grand Rapids: Baker, 1982.
Räisänen, Heikki. "Jesus and Hell." Pages 355-83 in *Jesus in Continuum*. Edited by Tom Holmén. Wissenschaftliche Untersuchungen zum Neuen Testament 289. Tübingen: Mohr Siebeck, 2012.
Reed, David A. "'Saving Judas' — A Social Scientific Approach to Judas's Suicide in Matthew 27:3-10." *Biblical Theology Bulletin* 35 (2005): 51-59.
Ridderbos, H. N. *Matthew*. Translated by Ray Togtman. Bible Student's Commentary. Grand Rapids: Zondervan, 1987.
Rigaux, Béda. "St. Peter in Contemporary Exegesis." Pages 147-79 in *Progress and Decline in the History of Church Renewal*. Concilium 27. New York: Paulist Press, 1967.

Bibliography of Secondary Literature Consulted

Robinson, Bernard P. "Peter and His Successors: Tradition and Redaction in Matthew 16:17-19." *Journal for the Study of the New Testament* 21 (1984): 85-104.
Sabourin, Leopold. *The Gospel according to St Matthew*. 2 vols. Bandra, Bombay: St. Paul Publications, 1982.
Sand, Alexander. *Das Evangelium nach Matthäus*. Regensburger Neues Testament. Regensburg: Pustet, 1986.
Schäfer, Ruth. *Paulus bis zum Apostelkonzil*. Wissenschaftliche Untersuchungen zum Neuen Testament. Second Series 179. Tübingen: Mohr Siebeck, 2004.
Schenk, Wolfgang. "'Das Matthäusevangelium' als Petrusevangelium." *Biblische Zeitschrift* Neue Folge 27 (1983): 58-80.
Schnackenburg, Rudolf. *The Gospel of Matthew*. Translated by Robert R. Barr. Grand Rapids: Eerdmans, 2002.
Schnelle, Udo. *Theology of the New Testament*. Translated by M. Eugene Boring. Grand Rapids: Baker Academic, 2009.
Schweizer, Eduard. *The Good News According to Matthew*. Translated by David E. Green. Atlanta: John Knox Press, 1975.
Senior, Donald. *What Are They Saying About Matthew?* New York: Paulist Press, 1983.
Sim, David C. "Matthew's Use of Mark: Did Matthew Intend to Supplement or to Replace His Primary Sources?" *New Testament Studies* 57 (2011): 76-92.
Simonetti, Manlio, ed. *Matthew 14–28*. Ancient Christian Commentary on Scripture, New Testament Ib. Downers Grove, Ill.: InterVarsity Press, 2002.
Smith, Barry D. *Jesus' Twofold Teaching about the Kingdom of God*. Sheffield: Sheffield Phoenix Press, 2009.
Smith, Terence V. *Petrine Controversies in Early Christianity*. Wissenschaftliche Untersuchungen zum Neuen Testament. Second Series 15. Tübingen: Mohr, 1985.
Stein, Robert H. "The Ending of Mark." *Bulletin for Biblical Research* 18 (2008): 79-98.
Stock, Augustine. "Is Matthew's Presentation of Peter Ironic?" *Biblical Theology Bulletin* 17, no. 2 (1987): 64-69.
Stock, Klemens. "Jesus und seine Jünger nach Markus." Pages 149-68 in *"Il Verbo di Dio è Vivo": Studi sul Nuovo Testamento in onore del Cardinale Albert Vanhoye, S.I.* Edited by José Enrique Aguilar Chiu et al. Analecta biblica 165. Rome: Pontifical Biblical Institute, 2007.
Streeter, Burnett Hillman. *The Four Gospels: A Study of Origins*. London: Macmillan, 1964.
Syreeni, Kari. "Peter as Character and Symbol in the Gospel of Matthew." Pages 106-52 in *Characterization in the Gospels: Reconceiving Narrative Criticism*. Edited by David Rhoads and Kari Syreeni. Journal for the Study of the New Testament: Supplement Series 184. Sheffield: Sheffield Academic Press, 1999.
Thiede, Carsten Peter. *Simon Peter: From Galilee to Rome*. Exeter: Paternoster, 1986.
Tresmontant, Claude. *The Gospel of Matthew: Original Reconstructed Translation and Notes*. Translated by K. D. Whitehead. Front Royal, Va.: Christendom Press, 1996.
Turner, David L. *Matthew*. Baker Exegetical Commentary on the New Testament. Grand Rapids: Baker Academic, 2008.
Van Cangh, J.-M. *Les sources judaïques du Nouveau Testament*. Bibliotheca ephemeridum theologicarum lovaniensium 204. Leuven: Leuven University Press, 2008.

Bibliography of Secondary Literature Consulted

Vanhoozer, Kevin J. *First Theology: God, Scripture and Hermeneutics*. Downers Grove, Ill.: InterVarsity Press, 2002.

Verheyden, Joseph. "Rock and Stumbling Block: The Fate of Matthew's Peter." Pages 263-311 in *The Gospel of Matthew at the Crossroads of Early Christianity*. Edited by Donald Senior. Bibliotheca ephemeridum theologicarum lovaniensium 243. Leuven: Peeters, 2011.

Volkmar, Gustav. *Die Religion Jesu und ihre erste Entwicklung nach dem gegenwärtigen Stande der Wissenschaft*. Leipzig: Brockhaus, 1857.

Wall, Robert W. "Peter, 'Son' of Jonah: The Conversion of Cornelius in the Context of Canon." *Journal for the Study of the New Testament* 29 (1987): 79-90.

Wallace, Daniel B. *Greek Grammar beyond the Basics: An Exegetical Syntax of the New Testament*. Grand Rapids: Zondervan, 1996.

Watson, Francis. *Gospel Writing: A Canonical Perspective*. Grand Rapids: Eerdmans, 2013.

Wiarda, Timothy. *Peter in the Gospels: Pattern, Personality and Relationship*. Wissenschaftliche Untersuchungen zum Neuen Testament. Second Series 127. Tübingen: Mohr Siebeck, 2000.

Wiefel, Wolfgang. *Das Evangelium nach Matthäus*. Theologischer Handkommentar zum Neuen Testament 1. Leipzig: Evangelische Verlagsanstalt, 1998.

Wilkins, Michael J. *The Concept of Disciple in Matthew's Gospel as Reflected in the Use of the Term Μαθητής*. Novum Testamentum Supplements 59. Leiden: Brill, 1988.

———. "Peter's Declaration concerning Jesus' Identity in Caesarea Philippi." Pages 293-381 in *Key Events in the Life of the Historical Jesus: A Collaborative Exploration of Context and Coherence*. Edited by Darrell L. Bock and Robert L. Webb. Grand Rapids: Eerdmans, 2009.

Wilcox, Max. "Peter and the Rock: A Fresh Look at Matthew xvi.17-19." *New Testament Studies* 22 (1975/1976): 73-88.

Witherington, Ben, III. *Matthew*. Smyth & Helwys Bible Commentary. Macon, Ga.: Smyth & Helwys, 2006.

Wright, N. T. *Paul and the Faithfulness of God*. 2 vols. Christian Origins and the Question of God 4. Minneapolis: Fortress, 2013.

Zahn, Theodor. *Das Evangelium des Matthäus*. 3rd ed. Kommentar zum Neuen Testament 1. Leipzig: Deichert, 1910.

CHAPTER 1

Introduction

The figure of Peter has always attracted the attention of biblical scholars as well as church historians, theologians, and lay Christians. But during the recent half century or so and in the wake of Oscar Cullmann's book on Peter,[1] the figure of Peter seems to have attracted more attention than ever, at least among biblical scholars.[2] Some of them troll for the historical Pe-

---

1. Oscar Cullmann, *Peter: Disciple, Apostle, Martyr: A Historical and Theological Study* (trans. Floyd V. Filson; 2nd ed.; Library of History and Doctrine; Philadelphia: Westminster, 1962).

2. Following is a partial list of recent books devoted to the figure of Peter: Jürgen Becker, *Simon Petrus im Urchristentum* (Biblisch-Theologische Studien 105; Neukirchen-Vluyn: Neukirchener Verlag, 2009); Markus Bockmuehl, *The Remembered Peter: In Ancient Reception and Modern Debate* (WUNT 262; Tübingen: Mohr Siebeck, 2010); Bockmuehl, *Simon Peter in Scripture and Memory: The New Testament Apostle in the Early Church* (Grand Rapids: Baker Academic, 2012); Christfried Böttrich, *Petrus: Fischer, Fels und Funktionäre* (Biblische Gestalten 2; Leipzig: Evangelische Verlagsanstalt, 2001); Raymond E. Brown et al., eds., *Peter in the New Testament: A Collaborative Assessment by Protestant and Roman Catholic Scholars* (Minneapolis: Augsburg; New York: Paulist, 1973); Richard J. Cassidy, *Four Times Peter: Portrayals of Peter in the Four Gospels and at Philippi* (Interfaces; Collegeville, Minn.: Liturgical Press, 2006); Peter Dschulnigg, *Petrus im Neuen Testament* (Stuttgart: Katholisches Bibelwerk, 1996); Christian Grappe, *Images de Pierre aux deux premiers siècles* (Études d'histoire et de philosophie religieuses 75; Paris: Presses Universitaires de France, 1995); Martin Hengel, *Saint Peter: The Underestimated Apostle* (trans. Thomas H. Trapp; Grand Rapids: Eerdmans, 2010); F. Lapham, *Peter: The Myth, the Man and the Writings: A Study of Early Petrine Text and Tradition* (JSNTSup 235; Sheffield: Sheffield Academic, 2003); René Laurentin, *Petite vie de saint Pierre* (Paris: Desclée de Brouwer, 1992); Arlo J. Nau, *Peter in Matthew: Discipleship, Diplomacy, and Dispraise* (GNS 36; Collegeville, Minn.: Liturgical Press, 1992); Pheme Perkins, *Peter: Apostle for the Whole Church* (Columbia:

Peter — False Disciple and Apostate according to Saint Matthew

ter swimming beneath the surface of the biblical texts. Other scholars use redaction, composition, or narrative criticism, or combinations thereof, to discover the literary Peters on the surface of the biblical texts. Yet other scholars, interested in so-called reception history, investigate the effects of Petrine biblical texts on later understandings of what we might call the ecclesiastical Peters.

The present study deals neither with the historical Peter nor with the received Peter — rather, with the particular and distinctive portrayal of Peter in the Gospel according to Saint Matthew (from now on "Matthew"). Because of the famous rock-, keys-, and binding-and-loosing passage, Matt 16:17-19, this evangelist's overall portrayal has drawn a disproportionate amount of attention; and the portrayal has been judged usually as more or less favorable toward Peter,[3] occasionally as more or less unfavorable toward him,[4] and increasingly as a mixture of the favorable and unfavorable.[5] Here, emphasis will fall on the unfavorable even to the extent of

---

University of South Carolina Press, 1994); Rudolf Pesch, *Die biblischen Grundlagen des Primats* (QD 487; Freiburg: Herder, 2001); Pesch, *Simon-Petrus: Geschichte und geschichtliche Bedeutung des ersten Jüngers Jesu Christi* (Päpste und Papsttum 15; Stuttgart: Anton Hiersemann, 1980); Timothy Wiarda, *Peter in the Gospels: Pattern, Personality and Relationships* (WUNT 2/127; Tübingen: Mohr Siebeck, 2000). Excluded from the foregoing list are books on a single passage, such as Matt 16:17-19, and all the many articles on Peter. For further bibliography, see Joseph Verheyden, "Rock and Stumbling Block: The Fate of Matthew's Peter," in *The Gospel of Matthew at the Crossroads of Early Christianity* (ed. Donald Senior; BETL 243; Leuven: Peeters, 2011), 264-65 nn. 3-5.

3. See, e.g., Brown et al., *Peter in the New Testament*, 75. Christoph Kähler even describes Matthew as "ein Petrusevangelium" ("Zur Form- und Traditionsgeschichte von Matth. xvi. 17-19," *NTS* 23 [1976/1977]: 36-58, esp. 56-57); also Wolfgang Schenk, "Das 'Matthäusevangelium' as Petrusevangelium," *BZ* nf 27 (1983): 58-80, esp. 71-73, 78; Michael Goulder, *St. Paul versus St. Peter: A Tale of Two Missions* (Louisville: Westminster John Knox, 1995), 31.

4. Cf. Peter Dschulnigg's suggestion that Matthew wants to undermine a false idealization of Peter, due perhaps to Matt 16:16-18 ("Gestalt und Funktion des Petrus im Matthäusevangelium," SNTSU: Serie A14 [1989]: 178). As part of his extreme version of the old Tübingen hypothesis, Gustav Volkmar went so far as to describe Matthew as a "judenchristlich = *paulinische* Evangelium" because of negativity toward Peter in this Gospel (*Die Religion Jesu und ihre erste Entwicklung nach dem gegenwärtigen Stande der Wissenschaft* [Leipzig: Brockhaus, 1857], 360-61, 384 [emphasis added]).

5. See Kari Syreeni's statement that Matthew's "portrayal of Peter is much more opaque and contradictory" than "Matthew's Gospel as a whole" ("Peter as Character and Symbol in the Gospel of Matthew," in *Characterization in the Gospels: Reconceiving Narrative Criticism* [ed. David Rhoads and Kari Syreeni; JSNTSup 184; Sheffield: Sheffield Academic, 1999], 107 n. 7). Ulrich Luz writes similarly, "On the whole there is a striking 'ambivalence' in Peter's

Introduction

proposing that Matthew portrays Peter as a *false* disciple of Jesus, a disciple who went so far as to apostatize; that Matthew does so to warn Christians against the loss of salvation through falsity-exposing apostasy; that this warning fits the Matthean theme of apostasy-inducing persecution; and that the danger of apostasy fits the further Matthean theme of the ongoing presence of false disciples in the church, a present form of Jesus the Son of Man's kingdom, till the end.[6]

To be sure, Matthew does not pronounce an explicit judgment on Peter as a false disciple. He simply presents evidence of Peter's falsity. This avoidance of an explicit judgment conforms to the prohibition of weeding out tares, representative of false disciples, from among wheat, representative of true disciples, though the tares, which were originally indistinguishable from the wheat, became recognizable as tares even before harvesttime, representative of the consummation (Matt 13:24-30, 37-43).[7] That is to say, the avoidance of an explicit judgment while presenting evidence of falsity keeps Matthew from disobeying Jesus' prohibition of judgment (Matt 5:22; 7:1-2).[8] By contrast, Jesus pronounces judgment against Judas

---

behavior [in Matthew]. He is confessor *and* tempter, denier *and* penitent, courageous *and* weak" (*Matthew 8–20* [ed. Helmut Koester; trans. James E. Crouch; Hermeneia; Minneapolis: Fortress, 2001], 366 [emphasis original]; cf. Pope Gregory the Great's highlighting the faults of Peter to exhort Peter's ecclesiastical heirs to humility [George E. Demacopoulos, *The Invention of Peter: Apostolic Discourse and Papal Authority in Late Antiquity* (Philadelphia: University of Pennsylvania Press, 2013), 135-39, 162]). Verheyden acknowledges the ambivalence, but plays down the unfavorable for emphasis on the favorable ("Rock and Stumbling Block," 268-73). Others have dealt sufficiently well with portrayals of Matthew's Peter as a typical disciple (a view associated esp. with Georg Strecker) or as a kind of supreme rabbi who guaranteed and transmitted traditions of Jesus (a view associated esp. with Reinhart Hummel [see references in John R. Markley, *Peter — Apocalyptic Seer: The Influence of Apocalyptic Genre on Matthew's Portrayal of Peter* (WUNT 2/348; Tübingen: Mohr Siebeck, 2013), 2]).

6. Contrast the statement of Hans Kvalbein that Matthew's portrayal of Peter's "weaknesses and failures ... makes it easier for all believers to identify with him" ("The Authorization of Peter in Matthew 16:17-19: A Reconsideration of the Power to Bind and Loose," in *The Formation of the Early Church* [ed. Justein Ådna; WUNT 183; Tübingen: Mohr Siebeck, 2005], 168). Similarly, Samuel Byrskog says that the failures of a historic hero like Peter may make his position stronger in the group by the group's ongoing activities of social remembering, thus vindicating him post-failures ("A New Quest for the *Sitz im Leben*: Social Memory, the Jesus Tradition and the Gospel of Matthew," *NTS* 52 [2006]: 332-33).

7. See below, pp. 74-76, on the tares as representative of false disciples, not the wicked in general, and on the wheat as representative of true disciples.

8. See further Robert H. Gundry, *Matthew: A Commentary on His Handbook for a Mixed Church under Persecution* (2nd enl. ed.; Grand Rapids: Eerdmans, 1994), 84-85, 119-21.

Iscariot as a false disciple, for he has the judgmental authority to do so (see Matt 26:24-25).

Matthew's Petrine texts will undergo treatment seriatim with the use of redaction, composition, and narrative criticisms (though without their terminological paraphernalia).[9] Assumptions underlying this treatment are as follows: (1) Whether by way of drawing on oral traditions, presently unknown written sources, or his own predilections, Matthew redacted Mark by way of both revisions of Markan materials and additions to and subtractions from these materials. (Those who believe that Mark redacted Matthew may interpret Mark's portrayal of Peter as a rehabilitation of him, as in Luke-Acts and John 21.[10]) (2) Matthew wrote for first-time auditors. (3) They may or may not have known his sources, but would have detected his emphases even without such knowledge. (4) He wrote with the purpose and expectation that they would detect his emphases. (5) He wrote with the further expectation that they would hear his Gospel read to them in a single session, or at least in big chunks, so as to gain at least part of their understanding from narratival progress in the Gospel.[11] (6) He wrote with the yet further expectation that repeated readings would confirm or correct initial impressions and foster new ones according to his intentions. (7) The translations into Greek of Ἐμμανουήλ in Matt 1:23 and of ηλι ηλι λεμα σαβαχθανι in Matt 27:46 show that the evangelist did not expect his audience to understand Hebrew or Aramaic, so that — whatever the historical Jesus may have meant in those languages

---

9. Cf. Perkins's favoring "an eclectic method of analysis that combines results of redaction criticism and narrative criticism" (*Peter*, 54).

10. See Brown et al., *Peter in the New Testament*, 109-28. Luke could have rehabilitated Peter not only vis-à-vis Mark but also in contradiction of Matthew's portrayal of him if Luke knew and used Matthew, as argued, e.g., by Robert H. Gundry, "Matthean Foreign Bodies in Agreements of Luke with Matthew Against Mark: Evidence That Luke Used Matthew," in *The Four Gospels 1992: Festschrift Frans Neirynck* (ed. F. Van Segbroeck et al.; BETL 100; Leuven: University Press/Peeters, 1992), 1467-95; Gundry, "A Rejoinder on Matthean Foreign Bodies in Luke 10,25-28," *ETL* 71 (1995): 139-50; Gundry, "The Refusal of Matthean Foreign Bodies to Be Exorcised from Luke 9,22; 10,25-28," *ETL* 75 (1999): 104-22; Michael F. Bird, *The Gospel of the Lord: How the Early Church Wrote the Story of Jesus* (Grand Rapids: Eerdmans, 2014), 154-87. Given parallels between and unique to Luke and John, the latter may have extended Luke's rehabilitation of Peter, especially in John 21:15-17.

11. Compare the use of reader-response criticism and discourse analysis by Fred W. Burnett, "Characterization in Matthew: Reader Construction of the Disciple Peter," *McKendree Pastoral Review* 4 (1987): 13-43; Burnett, "Characterization and Reader Construction of Characters in the Gospels," *Semeia* 63 (1993): 3-28, esp. 20-23; also Kari Syreeni, "Peter as Character and Symbol," 106-52.

Introduction

— an untranslated Semitic substratum does not determine the meaning of Matthew's Greek text.[12]

To the texts, then.

---

12. To accommodate his apparently Aramaic- and Hebrew-ignorant audience, Matthew even avoids κορβᾶν despite Mark's provision of a translation (Matt 15:5; par. Mark 7:11). He also omits ταλιθα κουμ (Mark 5:41) in 9:25, and in 15:29-31 omits the parallel in Mark 7:32-36 that features εφφαθα. Semitic personal names and place names whose meanings carry no significance get no translation, naturally. Neither does ῥακά in Matt 5:22, because the next clause contains μωρέ as basically synonymous, so that Matthew does not need to translate. Similarly, he does not translate μαμωνᾷ in 6:24; but the preceding context features "treasure(s)" (θησαυρ-), so that again he does not need to translate for his audience ignorant of Aramaic and Hebrew. In 21:9, finally, Matthew does not translate ὡσαννά, but almost certainly because it had lost the meaning "Save, please," in favor of an ejaculatory acclamation, as the narrative makes clear. Boxall observes, "The removal of Aramaic words (which is not in fact consistently applied across the Gospel . . .) is evidence only that the intended audience are Greek-speakers, not that they are non-Jews" (*Discovering Matthew: Content, Interpretation, Reception* [London: SPCK, 2014], 70).

CHAPTER 2

Peter in Matthew Prior to Matthew 16:13-23

Matthew 4:18-20 (par. Mark 1:16-18)

In 4:18-20 Matthew introduces Peter under the common personal name "Simon" (Greek for the Semitic "Symeon") and then adds "the one called Peter" (not in the par. Mark 1:16). This addition joins both the unusualness of "Peter" as a personal name, the mention of these two names ahead of "Andrew his brother," and the calling of Andrew "his brother" rather than vice versa ("Peter, the brother of Andrew") to make Peter prominent. At this point "Peter" appears to be an ordinary name meaning "stone," as πέτρος usually means in Greek — only unusually meaning "rock." Despite making Peter more prominent than Andrew, Matthew cannot have expected his first-time auditors to consider "Peter" an honorific name.[1] Whether in 16:17-19 Jesus will interpret the name as honorific remains to be seen; and neither there nor here is it said that Jesus conferred the name on Simon, as might have been expected for an honorific name.[2] But instead

---

1. So, correctly, Syreeni, "Peter as Character and Symbol," 121.

2. It is doubtful that first-time auditors would ask themselves, "Called Peter by whom?" instead of assuming simply that "Peter" was a name alternative to "Simon" (against Burnett, "Characterization in Matthew," 14). In any event, Matthew calls him Peter also in 8:14; 10:2; 14:28, 29; 15:15; 16:16 before Jesus does in 16:18; and in 16:18 the statement "You are Peter" is most naturally understood as the recognition of a name already given rather than as the conferral of a new name (contrast Mark 3:16; Luke 6:14; John 1:42). So even from an authorial standpoint 4:18 hardly anticipates 16:18; and auditors of Matthew have no reason, and will have no reason, to think of "Peter" as an honorific name bestowed on Simon by Jesus. See Bockmuehl, *The Remembered Peter*, 85, against W. D. Davies and Dale C. Allison

of describing Andrew as "the brother of Simon" (Mark 1:16), Matthew describes Andrew as "his brother," i.e., the brother of "Simon, the one called Peter," so that the last-mentioned name, "Peter," and its bearer gain further prominence. Peter and Andrew's immediately leaving their nets and following Jesus in obedience to Jesus' command strikes a favorable note. In this case, however, Peter enjoys no advantage; for Andrew and, in the next episode, James and John do the same, just as Jesus says Andrew as well as Peter will become a fisher of human beings.

Matthew 8:14-15 (par. Mark 1:29-31; Luke 4:38-39)

In 8:14-15 Matthew substitutes "Peter" for Mark's "Simon" (1:29; so too Luke 4:38), but Peter himself does not make an appearance. Only his house and his mother-in-law do. For all we know, he was absent, because in contrast with Mark 1:16-21 and 1:29-31, which have Simon, Andrew, James, and John accompany Jesus into Simon's house and all get served by Simon's mother-in-law once she is healed (so too Luke 4:39 for the latter), Matthew mentions only Jesus' entrance into the house and getting served. So along with Andrew, James, and John, Peter fades out of the picture. It might be thought that Matthew's substituting "Peter" for "Simon" and mentioning Peter as the house owner while the other disciples go unmentioned somehow highlights Peter.[3] But the substitution merely reflects "the one called Peter" in 4:18, where there was no indication of Jesus' conferring on Simon an honorific name; and the mention of Peter as the house owner simply prepares for the healing of his mother-in-law.[4]

Jr., *A Critical and Exegetical Commentary on the Gospel according to Saint Matthew* (3 vols.; ICC; Edinburgh: T. & T. Clark, 1988-1997), 2:623-25. Davies and Allison ask whether the present tense in "You are Peter" does not "point to an event taking place as Jesus speaks." But the verb "are" references a current state of being, not an event. Davies and Allison also argue that "no one else in the story uses 'Peter' until [Jesus does in] 16.17." Only Matthew the narrator does. But when he does, there is no indication of a name-*giving*, only of a name-*recognizing*. Besides, Matthew's audience should not be expected to make a careful distinction between characters in the story and the narrator. Audiences tend to merge a narrator right into his or her story.

3. So Syreeni, "Peter as Character and Symbol," 123, though he recognizes that other features of Matthew's text "make Peter's explicit role . . . even more marginal than in Mark's narrative." Actually, Peter plays no *role* at all in Matt 8:14-15.

4. That Peter has two names, owns a house entered by Jesus, and through marriage has a mother-in-law living or staying in his house does make him a more "round" character

Peter — False Disciple and Apostate according to Saint Matthew

Matthew 10:2-4 (par. Mark 3:16-19; Luke 6:13d-16)

In contrast with 8:14-15, Peter attains some prominence in 10:2-4. Here, as elsewhere in the NT, he heads a list of the twelve apostles. But without parallel elsewhere, Matthew also gives Peter the description "first" (πρῶτος, which might make a wordplay with Πέτρος[5]). On the other hand, Matthew replaces the statement "And he [Jesus] put on Simon [the] name 'Peter'" (Mark 3:16) with the phrase "Simon, the one called 'Peter.'" Echoing 4:18 exactly, this replacement takes away any honorific name-giving by Jesus; and the advancement of Andrew from fourth place (so Mark 3:17-18) to second place with "and Andrew his brother" (so too Luke 6:14), which also echoes 4:18 exactly (for which Luke has no parallel), lessens the concentration on Peter[6] and forestalls an interpretation of Peter as the chronologically first disciple called by Jesus. For Andrew was called at the very same time.[7] At this point, then, Peter's

---

than his fellow disciples, but does not speak well or ill of him. His prominence in these respects leans in neither direction. On his own initiative Jesus enters more than once into synagogues full of antagonistic crowds (12:9-14; 13:53-58). Since those entries do not imply the worthiness of these synagogues, it seems doubtful to say his entering "on his initiative ... Peter's house implies that Peter's household is worthy of Jesus' presence" (against Burnett, "Characterization in Matthew," 17). Peter Dschulnigg notes the contrast with Jesus' not entering the house of the "heidnischen" centurion in 8:5-13 ("Gestalt und Funktion," 163). But there it was the centurion who declared himself unworthy to have Jesus enter. Jesus declared himself quite happy to enter the house of this heathen: "I will come and heal him [the centurion's servant]" (8:7).

5. Augustine Stock, "Is Matthew's Presentation of Peter Ironic?" *BTB* 17 (1987): 67-68, in dependence on B. Van Iersel.

6. Against Becker, *Simon Petrus im Urchristentum*, 81-82.

7. Correctly, Theodor Zahn, *Das Evangelium des Matthäus* (3rd ed.; Kommentar zum Neuen Testament 1; Leipzig: Deichert, 1910), 394; Paul Gaechter, *Das Matthäus Evangelium* (Innsbruck: Tyrolia, 1963), 318; Hubert Frankemölle, *Matthäus* (2 vols.; Düsseldorf: Patmos, 1994-1997), 2:74, 218-19; Burnett, "Characterization in Matthew," 19; Davies and Allison, *Matthew*, 2:154; Ulrich Luz, *Matthew 8–20*, 367; John P. Meier, *A Marginal Jew: Rethinking the Historical Jesus* (3 vols.; ABRL; New York: Doubleday, 2001), 3:222. An astonishingly large number of interpreters mistakenly posit a chronological firstness for Peter. They include, among others, P. Hoffmann, "Der Petrus-Primat im Matthäusevangelium," in *Neues Testament und Kirche* (ed. J. Gnilka; Freiburg: Herder, 1974), 108-9; Rudolf Pesch, *Simon-Petrus*, 9, 141, 143 (though see pp. 15-21 for an inclusion of Andrew); Pesch, *Die biblischen Grundlagen des Primats*, 25-29, 31, 96-97, 106; Perkins, *Peter*, 66; Syreeni, "Peter as Character and Symbol," 125; Hans Kvalbein, "Authorization of Peter," 610; Cassidy, *Four Times Peter*, 5, 71; Wolfgang Kraus, "Zur Ekklesiologie des Matthäusevangeliums," in *The Gospel of Matthew at the Crossroads of Early Christianity* (ed. Donald Senior; BETL 243;

firstness remains undefined. As often remarked, the absence of "second," "third," and so on down the list of apostles probably rules out a reference to mere firstness on the list. Such firstness is so obvious that pointing it out would seem superfluous, if not demeaning to an audience.[8] Perhaps, then, "first" looks forward to Peter's prominence among the Twelve and functioning as their spokesman, even their leader, at least the first among equals, with a possible anticipation of 16:17-19: Peter as the Rock who has the keys of the kingdom and the authority of binding and loosening (cf. the substitution of "great" in Matt 22:36 for "first" in Mark 12:28, and the pairing of "great" and "first" in Matt 22:38).[9] We shall see when arriving at that passage. Seemingly overlooked, however, has been the ominous use of "first" in Matt 19:29-30, where the many "first ones" who "will be last ones" contrast with those who "will inherit eternal life," as illustrated by the uniquely Matthean parable in 20:1-16, which begins with an explanatory γάρ, "For," and attracts a correctly interpretive variant reading at the end of v. 16: "For many are called, but few are chosen" (see the text-critically secure 22:14, where not being chosen means damnation according to 22:13 [cf. Luke 13:23-30]). Especially in view of Peter's failure in 26:69-75 to heed Jesus' command in 10:26-31 not to fear antagonists, the possibility that "first Peter" in 10:2 augurs for Peter the fate of the first who will be last, and therefore lost, should be kept open.

Leuven: Peeters, 2011), 230; Wolfgang Wiefel, *Das Evangelium nach Matthäus* (THKNT; Leipzig: Evangelische Verlagsanstalt, 1998), 190. Jack Dean Kingsbury posits a chronological firstness for Peter in the framework of salvation history ("The Figure of Peter in Matthew's Gospel as a Theological Problem," *JBL* 98 [1979]: 70-71, 74, 76, 80-82). So too Burnett, "Characterization in Matthew," 19.

8. See, e.g., M-J. Lagrange, *Évangile selon Saint Matthieu* (7th ed.; EBib; Paris: Gabalda, 1948), 195; Alan Hugh McNeile, *The Gospel According to St. Matthew* (New York: St. Martin's, 1965), 131; Michael J. Wilkins, *The Concept of Disciple in Matthew's Gospel as Reflected in the Use of the Term Μαθητής* (NovTSup 59; Leiden: Brill, 1988), 201.

9. So Alfred Plummer, *An Exegetical Commentary on the Gospel according to St. Matthew* (1915; repr., Grand Rapids: Baker, 1982), 147; Brown et al., *Peter in the New Testament*, 105; W. F. Albright and C. S. Mann, *Matthew: Introduction, Translation, and Notes* (AB; Garden City, N.Y.: Doubleday, 1971), 117; Walter Grundmann, *Das Evangelium nach Matthäus* (2nd ed.; THKNT; Berlin: Evangelische Verlagsanstalt, 1971), 287; Wilkins, *Concept of Disciple*, 201; Davies and Allison, *Matthew*, 2:154; Syreeni, "Peter as Character and Symbol," 125; Meier, *A Marginal Jew*, 3:222; and esp. Samuel Byrskog, *Jesus the Only Teacher: Didactic Authority and Transmission in Ancient Israel, Ancient Judaism and the Matthean Community* (ConBNT 24; Stockholm: Almqvist & Wiksell International, 1994), 250-51; R. T. France, *The Gospel of Matthew* (NICNT; Grand Rapids: Eerdmans, 2007), 378.

Peter — False Disciple and Apostate according to Saint Matthew

Matthew 14:22-33 (par. Mark 6:45-52; John 6:16-21)

To the story of Jesus' walking on the sea (Matt 14:22-27) Matthew adds without parallel the episode of Peter's walking on the waters, sinking into them, and being rescued by Jesus (vv. 28-33). How does Peter fare here in the way Matthew presents him, and in the way Matthew's audience is likely to have perceived him? In view of nondisciples' addressing Jesus with "Lord" (8:2, 6, 8; 15:22, 25, 27; 17:15; 20:30, 31, 33) and in view of false disciples' addressing Jesus at the Last Judgment with "Lord, Lord" (7:21-22; 25:11 [this latter unparalleled]), it is too much of a stretch to regard Peter's addressing him with "Lord" (14:28, 30) as an implied confession of faith in Jesus' deity or messiahship. Peter will not confess Jesus' messiahship and divine sonship till 16:17-19, and it will be the other disciples who confess the divine sonship here in 14:33. The present address arises out of fear and doubt (vv. 26-28). For Peter's "*if* you are [Jesus]" (v. 28) questions Jesus' immediately preceding assurance, "I am [Jesus]" (v. 27), so that the episode begins with Peter's doubt just as it will proceed with it in vv. 30-31.[10] "If you are [Jesus]" may even recall the devil's first two temptations of Jesus, which began, "If you are the Son of God" (Matt 4:3, 6), so that Peter's request, "Command me to come to you on the waters," looks like the devil's tempting Jesus to test his divine sonship with a stunt (4:5-6). Only here Peter would be testing Jesus' self-identification with a

---

10. See Jeffrey A. Gibbs, *Matthew 11:2–20:34* (Concordia Commentary; Saint Louis: Concordia, 2010), 762 n. 21, against the meaning, "*since* you are [Jesus]," for which an introductory ἐπεί or ἐπειδή rather than εἰ would be likely, especially given the fear of Peter and his fellow disciples (against Carsten Peter Thiede, *Simon Peter: From Galilee to Rome* [Exeter: Paternoster, 1956], 29-30; also against Cassidy's statement, "Seemingly Peter knows that it is Jesus" [*Four Times Peter*, 71]). On Peter's doubting right from the start, see John Calvin, *Commentary on a Harmony of the Evangelists: Matthew, Mark, and Luke* (trans. William Pringle; 3 vols.; Grand Rapids: Eerdmans, 1949), 2:240; Syreeni, "Peter as Character and Symbol," 127 n. 48. By inferring Peter's "enthusiasm for Jesus" and Jesus' approval of Peter's request when saying, "Come," Wiarda overlooks the doubt in "if you are [Jesus]" (*Peter in the Gospels*, 91-93; cf. Boxall's interpreting Peter in this passage as both a positive example and a negative example [*Discovering Matthew*, 141-42]). But Wiarda is on target in noting that Jesus' later rebuke "comes in a climactic position following the description of Jesus rescuing Peter." On the interpretation of Peter's asking to walk on the waters as blasphemous because only divinity does so appropriately, see Rachel Nicholls, *Walking on the Water: Reading Mt. 14:22-23 in the Light of Its Wirkungsgeschichte* (Biblical Interpretation Series 90; Leiden: Brill, 2008), 194. Nicholls downplays Peter's doubt in favor of "the beginning of a new adjustment to a bigger picture of who Jesus is" (p. 91).

stunt of Peter's own.¹¹ In any case, it goes too far to cast Peter's request as an admirable example of discipular desire to obey Jesus' commands. The content of the request bespeaks doubt more than desire, because the desire arises out of the doubt.

Jesus' enabling Peter to walk on the waters has the purpose, then, of erasing Peter's doubt. But as shown by Peter's subsequently starting to drown and by Jesus' following question, "You of little faith, why did you doubt?" the doubt persisted — or at least revived.¹² Moreover, Peter's becoming "afraid" at seeing "the strong wind" constituted a disobedience of Jesus' earlier command not to be afraid (v. 27); and Jesus' statement in Matt 18:6 that it is advantageous for whoever "snares" (σκανδαλίσῃ) one of the little ones who believe in him to have an upper millstone hung around his neck and "be drowned [καταποντισθῇ] in the depth of the sea" may retrospectively highlight a danger of damnation in Peter's starting "to drown" (καταποντίζεσθαι).¹³ "He screamed" (ἔκραξεν) recollects v. 26, where the disciples "screamed from fear" (ἀπὸ τοῦ φόβου ἔκραξαν). This addition of disobedient fear to doubt overwhelms whatever faith in Jesus' power to save him may be implied in Peter's screaming for rescue.¹⁴ To stop him

---

11. Syreeni notes this curious echo and suggests that it prepares the reader for Peter's playing the tempter's role in Matt 16:22-23 ("Peter as Character and Symbol," 127). See also France, *Matthew*, 567-68.

12. Warren Carter comments perceptively that Peter "did not have enough faith in Jesus' word to *persevere*" (*Matthew and the Margins: A Sociopolitical and Religious Reading* [The Bible and Liberation Series; Maryknoll, N.Y.: Orbis, 2000], 312 [emphasis added]). Cf. Matt. 24:13.

13. See Gundry, *Matthew*, 361-62.

14. Does Matthew want his audience to sympathize with Peter's fear of the strong wind (as thought by Wiarda, *Peter in the Gospels*, 93-94)? Hardly, given the following citation of Jesus' rebuke, which also undermines the notion that "for Matthew, the disciple in this life is always caught between faith and doubt" (John P. Meier, *Matthew* [New Testament Message 3; Wilmington, Del.: Michael Glazier, 1980], 165). That little faith is not distinctive of Peter in Matthew (see 6:30; 8:26; 16:8; 17:20) does not lessen its danger. Correctly, "Jesus is there to save [Peter] *despite* inadequate faith" (Davies and Allison, *Matthew*, 2:509 [emphasis original]). Incredibly, Udo Schnelle writes that Peter's "conduct is held up as a didactic example of the *right* relation of faith and doubt" (*Theology of the New Testament* [trans. M. Eugene Boring; Grand Rapids: Baker Academic, 2009], 451 [emphasis added]). Almost as incredibly, Luz writes that though Matthew does not declare doubt essential to faith, "neither does he condemn it" (*Matthew 8–20*, 321). Lagrange downplays the seriousness of little faith by writing that Jesus rebukes Peter's doubt "sans plus" (*Matthieu*, 294), as does Zahn with a parenthetical exclamatory phrase: "Der Kleinglaube (nicht der Unglaube!) des Petrus wird getadelt" (*Matthäus*, 308). Because the verb for doubting, δίσταξεν, means "to be of

from drowning, Jesus takes hold of him. This rescue is often considered a symbol of ultimate salvation for disciples who out of little faith succumb to fear and doubt.[15] But the verb of salvation that Peter used (σῶσόν με) is not repeated in regard to Jesus' action (rather, ἐπελάβετο αὐτοῦ, "took hold of him"), so that Jesus' question, "You of little faith, to what end did you doubt?" casts doubt on such a symbolism and — in view of the possibility that Peter will be among those who doubt Jesus' resurrection (Matt 28:17) — leaves open the questions of reinvigorated faith and ultimate salvation. Yes, little faith does not equate with a total lack of faith. But is little faith enough to count as saving faith (cf. 10:22; 24:13)? Whatever the answer, Jesus' last word underscores Peter's little faith and doubt, not faith in Jesus' power to save him from drowning. There is not even partial praise, only rebuke.[16]

Though Jesus and Peter get into the boat, "the ones in the boat" are most naturally understood as the disciples *already* there and hence exclusive of Peter as well as Jesus.[17] Hence Peter is not included among those

---

two minds," France distinguishes between Peter's trustful mind, consisting in "intellectual conviction," and distrustful mind, consisting in "the evidence of his senses" when seeing the strong wind (*Matthew*, 570-71). But he had *seen* Jesus walking on the sea, *heard* Jesus' command to come, and *felt* himself walking on the waters. So the evidence of his senses inclined at least as much toward faith as toward doubt.

15. So, e.g., Gundry, *Matthew*, 300; Pesch, *Simon-Petrus*, 136-37, 141-42; Cassidy, *Four Times Peter*, 220.

16. For εἰς τί as meaning not "why?/because of what?" but "to what end?/what was the point [of doubting on having come so far]?" see D. A. Carson, "Matthew," in *The Expositor's Bible Commentary* (ed. Tremper Longman III and David E. Garland; 13 vols.; rev. ed.; Grand Rapids: Zondervan, 2010), 9:395; Robert H. Gundry, *Commentary on the New Testament* (Grand Rapids: Baker Academic, 2010), 66.

17. So Syreeni, "Peter as Character and Symbol," 126; John Paul Heil, *Jesus Walking on the Sea: Meaning and Gospel Functions in Matt 14:22-33, Mark 6:45-52, and John 6:15b-21* (AnBib 87; Rome: Biblical Institute Press, 1981), 66; against Wiefel, *Matthäus*, 278. Frankemölle thinks it unclear whether Peter is included among "the ones in the boat" (*Matthäus*, 2:200). Contrastively, J. Andrew Overman avers that "they" who got into the boat included the other disciples as well as Peter, even though those disciples had not gotten out of the boat and as though "they" were not just Jesus and Peter (*Church and Community in Crisis: The Gospel according to Matthew* [The New Testament in Context; Valley Forge, Pa.: Trinity Press International, 1996], 221-22). But treating Peter as a symbol of all disciples fails to justify such an understanding of this Matthean text. Gibbs favors the translation "and they worshiped him in the boat" (oἱ as the subject) over the usual translation "and the ones in the boat worshiped him" (oἱ as governing the prepositional phrase) (*Matthew 11:2–20:34*, 758). Pesch thinks that Jesus' enabling Peter to walk on the waters, not just Jesus' doing so, induced the other disciples to confess Jesus as God's Son (*Die biblischen Grundlagen*, 35).

who of their own accord presently confess Jesus as "truly God's Son." For Peter, that confession awaits 16:16-17, where Jesus will attribute it to divine revelation rather than to "flesh and blood," such as Peter's or that of the other disciples.[18]

Matthew 15:12-20 (par. Mark 7:17-23)

In 15:12 Matthew replaces the disciples' inquiry about "the parable" concerning what does and does not defile a person (so Mark 7:17) with their inquiry whether Jesus knows that the Pharisees were offended by his parabolic statement. Jesus' answer in Matt 15:13-14, which includes a description of the Pharisees as "blind guides," implies that he does know they were offended. Thus his knowledge concerning the Pharisees highlights by contrast the next-mentioned ignorance of the disciples concerning the parable. According to Mark 7:17 "the disciples" inquired about the parable, but Matt 15:15 makes Peter alone their spokesman. Jesus' answer, "Are you [plural] too still ignorant?" (Matt 15:16 par. Mark 7:18 with one difference) references the disciples' ignorance; but Peter's ignorance stands out because he took the lead in betraying ignorance. In both Matthew and Mark, "you too" draws a parallel between the disciples and the Pharisees in regard to their shared ignorance. But Matthew replaces Mark's "Are you too *thus* [οὕτως] ignorant?" with "Are you too *still* [ἀκμήν] ignorant?" Mark's οὕτως, "thus/in this way," has to do with manner and probably attributes the disciples' ignorance to the same regard of "the elders' tradition" (Matt 15:2 par. Mark 7:5) that the Pharisees and scribes have and that contradicts "the commandment/word of God" (Matt 15:3, 6; par. Mark 7:8, 13). Matthew's adverbial accusative ἀκμήν, "still," has to do with chronology, not manner; comes from ἀκμή, "acme, the highest point of anything"; occurs seldom; and appears for the first time in the Greek text of Jesus' answer.[19] For these reasons it carries a great deal of emphasis. It was *high* time for Peter and his fellow disciples to have reached an understanding

---

18. Cf. the comment of Eduard Schweizer that "this confession [of the other disciples in 14:33] in fact depreciates the confession of Peter in 16:16" (*The Good News According to Matthew* [trans. David E. Green; Atlanta: John Knox Press, 1975], 321). It is unclear how Grundmann concludes that Matthew converts the disciples' ignorance (so Mark 6:52) into Peter's little faith (*Matthäus*, 367) — rather, into the other disciples' confession of Jesus' divine sonship.

19. See France, *Matthew*, 574 n. 11.

that would have made Jesus' explanation of the parable unnecessary. So Matthew makes Peter representative of blameworthy ignorance.[20] "It is exceptional for Matthew to state that the disciples do not understand."[21] Usually, in fact, he turns their ignorance into understanding (see, e.g., Matt 13:51; 16:12; 17:13, 23; and pars.).[22]

Worsening this blameworthy ignorance, spearheaded as it is by Peter, is Matthew's having inserted — without parallel and between the disciples' question in v. 12 and Peter's request in v. 15 — Jesus' statements in vv. 13-14, "Every plant that my heavenly Father did not plant will be uprooted. Leave them [the Pharisees]! They are blind guides. And if a blind person is leading a blind person, both will fall into a pit." That is to say, Jesus compares the Pharisees to plants rather like the tares that will be uprooted at the Last Judgment and thrown into the fire of eternal punishment (Matt 13:24-30, 36-43).[23] This insertion exacerbates to the nth degree the parallel between Peter's and the other disciples' ignorance and that of the Pharisees and scribes. Therefore attempts to laud Peter as the spokesman of the disciples and as the primary recipient and guarantor of Jesus' teaching — these attempts fail to convince.[24]

---

20. Against Gundry, *Matthew*, 308.

21. Schweizer, *Matthew*, 327. But Schweizer mistakenly says that Matthew has turned Jesus' statement in Mark into a question and thus toned down the rebuke, so that "Jesus is not horrified or dismayed (as in Mark) that they [the disciples] don't [understand]." Mark's text contains a question just as Matthew's does, however.

22. See also Gundry, *Matthew*, 683, and pages listed for "Understanding."

23. For more detail, see Gundry, *Commentary on the New Testament*, 68.

24. Correctly, Daniel Patte, *The Gospel according to Matthew: A Structural Commentary on Matthew's Faith* (Philadelphia: Fortress, 1987), 219; Wilkins, *Concept of Disciple*, 184-85; Syreeni, "Peter as Character and Symbol," 127-28; against Wolfgang Schenk, "Das 'Matthäusevangelium als Petrusevangelium," 70; Pesch, *Simon-Petrus*, 142-43; Davies and Allison, *Matthew*, 2:534; Perkins, *Peter*, 67.

CHAPTER 3

Peter in Matthew 16:13-23

Matthew 16:13-20 (par. Mark 8:27-30; Luke 9:18-21)

Though Matt 16:13-23 centers on Jesus as the Christ and God's Son and on the necessity of his coming death and resurrection, Peter figures in the passage even more prominently than usual.[1] Since the present treatment deals with the way Matthew portrays Peter, questions of historicity, integrity, and chronological misplacement need no discussion here.[2] More

---

1. See the comment of Béda Rigaux that of the Peter-primary texts in Matt 16:16-19; Luke 22:31-32; John 21:1-14, "the first is by far the most important and most crucial" ("St. Peter in Contemporary Exegesis," in *Progress and Decline in the History of Church Renewal* [Concilium 27; New York: Paulist Press, 1967], 166). For hermeneutical analysis from a conservative Protestant point of view, see Gerhard Maier, "The Church in the Gospel of Matthew: Hermeneutical Analysis of the Current Debate," in *Biblical Interpretation and the Church: Text and Context* (ed. D. A. Carson; Exeter: Paternoster, 1984), 45-63.

2. For representative defenses of authenticity, see Cullmann, *Peter*, 193; Gaechter, *Matthäus*, 522-23; Michael J. Wilkins, "Peter's Declaration concerning Jesus' Identity in Caesarea Philippi," in *Key Events in the Life of the Historical Jesus: A Collaborative Exploration of Context and Coherence* (ed. Darrell L. Bock and Robert L. Webb; Grand Rapids: Eerdmans, 2009), 293-381; Benjamin L. Merkle, "The Meaning of Ἐκκλησία in Matthew 16:18 and 18:17," *BSac* 167 (2010): 281-91. For representative arguments against symmetry and Semitisms as necessarily indicating authenticity, see Kähler, "Zur Form- und Traditionsgeschichte," 38-40; Bernard P. Robinson, "Peter and His Successors: Tradition and Redaction in Matthew 16:17-19," *JSNT* 21 (1984): 86-87; Gundry, *Matthew*, 331-37. Mark Adam Elliott provides a survey of older debate over authenticity (*The Survivors of Israel: A Reconsideration of the Theology of Pre-Christian Judaism* [Grand Rapids: Eerdmans, 2000], 642-48). See also the survey in Davies and Allison, *Matthew*, 2:603-15. Tord Fornberg's hypothesis of a pre-Matthean portrayal of Peter as a high priestly figure is likewise irrelevant to the present

particularly, since Matthew is writing for an audience who need Greek translations of Semitic expressions (see the introductory comments above on pp. 4-5), questions of Aramaic substrata need little or no discussion. What counts is what Matthew expected an audience competent in Greek but not in Aramaic to understand from his Greek text.

In v. 16 Matthew refers to "Simon Peter." The use of "Simon" prepares for Jesus' addressing Peter with "Simon bar Jonah" (v. 17, unique to Matthew along with vv. 18-19). Matthew reserves "Peter" for Jesus' statement "You are Peter" (v. 18).[3] That statement would sound redundant if Matthew had used in v. 16 the full expression "Simon, the one called Peter," which appeared in 4:18; 10:2.

Matthew borrows Peter's confession, "You are the Christ," from Mark 8:29, and then adds "the Son of the living God" (v. 16). For its part, this addition conforms the confession to that of the disciples other than Peter in 14:33.[4] In effect, then, Matthew has Peter playing catch-up to his fellow disciples. In v. 17 Jesus responds by pronouncing Peter "Blessed," but not because Peter recognized on his own the messiahship and divine sonship of Jesus, as the other disciples *had* recognized Jesus' divine sonship on their own in 14:33. Ἀληθῶς and the prior position of θεοῦ in those disciples' confession, **ἀληθῶς θεοῦ** υἱὸς εἶ, "*Truly* you are *God's* Son," actually carried more emphasis than does Peter's confession, σὺ εἶ ... ὁ υἱὸς τοῦ θεοῦ, "You are ... the Son of God," to which the addition of τοῦ ζῶντος, "the living," lessens emphasis on "the Son" in favor of emphasis on "God" as well as conforming to OT and other Jewish usage, e.g., in 26:63; Deut 5:26; Josh 3:10; 1 Sam 17:26; Ps 42:2; Jer 10:10; Hos 1:10; *Jub.* 1:25; *Sib. Or.* 3:763; *T. Job* 37:2; *T. Sol.* 1:13).

Jesus attributes Peter's confession to a revelation by Jesus' Father in heaven.[5] So Peter gets no credit, and the Father in heaven is identified as

---

concern with Matthew's portrayal of Peter in 16:17-19 ("The Figure of Peter in Matthew and 2 Peter," *Indian Theological Studies* 32 [1995]: 237-49).

3. See the comments above on 4:18-20 and Gundry, *Matthew,* 334-35; Bockmuehl, *Simon Peter in Scripture and Memory,* 21-23, 26, 71, that Matthew does not have Jesus giving Simon the name "Peter" here because Simon confessed Jesus to be the Christ — against comments such as those by Cullmann (*Peter,* 22), Kvalbein ("Authorization of Peter," 152), and Bart D. Ehrman (*Peter, Paul, and Mary Magdalene: The Followers of Jesus in History and Legend* [New York: Oxford University Press, 2006], 15).

4. See the comments above on 14:33 that Peter did not join in the confession there.

5. Cf. Matt 11:25-27, though there Jesus says nothing about the Father's revealing the Son (against Boxall, *Discovering Matthew,* 140; also against Frankemölle, who extends the Father's revelation to all the Twelve [*Matthäus,* 2:200]). Surprisingly, Leopold Sab-

Jesus' rather than Peter's, as is appropriate in view of Jesus as "the Son of the living God." "Flesh and blood did not reveal [this] to you" furthers the emphasis on God as the revealer in opposition to any insight on Peter's part. Not even hearing the confession of Jesus' divine sonship by the "flesh and blood" of the other disciples in 14:33 had informed Peter successfully (cf. Gal 1:15-17, where Paul says that because of divine revelation he did not consult with "flesh and blood" such as that of those who were apostles before him). Peter was too obtuse. As in the later case of Paul, it took a direct revelation from God the Father to convince him that Jesus was the Christ, the Son of the living God.[6] Because of this revelation, Jesus pronounces a beatitude on Peter. But lest the beatitude be given too much weight, it should be noted that the disciples on whose eyes and ears Jesus pronounced a beatitude because they see and hear (13:16) included Judas Iscariot. There and here in 16:17, "Blessed" means "Privileged." In both instances, ultimate fate is determined by what is done with the privilege, not by the privilege as such.[7]

Still in v. 17 Βαριωνᾶ, usually translated "Bar Jonah," gets no explanation or translation into Greek and therefore remains mysterious in meaning to an Aramaic-ignorant audience; consequently it functions as a mere substitute for "Peter."[8] "And I say to you" (v. 18) puts Jesus' following

---

ourin opines that "Peter needed no special revelation to recognize Jesus' messiahship" (*The Gospel according to St Matthew* [2 vols.; Bandra, Bombay: St Paul Publications, 1982], 2:671).

6. The alternation between "Christ" and "Son of God" thus far in Matthew demonstrates the basic synonymity of these two terms (see 1:1, 16, 17; 2:4; 4:3, 6; 8:29; 11:2; 14:33; plus later passages, esp. 26:63) (against Kvalbein, who suggests that "the Christ" in 16:16 is an advance on "God's Son" in 14:33 ["Authorization of Peter," 151]). As do others, Larry R. Helyer observes that the apostles' confession in 14:33 "seems to upstage Peter's confession at Caesarea Philippi" (*The Life and Witness of Peter* [Downers Grove, Ill.: InterVarsity Press, 2012], 42 n. 28). France tries to blunt this observation by describing the confession in 14:33 as instinctive, and the one in 16:16 as deliberate (*Matthew*, 571). But Matthew's Jesus describes Peter's confession as derivative, not deliberate (cf. Becker's argument that "in keinem Fall will Matthäus einer Oberhoheit des Petrus über die anderen Apostel" [*Simon Petrus im Urchristentum*, 104]). Because of the confession in 14:33, Davies and Allison wonder why the confession in 16:16 "is treated as a break-through attributable only to divine revelation" and resort to suggesting an imperfect assimilation by Matthew of two different traditions (*Matthew*, 2:621).

7. Against Brown et al., *Peter in the New Testament*, 87, 89, 106-7, where Jesus is mistakenly said to have lauded Peter.

8. But see Gundry, *Matthew*, 332, and Robinson, "Peter and His Successors," 80-91, for a possible theological implication underlying "Bar Jonah"; and for a general discussion,

statement in parallel with the Father's revelation. As regularly noted, σὺ εἶ Πέτρος, "You are Peter," parallels σὺ εἶ ὁ χριστός, "You are the Christ," though the parallel is inexact because "Peter" is a personal name whereas "the Christ" is a title. There follows a wordplay on Πέτρος: καὶ ἐπὶ ταύτῃ τῇ πέτρᾳ οἰκοδομήσω μου τὴν ἐκκλησίαν, "and on this rock I will build my church."[9]

A wordplay does not require synonymity between different words, or even between words only slightly different from each other (as are Πέτρος and πέτρα). In a wordplay such words may carry different meanings, even completely different meanings. So other things being equal, πέτρα could either mean the same as Πέτρος despite their difference in gender (feminine and masculine, respectively),[10] or carry a different meaning despite their sharing the same stem (πετρ-). In both instances the wordplay would work.[11] So statements to the effect that the wordplay works, or works well, only in an underlying Aramaic ("You are כיפא

Gérard Claudel, *La Confession de Pierre: Trajectoire d'une Péricope Évangélique* (EBib n.s. 10; Paris: Gabalda, 1988), 327-30.

9. "It has been suggested," notes Craig Evans, "that the naming of Simon and the declaration that he was the foundation of a new people of God follow an Old Testament pattern. Abraham and Jacob are the only persons in the Hebrew Bible whose names are changed [Gen 17:1-8; 32:22-32].... Of special interest is that the change of their names was related to their roles as founders of a new nation, or new people" (*Matthew* [NCBC; New York: Cambridge University Press, 2012], 313-14). Evans goes on to say that "only Abraham is later associated with a rock foundation," and cites in support Isa 51:1-2: "Look to the rock from which you were hewn, and to the quarry from which you were dug. Look to Abraham your father and to Sarah who bore you" (see also Davies and Allison, *Matthew*, 2:623-24). Several difficulties attend this suggestion: (1) Unlike the other evangelists, Matthew does not say that Jesus gave Simon the nickname "Peter" on this or any other occasion. (2) It is disputed whether Jesus pronounces Peter the rock-foundation of the church (see, e.g., Evans's own identification of "this rock" with "Peter's confession and leadership" rather than with Peter himself, an identification already broached by none other than Pope Gregory the Great in his exhortation, "Establish your life on the rock of the Church, which is to say, on the confession of St. Peter" [*Epistle* 4.33, quoted by Demacopoulos in his book *The Invention of Peter*, 149]). (3) Isaiah's rock quarry hardly counts as a foundation. (4) The inclusion of Sarah in Isaiah's rock-quarry has no counterpart in Jesus' statement. (5) Isaiah's reference to Sarah's giving birth interprets the rock quarry in terms of parentage rather than building (so, correctly, Sabourin, *Matthew*, 2:672).

10. See McNeile's statement, "Πέτρος 'stone' is not intended to differ in meaning [from πέτρα], but was chosen because the masc. was more suitable for a man's name.... Thus the word-play need not have originated only in the Greek" (*Matthew*, 241).

11. For further discussion of wordplay, see Chrys C. Caragounis, *Peter and the Rock* (BZNW 58; Berlin: de Gruyter, 1989), 44-57, 108-12; Byrskog, *Jesus the Only Teacher*, 250.

['Rock'], and on this כיפא ['rock'] . . ."), do not stand scrutiny.¹² Neither do statements to the effect that the wordplay works, or works well, only in Greek.¹³

Debates continue over whether כיפא means bedrock, suitable for a foundation, and over whether v. 18, or vv. 17-19, rest on an Aramaic substratum; but for Matthew's present text, that debate is irrelevant to an audience that does not know Aramaic. (Matthew could have quoted Jesus as saying, σὺ εἶ Κηφᾶς,¹⁴ ὅ ἐστιν μεθερμηνευόμενον πέτρα [cf. 1:23], καὶ ἐπὶ σοὶ οἰκοδομήσω μου τὴν ἐκκλησίαν, "You are Cephas, which translated means 'bedrock,' and on you I will build my church," but Matthew did not quote Jesus thus.) Debate continues also over whether Πέτρος and πέτρα are interchangeable in meaning (so that Πέτρος as well as πέτρα can refer to bedrock), or whether Πέτρος means, exclu-

---

12. Against, e.g., John A. Broadus, *Commentary on the Gospel of Matthew* (An American Commentary on the New Testament; Philadelphia: American Baptist Publication Society, 1886), 355; Rudolf Bultmann, *The History of the Synoptic Tradition* (trans. John Marsh; rev. ed.; Peabody, Mass.: Hendrickson, 1963), 139. J.-M. Van Cangh argues that an Aramaic wordplay on one word (כיפא) with two meanings ("stone" and "rock") "n'est pas évident en grec" (*Les sources judaïques de Nouveau Testament* [BETL 204; Leuven: Leuven University Press, 2008], 608 [with M. Van Esbroeck]). Similarly, Grundmann says that "ein Wortspiel, dessen Sinn freilich allein im Aramäischen rein erscheint, insofern zweimal das Wort kepha verwendet wird, während die griechische Übersetzung zwischen dem vorher nicht zu belegenden Petros und der πέτρα differenzieren muss" (*Matthäus*, 387; so too Joachim Gnilka, *Das Matthäusevangelium* [2 vols.; HTKNT; Freiburg: Herder, 1988], 2:48; Barry D. Smith, *Jesus' Twofold Teaching about the Kingdom of God* [Sheffield: Sheffield Phoenix Press, 2009], 226 n. 151; Meier, *Matthew*, 179; Cullmann, *Peter*, 212).

13. Against, e.g., Peter Lampe, "Das Spiel mit dem Petrusnamen — Matt. XVI. 18," *NTS* 25 (1978/1979): 240-43; Lampe, "Peter (the Disciple)," in *Religion Past and Present: Encyclopedia of Theology and Religion* (ed. Hans Dieter Betz et al.; 13 vols.; Leiden: Brill, 2011), 10:2; Becker, *Simon Petrus im Urchristentum*, 87; Ruth Schäfer, *Paulus bis zum Apostelkonzil* (WUNT 2/179; Tübingen: Mohr Siebeck, 2004), 218; Luz, *Matthew 8–20*, 359; Caragounis, *Peter and the Rock*, 48. Caragounis observes, "It is obvious that a word-play is inconceivable when the same word is used twice with the same meaning," as in "the supposed כיפא-כיפא." To this observation proponents of an Aramaic wordplay might retort that the first כיפא would have functioned, whether or not for the first time, as a personal name, the second differently as a common noun (cf. the overly confident statement, "On that [Aramaic] level, precisely because of the Aramaic identity of *Kephā'/kephā'*, there can be no doubt that the rock on which the church was to be built was Peter" [Brown et al., *Peter in the New Testament*, 92]). If a second כיפא referred to Simon and if πέτρος could at least occasionally mean bedrock, it might be asked why Matthew's text does not read ἐπὶ τούτῳ τῷ πέτρῳ. Dschulnigg thinks πέτρα *interprets* Πέτρος as bedrock (*Petrus im Neuen Testament*, 40).

14. -ς is added for the Greek transliteration, as elsewhere in the NT.

sively or usually, "stone," whereas πέτρα means, exclusively or usually, "bedrock."[15]

To rehearse here those lexicographical debates would likely prove to be labor lost — and beside the point, given what follows in the present discussion. More decisive is the switch from the second-person pronoun "*You are Peter*" to the third-person nominal phrase "on *this bedrock,*" rather than sticking to the second-person pronoun with "on *you,*" which would clearly imply the meaning "bedrock" for "Peter/Πέτρος." As it is, the switch implies a difference between Peter and the bedrock.[16] At the level of Matthew's Greek text, then, a wordplay does not require that Πέτρος and πέτρα have the same referent. Different referents could just as well play on the similarity of Πέτρος and πέτρα. Indeed, the contrast in genders and the shift from second person to third person favor a difference in referents.

Even more decisively, ἐπὶ ταύτῃ τῇ πέτρᾳ οἰκοδομήσω, "on this bedrock I will build," recalls the wise man in 7:24, ὅστις ᾠκοδόμησεν . . . ἐπὶ τὴν πέτραν, "who built . . . on the bedrock."[17] And what was that bedrock?

---

15. Important for the lexicographical debates are Joseph A. Fitzmyer, *To Advance the Gospel* (New York: Crossroad, 1981), 112-24; Fitzmyer, "The Meaning of the Aramaic Noun כפא/כיפא in the First Century and Its Significance for the Interpretation of Gospel Passages," in *"Il Verbo di Dio Vivo": Studi sul Nuovo Testamento in onore del Cardinale Albert Vanoye, S.I.* (AnBib 165; Rome: Pontifical Biblical Institute, 2007), 35-43; P. Lampe, "Das Spiel mit dem Petrusnamen," 227-45; Caragounis, *Peter and the Rock,* passim; Bockmuehl, *The Remembered Peter,* 148-57; Thomas Finley, "'Upon this Rock': Matthew 16:18 and the Aramaic Evidence," *Aramaic Studies* 4 (2006): 133-51.

16. See also Plummer, *Matthew,* 229 n. 1 ("If the promise had been absolutely personal and individual, we should have had ἐπί σοι rather than ἐπὶ ταύτῃ τῇ πέτρᾳ"); David Biven, "Matthew 16:18 — The Petros-Petra Wordplay: Greek, Aramaic, or Hebrew?" *Jerusalem Perspective* 46-47 (1994): 38 ("But if he [Peter] is the 'rock,' ταύτῃ is strange after the direct σὺ εἶ Π[έτρος]. It would be more natural if the Lord were speaking of him in the third person to the other disciples"); Cassidy, *Four Times Peter,* 38 ("Jesus could have clearly indicated Peter [by using 'on you'] had he wanted. The words 'and on this rock' following 'you are Peter' only make sense if Jesus was speaking *about* Peter to others. Since he is not, there must be a switch to a subject other than Peter"); P. Lampe, "Das Spiel mit dem Petrusnamen," 242 ("Man könnte genauso gut sagen: du bist Fels, *auf dir* . . ." [emphasis original]); Caragounis, *Peter and the Rock,* 88-90 ("In normal syntax a phrase like ἐπὶ ταύτῃ τῇ πέτρᾳ can only refer to something outside of the speaker and his interlocutor"). Caragounis goes on to suggest σὺ εἶ ὁ Πέτρος ἐφ' ᾧ οἰκοδομήσω . . . , "You are Peter, on whom I will build . . . ," as another way it could have been made clear that Peter is the church's foundation.

17. Against Joseph A. Burgess, *History of the Exegesis of Matthew 16:17-19 from 1781 to 1965* (Ann Arbor: Edwards Brothers, 1976), 19 n. 46, 58-59. The recollection of 7:24, where bedrock is clearly in view, undermines the interpretation of 16:18 by Davies and Allison that Jesus is speaking about the cornerstone of a foundation (*Matthew,* 2:626). Furthermore, the

It was μου τοὺς λόγους τούτους, "these my [Jesus'] words" (see also 7:26).[18] Not only do both passages feature building on bedrock. So too do both passages feature the demonstrative pronoun: "these" in 7:24, where it is distinctive of Matthew over against the parallel in Luke 6:47, and "this" in Matt 16:18. Given the shifts both from the masculine gender to the feminine gender and from the second person to the third, Matthew's audience will have naturally equated "*this* bedrock" with "the bedrock" which consisted of "*these* words" of Jesus.

It is argued against this equation that 16:18 is too far removed from 7:24 for Matthew's intended audience to have connected the two passages.[19] At least in part, this argument probably arises out of the modern practice of reading and studying only short sections of Scripture at a time, whereas ancient audiences normally listened to long stretches, even the whole of a book like Matthew, in a single session.[20] As a result, those audiences would still have in mind 7:24 when listening to 16:18. In fact, it takes less than an hour for an oral reading from the earlier passage to the later one. Even modern commentators who engage in piecemeal study often relate the two passages to each other, though unfortunately failing to reap the interpretive harvest that "this bedrock" refers to "these my words" of Jesus.[21]

---

wise man in 7:24 is an obedient *disciple* of Jesus, so that the house that the wise man builds cannot represent the church as a temple built by *Jesus*, a Solomonic son of David (against Michael Patrick Barber, "Jesus as the Davidic Temple Builder and Peter's Priestly Role in Matthew 16:16-19," *JBL* 132 [2013]: 936, 939-42). (Barber favors a recollection of 7:24 in 16:18.)

18. According to Sabourin, "The rock upon which the wise man builds his life is less the words of Jesus than the doing which these words describe" (*Matthew*, 1:438). Not so! The *building* represents the doing, whereas the *bedrock* represents the words.

19. For example, David L. Turner argues that "the distance of 7:24 from 16:18 renders such an allusion extremely subtle at best" (*Matthew* [BECNT; Grand Rapids: Baker Academic, 2008], 406). See also Wilkins, *Concept of Disciple*, 190; Ben Witherington III, *Matthew* (Smyth & Helwys Bible Commentary; Macon, Ga.: Smyth & Helwys, 2006), 406.

20. See Ulrich Luz, *Studies in Matthew* (trans. Rosemary Selle; Grand Rapids: Eerdmans, 2005), 3-5 with 14-17.

21. For a particularly pertinent example, see France, *Matthew*, 621-22 n. 26; but also Caragounis, *Peter and the Rock*, 107 ("A connection between both 16:18 and 7:24 is inescapable"); Wallace W. Bubar, "Killing Two Birds with One Stone: The Utter De(con)struction of Matthew and His Church," *BibInt* 3 (1995): 146 ("Does this passage [Matt 16:17-19] not immediately prompt the reader to recall a certain parable about two builders?"); Zahn, *Matthäus*, 326; Davies and Allison, *Matthew*, 2:611; Rigaux, "St. Peter in Contemporary Exegesis," 155. Bockmuehl relates 16:18 interpretively to 7:24 by way of saying that "Jesus *himself* is . . . the epitome of the wise man . . . who built upon the rock" (*Simon Peter in Scripture and Memory*, 76). But Bockmuehl regards Peter as the rock in 16:18, whereas Jesus' words are the rock in

Peter — False Disciple and Apostate according to Saint Matthew

In addition to my recent work,[22] plus a passing suggestion by Burnett,[23] a happy exception to this failure was Jacques Lefèvre d'Etaples (1522), who emphasized *verba mea* of Jesus in exegeting Matt 16:18. According to John E. Bigane III, Lefèvre "is the only sixteenth century exegete to make the movement from the 'petra' of Mt. 16:18 back to the 'petra' of Mt. 7:24-25," though "medieval commentary on the rock of Mt. 16:18 also had in mind the rock of Mt. 7:24-25." Yet "[previous] exegesis going back to Origen had made the movement in the other direction, that is, from Mt. 7:24-25 to Mt. 16:18."[24] Meanwhile, modern commentators regularly expect Matthew's audience to have connected ὕπαγε ὀπίσω μου, σατανᾶ, "Go behind me, Satan!" right here in our passage (v. 23) with ὕπαγε, σατανᾶ, "Go, Satan!" (4:10). A host of ancient copyists made this very connection by inserting in 4:10 ὀπίσω μου (see C² D L Z T 33 579ᶜ 892ᶜ 1241 1424 𝔐 b h l* sy⁽ˢ⁾,ᶜ,ʰ saᵐˢˢ boᵐˢˢ). So too do modern commentators regularly expect Matthew's audience to have connected Jesus' ἐγὼ μεθ' ὑμῶν εἰμι, "I am with you" (28:20), with μεθ' ἡμῶν ὁ θεός, "God [is] with us" (1:23).[25] The uniquely Matthean parable concerning the wise and foolish virgins (25:1-13) would surely have reminded Matthew's hearers of the parable concerning the wise and foolish builders (7:24-27). Yet these interrelated passages, among others, are sep-

---

7:24; and it is impossible to equate Peter with Jesus' words. As noted above, moreover, the wise man in 7:24 is an obedient disciple of Jesus, not Jesus himself.

22. Gundry, *Matthew*, 334; Gundry, *Commentary on the New Testament*, 72.

23. Burnett, "Characterization and Reader Construction," 24: "It could imply that Peter is the wise person who ... builds upon *the rock of Jesus' words.*" But in 16:18 Jesus, not Peter, is the builder; and the church is Jesus', not Peter's (also against Boxall, *Discovering Matthew*, 140).

24. John E. Bigane III, *Faith, Christ or Peter: Matthew 16:18 in Sixteenth Century Roman Catholic Exegesis* (Washington, D.C.: University Press of America, 1981), 81, with extensive quotations in nn. 57, 65-68 on pp. 98-100. See Luz, *Studies in Matthew*, 165-82, that the earliest interpretations did not identify the foundational rock in 16:18 with the person of Peter; Verheyden, "Rock and Stumbling Block," 279-311, that in general "Peter, let alone Matthew's Peter, did not dominate second-century literature; he managed to survive and pop up here and there"; and Demacopoulos's whole book *The Invention of Peter*, for a Foucauldian analysis of the "Petrine discourse" as it developed in late antiquity (e.g., p. 37: "It is perhaps surprising that we have so little evidence of the Roman bishops' attempts to employ the Petrine narrative for their own purposes before the middle of the fourth century").

25. See, e.g., Boxall, *Discovering Matthew*, 174 ("the Gospel's last and greatest *inclusio*"); cf. Dschulnigg's interrelating 7:24-27 and 28:20a (*Petrus im Neuen Testament*, 106) and the statement of Ulrich Luz, "The readers [of Matt 26:34] may think back to 10:32-33" (*Matthew 21–28* [ed. Helmut Koester; trans. James E. Crouch; Hermeneia: Minneapolis: Fortress, 2005], 389).

arated by longer stretches of text — almost the whole of the Gospel in the case of 1:23 and 28:20 — than that which separates 16:18 from 7:24![26]

The statement in Matt 16:18 that "the gates of hades will not overpower it [Jesus' 'church']" corresponds to the statement in 7:25 that "the rain descended and the streams came and the winds blew and they [the rain, streams, and winds] fell against that house; and it did not fall, for it had been founded on bedrock" and thereby cements the relation between these two passages.[27] In addition, the identification of "this bedrock" with "these words" of Jesus rather than with Peter fits the strong emphasis on Jesus' words that runs throughout this Gospel. As regularly observed, Matthew gathers those words into five discourses (chs. 5–7, 10, 13, 18, 24–25 [or 23–25, given his omitting the story of the widow's mite (Mark 12:41-44; par. Luke 21:1-4)]). His version of the Sermon on the Mount (chs. 5–7) is much longer than Luke's parallel version in the Sermon on the Plain (Luke 6:20-49). Matthew's version of Jesus' missional instructions in ch. 10 is much fuller than the parallel passages in Mark and Luke. In ch. 13 Matthew adds parables that do not appear in the Markan and Lukan parallels. The

---

26. The suggestion that "*this* rock" draws an equation of the rock with "Peter" (Brown et al., *Peter in the New Testament*, 91 n. 211; Byrskog, *Jesus the Only Teacher*, 278) suffers from a lack of appreciation for the shift from second person to third and for the parallel with the demonstrative pronoun in 7:24, 26 (Byrskog having to admit, moreover, that "interpreting 16:18 together with 7:24f has the advantage of taking seriously the semantic field provided by the Matthean narrative itself"). Given the shift and the parallel, one could even wonder whether Matthew inserted vv. 17-19 into Markan material to *oppose* any notion that Peter is the rock-foundation of the church. Wilkins thinks that a reference to Jesus' words would do away with wordplay (*Concept of Disciple*, 192 n. 91). It does not. The similarity between Πέτρος as a personal name meaning "stone" and πέτρα as a figure of speech for the bedrock of Jesus' words produces a fine wordplay. If Peter is not to be equated with πέτρα, it becomes pointless to say that "the reader does not know . . . what this function [as a bedrock] means," so that "this indeterminacy creates a gap and requires the reader's imagination to fill it" (Burnett, "Characterization and Reader Construction," 20). It also becomes pointless to get irony out of the contradiction between Peter as bedrock and his vacillation throughout Matthew (A. Stock, "Is Matthew's Presentation of Peter Ironic?" 66, 68, with dependence on B. Van Iersel). On the other hand, if Πέτρος means "rock" rather than "stone," Peter's vacillation might relate to the rocky soil in Matt 13:5-6, 20-21 (so Bubar, "Killing Two Birds," 147-49); Mark Goodacre, "The Rock on Rocky Ground: Matthew, Mark and Peter as Skandalon," in *What Is It That the Scripture Says? Essays in Biblical Interpretation, Translation and Reception in Honour of Henry Wansbrough OSB* (ed. Philip McCosker; New York: T&T Clark, 2006), 63, 66.

27. Cf. Evans, *Matthew*, 314, though he summarily dismisses the likelihood of a reference to "death by martyrdom" (see below).

discourse in ch. 18 includes considerable material not found in Mark and Luke. Matthew's version of the Olivet Discourse (chs. 24-25) runs a whole chapter longer than what is found in the Markan and Lukan parallels and contains distinctive material.

Jesus is the disciples' "one teacher" (23:8), so that they are commissioned to teach converts to observe "all things whatever" that he has commanded in his many words as recorded in Matthew (28:20, both passages being unique to this Gospel). And as widely recognized, Matthew habitually reduces narratival material, as compared with Markan parallels, so as to make prominent the words of Jesus that are embedded within the narratives.[28] That is to say, the identification of the bedrock with Jesus' words fits one of Matthew's overall emphases perfectly, as evident also in the uniquely Matthean references to "these words" of Jesus in 7:28; 19:1; and to "all these words" of his in 26:1 (N.B. again the use of the demonstrative pronoun, as in 7:24, 26; 16:18).

This identification also fits perfectly the immediately following subject matter of 16:13-23, viz., Jesus' giving the keys (τὰς κλεῖδας) of heaven's kingdom to Peter, so that whatever he binds on the earth will have been bound in heaven, and whatever he loosens on the earth will have been loosened in heaven. For the figure of keys represents Jesus' words just as the figure of bedrock does (cf. "the key of knowledge" in Luke 11:52). To use the keys will be to teach these words to future disciples (see 28:20 again). The Great Commission will expand the authority to use these keys to include the other apostles along with Peter just as 18:18 will also expand the authority to bind and loosen to include all of them together. Judas Iscariot included! So if reception of this authority will not guarantee Judas Iscariot's salvation, it will not guarantee the salvation of Peter either, or that of the remaining apostles.[29] False discipleship remains a possibility for them too. Since according to 23:8-12 Jesus is the apostles' sole teacher and instructor, their teaching in obedience to the Great Commission consists in *conveying* his words/commandments, not in interpreting them.[30]

---

28. See, e.g., John Nolland, *The Gospel of Matthew* (NIGTC; Grand Rapids: Eerdmans, 2005), 10; Ulrich Luz, *Matthew 1-7: A Commentary* (trans. Wilhelm C. Linss; Minneapolis: Augsburg, 1989), 49; Boxall, *Discovering Matthew*, 35. On Jesus as the one teacher in Matthew, see Byrskog, *Jesus the Only Teacher*, 197-308. Though Byrskog ties "this rock" to the person of Peter, he also (and confusingly) ties it to "the foundational teaching [cf. Matthew's references to Jesus 'words'] that Jesus has given once and for all" (p. 253).

29. See below on the question of Judas Iscariot's salvation.

30. Against Kraus's statement, "Durch seine [Peter's] verbindliche *Auslegung* der Lehre

To "bind" means, then, to teach Jesus' words prohibiting behavior that calls for church discipline and, failing that, bars entrance into the kingdom of heaven. By the same token, to "loosen" means to teach Jesus' words concerning behavior conducive to entering that kingdom (cf., e.g., 5:19-20; 18:15-18; and contrast the hypocritical scribes' and Pharisees' shutting off [κλείετε] entrance into the kingdom of heaven with "the leaven" of their own "teaching" [16:5-12; 23:13], though people should "do and observe" all that they say when sitting "in the chair of Moses" to quote *his* words [23:2-3]).[31] Because of derivation from Jesus' words, the behaviors bound and loosened on earth will have already been bound and loosened in heaven.[32] So the words of Peter carry no authority of his own.

Peter's having the keys guarantees his entrance into the kingdom no more than the sitting of the scribes and Pharisees in the chair of Moses guarantees entrance for them. On the contrary, they not only shut off entrance for others — apparently with keys, for κλείετε, "shut off," is cognate to κλείδας, "keys" — but also they themselves do not enter. Ah, but what about Jesus' "giv[ing] the keys [κλεῖδας] of the kingdom of heaven" to Peter (Matt 16:19a; cf. Isa 22:22)? Well, those "hypocrites" — the "scribes and Pharisees" — "close [κλείετε] the kingdom of heaven in front of people" and do not themselves enter it (ὑμεῖς γὰρ οὐκ εἰσέρχεσθε [Matt 23:13]). So why should not Peter, if he turns out to be a false disciple, fail to enter the kingdom just as the scribes and Pharisees fail to enter despite their having the power of opening and closing?

To use 7:24-25 for an equation of Peter and the rock-foundation of the church, Overman says that "the term 'rock' is elsewhere used by Matthew to describe the person who depends on the teachings of Jesus (7:24 ff.)."[33]

Jesu öffnet er den Menschen das Himmelreich" ("Zur Ekklesiologie," 230 [emphasis added]). Byrskog correctly describes Jesus' teaching as "given once and for all" (*Jesus the Only Teacher*, 253) and Jesus' words and deeds as needing to be transmitted "as if they were isolated from the utterances and actions of other persons inside and outside of the community" (p. 307). If isolated even from the words of teachers inside Matthew's community, the transmission excludes interpretation and consists only in conveyance. Yet Byrskog goes on to speak (again confusingly) about "an elaboration that enhanced the Jesus-sayings" (pp. 397-98) in possible contradiction of the book-title, *Jesus the Only Teacher*.

31. Cf. Gibbs, *Matthew 11:2–20:34*, 822-23; Davies and Allison, *Matthew*, 2:639; Luz, *Matthew 8–20*, 454-55.

32. See Carson, "Matthew," 422-25, for a convincing argument in favor of "will have been . . ." rather than "will be . . ." (also France, *Matthew*, 626-27; Gibbs, *Matthew 11:2–20:34*, 807-9).

33. Overman, *Church and Community in Crisis*, 240.

Wrong! In 7:24-25 the rock represents Jesus' *words/teachings*, not the *person* of the builder. Oppositely to Overman, Cassidy states, "Clearly, the reference points for 'rock' are different in each passage [7:24-25 and 16:18]," and "without the foundation of a church there is no reason for the name 'Peter' to exist."[34] But Jesus' proceeding in 16:19 to use "keys" as a figure for Jesus' words favors a reference to Jesus' words in 16:18 as well as in 7:24-25, so that the reference points are *not* clearly different; and a nonequative wordplay between Πέτρος and πέτρᾳ suffices to justify the "exist[ence]" of "Peter" in the passage. Furthermore, an equation between Πέτρος and πέτρᾳ makes it passing strange that Matthew, as noted before, is the only one of the evangelists not to make Jesus responsible for giving the name "Peter" to Simon (contrast again Mark 3:16; Luke 6:14; John 1:42).

Matthew 16:21-23 (par. Mark 8:31-33; Luke 9:22)

The question now arises whether vv. 21-23 should be separated off from vv. 13-20. To do so would be to insulate somewhat (but not entirely) the beatitude on Peter in vv. 17-19 from Jesus' scathing response to him in vv. 21-23. The case for a separation rests mainly on the parallel of Ἀπὸ τότε ἤρξατο ὁ Ἰησοῦς, "From then [on], Jesus began," plus an infinitive (v. 21) and the same construction in 4:17, and on the judgment that 4:17 starts a new section of Matthew in which Jesus engages in preaching. Similarly, it is argued, 16:21 starts a new section in which he engages in predicting his death and resurrection. On the other hand, his move to Capernaum in 4:12-16 could just as easily be considered the start of a new section; and 4:17–16:20 contains a good deal more than preaching, viz., miracles, exorcisms, and private instruction, none of which are covered by the statement that "Jesus began to preach and to say, 'Repent, for the kingdom of heaven has drawn near.'" Furthermore, 16:21–28:20 contains more than passion-and-resurrection predictions, viz., the transfiguration, an exorcism, a miracle, and the triumphal entry as well as continued verbal ministry of various sorts and an account of Jesus' death and resurrection. So it is better to say that both 4:17 and 16:21 indicate the start of new but not exclusive activities — preaching and predicting, respectively — rather than a major structural break.

There are, in fact, indications that the phrase ἀπὸ τότε links rather

---

34. Cassidy, *Four Times Peter*, 74-75.

than delinks the following to the preceding (cf. the omission of καὶ ἤρξατο in Luke 9:22). In 4:17 ἀπὸ **τότε**, "From *then* [on]," builds on Jesus' foregoing move to Capernaum. In 16:21 the same phrase builds on Peter's foregoing confession of Jesus' messiahship and divine sonship, and also on Jesus' having put a gag order on the disciples in regard to his being the Christ (v. 20). Which is to say that the following passion-and-resurrection prediction grows out of a need to correct the disciples' notion of Jesus' messiahship that Peter has just now confessed on their behalf.[35] Moreover, by inserting εἰς Ἱεροσόλυμα **ἀπελθεῖν**, "to go *away* to Jerusalem" (not in Mark), Matthew deliberately locates vv. 21-23 still in τὰ μέρα Καισαρείας τῆς Φιλίππου, "the district of Caesarea Philippi," and thus links vv. 21-23 with vv. 13-20. As to Jerusalem, Boxall argues that since Jesus leaves Galilee for Judea and Transjordan not till 19:1, the present start of his passion-and-resurrection predictions hardly marks a crucial break at 16:21.[36] Moreover again, welding vv. 13-20 to vv. 21-23 are the antithetic parallels between "You [Jesus] are the Christ, the Son of the living God" (v. 16) and "You [Peter] are my snare" (v. 23), and between "flesh and blood did not reveal [this] to you — rather, my Father in heaven" (v. 17) and "you are not thinking the things of God — rather, the things of human beings" (v. 23).[37]

What sort of light, then, does this linkage of vv. 21-23 with vv. 13-20 cast on Peter? Not at all a good light! For to make creditable Peter's rebuke of Jesus, Matthew omits the indication in Mark 8:32 that Jesus "was stating the matter plainly" (καὶ παρρησίᾳ τὸν λόγον ἐλάλει).[38] Then, after adopting

---

35. Boxall notes that "16:21-23 continues the conversation with Peter begun in 16:13-20.... There is a further difficulty with focus on *apo tote*: it occurs again at 26:16 ('And from that moment he [Judas Iscariot] began to look for an opportunity to betray him [Jesus]'), without introducing a significant transition in the narrative" (*Discovering Matthew*, 39).

36. Boxall, *Discovering Matthew*, 11.

37. See Frans Neirynck, *Evangelica II: 1982-1991, Collected Essays* (ed. F. Van Segbroeck; BETL 99; Leuven: Leuven University Press, 1991), 141-55, 161-82, esp. 166-77. Also in favor of linking vv. 21-23 with vv. 13-20, see Dschulnigg, "Gestalt und Funktion," 170; Dschulnigg, *Petrus im Neuen Testament*, 44 n. 49; against Claudel, *La Confession de Pierre*, 177-79; Michael Goulder, *St. Paul versus St. Peter*, 18; Gibbs, *Matthew 11:2–20:34*, 809 n. 13. Gibbs appeals to a parallel between pericope-ending commands to silence in 8:4; 9:30 and a similar command in 16:20. But 9:30 does not end a pericope; 9:31 does. Even in 8:4 the command to silence is followed by two further commands.

38. Against my own previous statement that because the plainness of Jesus' speech in Mark makes Peter's obtuseness inexcusable, "Matthew's omission lightens the onus on Peter" (Gundry, *Matthew*, 338).

Peter — False Disciple and Apostate according to Saint Matthew

Mark's statement that Peter "took [Jesus] to himself" (προσλαβόμενος), as opposed to appropriately following after Jesus, Matthew also adopts Mark's statement that Peter "*began to* rebuke him [Jesus]," which parallels the earlier, similarly shared statement that "Jesus *began to* show his disciples that he must go away to Jerusalem and suffer much." The parallel heightens Peter's contradiction of Jesus' prediction.

To heighten the contradiction further, Matthew then inserts on his own the direct quotation of a vehement protest by Peter: ἵλεώς σοι, κύριε, "Never, Lord!"[39] By itself, a literal translation such as "[May God act] mercifully toward you, Lord!" sounds well-wishingly pious on Peter's part.[40] But the introductory infinitive, ἐπιτιμᾶν, "rebuke," has already tilted toward brazenness. Imagine, a disciple rebuking his master! And Peter's expression is a Septuagintal negation.[41] Next, Matthew intensifies the negation by inserting οὐ μὴ ἔσται σοι τοῦτο, "By no means will this happen to you!" οὐ μή plus a future indicative produces a double negation, "the strongest way to negate something in Greek,"[42] so that this insertion underlines Peter's contradiction of Jesus' prediction.

The omission of Jesus' seeing his disciples (according to Mark) focuses the spotlight solely on Peter, to whom alone Jesus "turns," so that Matthew's audience will think only of Peter in connection with Jesus' response, which Matthew shares with Mark — ὕπαγε ὀπίσω μου, σατανᾶ, "Go behind me, Satan!" — and which in the case of Matthew recalls Jesus' command to Satan in 4:10: ὕπαγε, σατανᾶ (not in Mark).[43] Thus Jesus identifies his confessor with his tempter.[44] (The inserted ὀπίσω μου suits

---

39. See the earlier comments on 14:22-33 that κύριε does not necessarily constitute a true disciple's confession of faith.

40. So Gundry, *Matthew*, 338; Gibbs, *Matthew 11:2–20:34*, 830-33; Syreeni, "Peter as Character and Symbol," 131-32. Lagrange even praises Peter: "Son amour pour son Maitre répugnait à le voir soufrir, et cela était louable" (*Matthieu*, 331; similarly, Laurentin, *Petite vie de saint Pierre*, 42).

41. See 2 Kgdms 23:17; 1 Chron 11:19; Carson, "Matthew," 430, with bibliography.

42. Daniel B. Wallace, *Greek Grammar beyond the Basics: An Exegetical Syntax of the New Testament* (Grand Rapids: Zondervan, 1996), 468.

43. Goulder seems to think that Matthew drops Jesus' seeing his disciples to spare Peter a public scolding (*St. Paul versus St. Peter*, 18). But Mark's text has to do with *Jesus'* seeing, not with the other disciples' seeing.

44. So Hoffmann, "Der Petrus-Primat im Matthäusevangelium," 106-7; Frankemölle, *Matthäus*, 2:228; Plummer, *Matthew*, 232-33. The recollection of 4:10 undermines Claudel's appeal to various passages in the OT and QL for an ameliorating interpretation of σατανᾶ as an adversary rather than the prince of demons (*La Confession de Pierre*, 300-302, 304; cf.

the proper location of a disciple behind his master, as in 4:19 par. Mark 1:17.) It is sometimes argued that Matthew substitutes εἶπεν, "[Jesus] said," for Mark's ἐπετίμησεν, "[Jesus] rebuked," to soften Jesus' response.[45] But Matthew's εἶπεν, "[Jesus] said," replaces Mark's λέγει, "[Jesus] says," for a merely stylistic reason just as Matthew often turns a historical present in Mark into an ordinary aorist (see the very same change of λέγει in Mark 8:29 to εἶπεν as recently as Matt 16:16). Mark's ἐπετίμησεν disappears in Matthew as part of the omission of Jesus' seeing the disciples; and if with B* D e sy Or^mss ἐπετίμησεν is to be accepted in v. 20, where Jesus would then have "rebuked," i.e. warned, the disciples to tell no one he was the Christ, Matthew may not have wanted to triple up on that verb. Finally, before adopting from Mark Jesus' statement to Peter, "because you are not thinking the things of God; rather, [you are thinking] the things of human beings," Matthew adds σκάνδαλον εἶ ἐμοῦ, "You [Peter] are my snare."[46]

Markley, *Peter — Apocalyptic Seer*, 203 n. 142). Further attempts to dull the sharp edge of Jesus' response to Peter include the following: "Jesus nimmt nicht zurück, was er dem Bekenner zugesprochen hat" (Zahn, *Matthäus*, 555). (But one might consider v. 23 a retraction of vv. 17-19.) Willoughby C. Allen observes that Jesus' rebukes are sometimes softened (*A Critical and Exegetical Commentary on the Gospel According to S. Matthew* [ICC; Edinburgh: T. & T. Clark, 1907], 179-80). (But not here!) According to Brown et al., *Peter in the New Testament*, if Peter thinks "the things of human beings" (v. 23), "he can *become* a stone of stumbling" (p. 93, emphasis added). (But Jesus declares him to *be* a snare.) "This addition [of vv. 17-19] also moderates the severity of juxtaposing [in Mark] Peter's confession with the rebuke by Jesus when Peter fails to accept the prediction of Jesus' Passion" (Perkins, *Peter*, 52). (Why then does Matthew increase the severity of Jesus' rebuke as compared with Mark?) "He [Matthew] even sharpens that rebuke *somewhat* by having Jesus describe Peter as a 'stumbling block'" (Perkins, *Peter*, 71 [emphasis added to point up the attempted amelioration]). (What then of Jesus' addressing Peter with "Satan"?) Albright and Mann go so far as to say that Matthew's "interest in Peter's failure . . . does not detract from this [his] pre-eminence; rather, it emphasizes it"; for "had Peter been a lesser figure his behavior would have been of lesser consequence" (*Matthew*, 195). (But the greater the preeminence, the greater the detraction.) McNeile states the matter strongly, i.e., that Jesus treated Peter as "possessed" by Satan (*Matthew*, 245-46; cf. Pierre Bonnard's statement: "Ce frappe, dans cet incident, c'est la violence des termes dont se sert le Christ matthéen dans sa réponse à Pierre" [*L'Évangile selon Saint Matthieu* (2nd ed.; CNT; Paris: Delachaux & Niestlé, 1970), 248]; also Goodacre, "The Rock on Rocky Ground," 68). Under the false presupposition that Jesus declared Peter the bedrock-foundation of the church, Syreeni is flummoxed by the extreme ambivalence of vv. 13-23: "How can Peter be the foundation of the church and Satan in one character?" ("Peter as Character and Symbol," 129-30).

45. So, e.g., Claudel, *La Confession de Pierre*, 297-98, 304-5.

46. The phrase πέτραν σκανδάλου, "rock of stumbling," occurs in Rom 9:33; 1 Pet 2:8. Matthew does not connect πέτραν with σκάνδαλον, however. So it is doubtful that he

Unhappily for Peter, every other Matthean occurrence of σκάνδαλον refers to those who are condemned to a furnace-like hell of eternal fire (13:41-42 [uniquely Matthean]; 18:7-9); and σκάνδαλον occurs here in the emphatic initial position.[47] Frankemölle notes bluntly that for Matthew, σκάνδαλα belong in hell.[48]

---

intended a contrast between bedrock and a rock of stumbling, particularly not if (as argued above) v. 18 did not portray Peter as bedrock (against Cassidy, *Four Times Peter*, 77; Goodacre, "The Rock on Rocky Ground," 62; Meier, *Matthew*, 185).

47. The verb σκανδαλίζω has to do with nondisciples and apostates in its uniquely Matthean occurrences at 15:12; 17:27; 24:10, plus paralleled occurrences in 5:29, 30; 11:6; 13:21, 57; 18:6, 8, 9. The only exceptions appear in 26:31, 33, where the disciples are predicted to be snared and thus scattered because of Jesus' passion. But these exceptions derive from Mark 14:27, 29. H. N. Ridderbos makes the point that Jesus calls Peter a snare located in front of Jesus as opposed to a disciple following properly behind him (*Matthew* [trans. Ray Togtman; Bible Student's Commentary; Grand Rapids: Zondervan, 1987], 311). In relation to Jesus' statement in Matt 11:6, "Blessed is the one who is not scandalized by me," Goodacre says that here in 16:23 Peter is "scandalized by Jesus" ("The Rock on Rocky Ground," 66). But σκάνδαλον εἶ ἐμοῦ means the opposite, i.e., that Jesus is scandalized by Peter.

48. Frankemölle, *Matthäus*, 2:229.

CHAPTER 4

Peter from the Mount of Transfiguration through the Garden of Gethsemane

Matthew 17:1-8 (par. Mark 9:2-8; Luke 9:28-36a)

Peter figures next in Matt 17:1-8, an account of Jesus' transfiguration. Peter's participation shows, according to Cassidy, that "Jesus no longer regards him as 'Satanic' [as Jesus did in 16:23]."[1] Cassidy's point would carry more weight if Jesus had taken Peter alone up the Mount of Transfiguration. As it is, however, Jesus took James and John, too; and Matthew adds (in contrast with Mark and Luke) that John was James's brother. So Peter does not stand out from the other two disciples as rehabilitatedly privileged. Matthew simply takes the three from Mark. In fact, if the text-critical decisions in the twenty-eighth revised edition of Nestle-Aland's *Novum Testamentum Graece* are to be followed, it could be argued that Matthew's eliminating Mark's definite article from the names of James and John and keeping it only before Πέτρον welds these disciples together as a unit, so that Peter fades into the trio: "the Peter-and-James-and-John-his-brother" (compare the single definite article that regularly welds together "Pharisees and Sadducees" in Matthew). If the one definite article with "Peter" does make him stand out, on the other hand, it remains to be seen whether he stands out positively or negatively in the following narrative.

In Peter's response to Jesus' transfiguration and conversation with Moses and Elijah, Matthew changes Mark's historical present tense λέγει, "[Peter] says," to the ordinary aorist εἶπεν, "said," as he often does for a sty-

---

1. Cassidy, *Four Times Peter*, 78. So too Syreeni, "Peter as Character and Symbol," 133: "After six days (17.1), Jesus and the formerly satanic Peter are great friends again."

listic reason (see the foregoing comments on 16:23) and for conformity to his usual ἀποκριθεὶς εἶπεν (the participle having been borrowed from Mark 9:5). "Lord" replaces Mark's "Rabbi." This replacement has been considered a mark of Peter's due deference toward Jesus,[2] but see the foregoing comments on 14:28 that throughout Matthew both nondisciples and false disciples address Jesus with "Lord." Likewise considered a mark of Peter's due deference toward Jesus is Matthew's replacement of Mark's simple καί, "and," with εἰ θέλεις, "If you [Jesus] wish."[3] But the replacement simply makes up in advance for Matthew's coming shift from Mark's hortatory subjunctive, ποιήσωμεν, "let us make," to a future indicative, ποιήσω, "I will make." In other words, "If you wish" is no more deferential than "let us make."

With Peter's "*I* will make," as opposed to "let *us* make," Matthew turns Peter's foolish suggestion into a ridiculously egotistical declaration: Peter, and he alone, will make "here" three tents, one each for Jesus, Moses, and Elijah. Matthew's insertion of a non-Markan ὧδε, "here" — and doing so despite a paralleled occurrence of this very same adverb in Peter's preceding sentence — underlines the ridiculousness of making three tents on the "high mountain." In the Markan Peter's address to Jesus, moreover, "let *us* make three tents" inappropriately includes Jesus in the making of those tents, whereas Peter apparently means to include in his exhortation only James and John with himself. Matthew has picked up on this Markan inconcinnity, and in his revision puts the onus on Peter for the declaration that, Jesus willing, he will in fact make three tents.[4]

Only Jesus was transfigured. So Peter's proposal to make tents for Moses and Elijah as well as for Jesus amounts to, or at least comes close to, a denial of Jesus' uniqueness, which God the Father promptly affirms and which Peter should have known better than to deny even implicitly, given his earlier confession of Jesus' divine sonship (16:16).[5] Since tents are for

---

2. See, e.g., Davies and Allison, *Matthew*, 2:699; Syreeni, "Peter as Character and Symbol," 133; Donald A. Hagner, *Matthew 14–28* (WBC 33B; Dallas: Word, 1995), 490.

3. So again Davies and Allison, *Matthew*, 2:699; Syreeni, "Peter as Character and Symbol," 133; Hagner, *Matthew 14–28*, 490; also Pesch, *Simon-Petrus*, 42; Luz, *Matthew 8–20*, 399.

4. The declaration of Matthew's Peter, "*I* will make here three tents," falsifies both Kingsbury's claim that "Peter speaks up not only for himself but for James and John as well" ("The Figure of Peter," 71) and Gnilka's assertion that in order not to spoil the reference in 16:16-19 to God the Father's revelation to Peter, Matthew does not highlight Peter's foolish request (*Matthäusevangelium*, 2:95). The "I" in this request likewise undermines France's paraphrase: "We [James and John as well as Peter] are available to do what needs to be done" (*Matthew*, 649).

5. See esp. Patte, *Matthew*, 236-37; but also Gibbs, *Matthew 11:2–20:34*, 853, 857 n. 28; Carson, "Matthew," 437-38; Hagner, *Matthew 14–28*, 494.

dwelling, Peter's proposal also amounts to, or comes close to, another protest against Jesus' having predicted he was "go[ing] away to Jerusalem" to be killed and then raised (16:21-23).[6]

Bonnard speaks of Peter's total incomprehension of Jesus' transfiguration.[7] But Matthew omits both Mark's explanation, "For he [Peter] did not know what he should answer [in the sense of how he should respond]," and the broader explanation, "For they [all three disciples] had become terrified." So other commentators treat these Matthean omissions as sparing of Peter.[8] The omissions do *not* spare Peter, however. They leave Peter without the excuse of ignorance and (shared) fear.[9] The omissions and Matthew's insertion, "While he [Peter] was still speaking" (cf. Luke 9:34), also allow God the Father's declaration-cum-command, "This is my Son, the Beloved One, in whom I am well pleased. Listen to him!" to butt up against Peter's egotistical malaprop as an abrupt and stringent correction of it. As Garland notes, Peter "is checked in midsentence."[10] (By saying that Peter "is not rebuked," Rudolf Schnackenburg fails to recognize in the Father's words a rebuke of the highest order.[11]) The command to listen to Jesus opposes listening to Moses and Elijah as they speak "with him" (v. 3). Matthew's additions of ἰδού, "behold!" and φωτεινή, "luminous" (in the description of the overshadowing cloud out of which God speaks), highlight the correction. All in all, then, Peter fares badly in this episode.

Matthew 17:24-27

Unique to Matthew's Gospel is the story of "Peter's Penny" in 17:24-27. The question asked of Peter by "the ones taking the double drachmas" looks forward to an affirmative answer: "Your teacher pays the double drachmas,

---

6. So Pesch, *Simon-Petrus*, 42; Ridderbos, *Matthew*, 319. Ridderbos softens Peter's implicit protest here in 17:4 by ascribing it to Peter's "desire to promote Christ's glory."

7. Bonnard, *Matthieu*, 255.

8. See Witherington, *Matthew*, 326; Nau, *Peter in Matthew*, 79; Syreeni, "Peter as Character and Symbol," 133; Hagner, *Matthew 14–28*, 493; France, *Matthew*, 649; Pesch, *Simon-Petrus*, 42; Luz, *Matthew 8–20*, 399 ("Unlike Mark, he [Matthew] is not interested in blaming Peter").

9. Cf. Lagrange, *Matthieu*, 335; Gaechter, *Matthäus*, 568.

10. David E. Garland, *Reading Matthew: A Literary and Theological Commentary on the First Gospel* (Reading the New Testament Series; New York: Crossroad, 1995), 182.

11. Rudolf Schnackenburg, *The Gospel of Matthew* (trans. Robert R. Barr; Grand Rapids: Eerdmans, 2002), 166.

doesn't he?" (οὐ plus an indicative mood of the Greek verb in a question). Peter's "Yes" fulfills the expectation. Highlighting this "Yes" are both the asyndeton with which the introductory λέγει, "he says," suddenly appears, the historical present tense of this verb, and the terseness of answering with a single word. One could describe Peter as impetuous in his answer.[12]

Matthew then writes that when Peter had entered the house (whether Jesus' or Peter's is hard to say in view of 4:12-13 and 8:14), "Jesus anticipated him by saying, 'How does it seem to you, Simon? From whom do the kings of the earth take custom dues and a poll tax? From their sons or from [sons] belonging to others?'" In other words, Jesus confronted Peter with a question before Peter had a chance to report to him. The brusqueness of this confrontation underscores Peter's ignorance of the reason Jesus pays the tax. The reason, as Jesus goes on to explain, is that despite being tax-exempt ("free"), to avoid snaring others — i.e., offending them with the result that they fall into damnation — payment will proceed.[13] As Meier notes, "Peter has not really understood the import of his first answer."[14] Jesus' question implies that Peter answered "Yes" erroneously on the ground of Jesus' legal obligation, whereas the God whose kingdom Jesus proclaims revealed Jesus' divine sonship earlier and privately to Peter (16:17) and in the meantime has declared him, in Peter's hearing, to be his beloved Son (17:5); and, as Jesus explains, kings' sons do not have to pay taxes. So Jesus "will Petrus korrigieren," and "die Tributabgabe nicht obligatorisch sein kann, weil sie nicht rechtmässig ist."[15] More than a little irony adheres to Jesus' telling the disciple whom in 16:23 he called "my snare" (σκάνδαλον ... ἐμοῦ) that the two of them will pay lest they "snare" (σκανδαλίσωμεν) others.[16]

---

12. Meier, *A Marginal Jew*, 2:881, though Meier describes Peter's answer as correct "thanks to the guidance of Jesus." Yet no thanks to Peter, Jesus' guidance was ex post facto.

13. The reason of not giving offense makes doubtful Gibbs's position that Jesus' coming self-sacrifice makes unnecessary any upkeep of the temple for the offering of animal sacrifices (*Matthew 11:2–20:34*, 884-85).

14. Meier, *A Marginal Jew*, 2:881.

15. Zahn, *Matthäus*, 362-63. Cf. Cassidy, *Four Times Peter*, 79: "Jesus will not allow Peter's simple 'yes' to stand as representative of his (Jesus') position." See also Carson, "Matthew," 446 ("Peter's defense of Jesus [v. 25] is misguided" [though "defense" may overstate the matter, because the tax-gatherers' question expected an affirmative answer]); Syreeni, "Peter as Character and Symbol," 135 ("His [Peter's] resolute 'yes' immediately proves to be problematic and provokes Jesus' critical comment").

16. Syreeni sees "mild irony" in Jesus' sending "Peter, formerly a fisherman, . . . to his pre-discipleship occupation for a while" ("Peter as Character and Symbol," 136). Perhaps

Laurentin exclaims, "Quel honneur pour Pierre!" because of Jesus' telling him to go catch a fish and pay the tax for both of them: "Bien plus, le Maître lui a manifesté plus avant sa confiance."[17] But the failure of Matthew to narrate Peter's obediently catching a fish and paying the tax for both himself and Jesus leaves the accent on the corrective nature of Jesus' instruction — viz., to avoid giving offense — rather than on any confidence Jesus had in Peter or on any honor bestowed by Jesus on Peter. It is likewise mistaken to say, "The episode also demonstrates that Peter has the authority to teach because he has turned to Jesus to resolve the question."[18] For Jesus confronted Peter, not vice versa; and Peter's earlier, confident "Yes" shows that he did not have in mind a question needing resolution.

In several ways Burnett is too easy on Peter when it comes to this episode: Since the tax collectors ask him a question, the reader has "an enhanced view of Peter," because "the reader knows that Peter not only has a dialogical relationship with Jesus but with other characters as well."[19] Peter's dialogue with other characters when he denies Jesus three times (26:69-74) will not "enhance" Peter, however; and Jesus' present correction of Peter's "Yes" would seem to eliminate any enhancement here too. So Burnett's modification that Peter's "status as a character ... is not enhanced as much as it could be since he is not asked *his* opinion" (emphasis added) does not go far enough. Nor does it go far enough to call Jesus' response an "interpretation" of what Peter said. Nor does the setting in a house cast a favorable light on Peter by implying "intimacy" between him and Jesus, any more than did the intimacy between the two when Jesus called him "Satan" and "my snare" (16:22-23).[20]

---

so, but it goes too far to say in addition that Jesus restored Peter here (pp. 136-37). Fishing for a fish hardly counts as an apostolic restoration. Nor should very much be made of Jesus' addressing Peter with "Simon" rather than "Peter," for nowhere else does Matthew's Jesus use "Peter" as an introductory address.

17. Laurentin, *Petite vie de saint Pierre*, 44-45; similarly, Pesch, *Simon-Petrus*, 141; France, *Matthew*, 729.

18. Perkins, *Peter*, 67; cf. Brown et al., *Peter in the New Testament*, 104-5.

19. Burnett, "Characterization in Matthew: Reader Construction of the Disciple Peter," 28-29.

20. With Burnett's notion of intimacy, cf. Markley's statement, "In this episode, Matthew portrays Peter individually as one who interacts with Jesus in the manner of an apocalyptic seer, receiving divine disclosure of halakah concerning payment of the temple tax" (*Peter — Apocalyptic Seer*, 186). Why not simple teaching by Jesus, as though he were a rabbi (cf. 23:8)?

Peter — False Disciple and Apostate according to Saint Matthew

Matthew 18:21-22 (par. Luke 17:3b-4)

In Luke 17:3b-4 Jesus is quoted as saying, "If your brother sins, reprimand him. And if he repents, forgive him. And if he sins against you seven times during a day and seven times turns to you, saying, 'I repent,' you shall forgive him." In 18:21-22 of his Gospel, Matthew puts these words, with differences, on Peter's lips and adds opposing words spoken by Jesus. As to the differences, an earlier reference to reprimanding a sinning brother (18:15-17) makes unnecessary a like reference here in Matthew. So it is missing. Peter, who plays no role in Luke's parallel, is said by Matthew to have approached Jesus and asked, "Lord, how many times shall my brother sin against me and I forgive him? Up to seven times?"[21] The contrast between a statement by Jesus (so Luke) and a question by Peter (so Matthew) makes Peter the butt of Jesus' corrective — indeed, contradictory — reply. "Seven is a common biblical number for completeness and goes well beyond the rabbinic maxim of forgiving three times (e.g., *b. Yoma* 85b, 87a)."[22] France thinks therefore that "Peter's proposal of up to seven times is probably intended to express the outer limits of generosity."[23] Going further, Calvin thinks Peter designed his question to show the absurdity of forgiving time after time because, in Peter's reasoning, repeated forgiveness fosters repeated offenses.[24] Yet forgiveness seven times overall is not so generous as seven times in a single day, or per day, as in Jesus' command according to Luke.[25] By comparison, then, Matthew's Peter falls below the Lukan Jesus' standard — and now very far below the Matthean Jesus' standard of "up to seventy times seven" (a probable reversal of Lamech's seventy-sevenfold revenge in Gen 4:24).

Asyndeton at the introduction of Jesus' reply (λέγει αὐτῷ ὁ Ἰησοῦς, "Jesus says to him") makes for an abruptness that emphasizes Jesus' corrective reply and thus Peter's mistake. The historical present tense of

---

21. See the comments on 14:28 that the address "Lord" does not necessarily imply true discipleship; also Burnett, "Characterization in Matthew," 27: "Peter's use of 'Lord' is no guarantee that he speaks for God (7:21-22; 16:22)."

22. Craig L. Blomberg, *Matthew* (The New American Commentary 22; Nashville: Broadman & Holman, 1992), 281. See *m. Yoma* 8:9 that the Day of Atonement is ineffective if a sinner has not appeased his fellow, and also for no second chance for repentance of a sin.

23. France, *Matthew*, 700.

24. Calvin, *Commentary on a Harmony of the Evangelists*, 2:363-64.

25. See Nolland, *Matthew*, 754.

λέγει, often changed by Matthew into an ordinary aorist but put forward here, likewise emphasizes Jesus' corrective reply and thus Peter's mistake. Even further such emphasis derives from the forward position of οὐ, "not" — οὐ λέγω σοι ἕως ἑπτάκις, "I do *not* say to you 'up to seven times'" — where we might have expected λέγω σοι οὐ ἕως ἑπτάκις, "I say to you 'not up to seven times.'"[26] These multiple emphases on Peter's mistake and Jesus' correction attain their maximum, finally, in the strong adversative ἀλλ', "rather," that introduces Jesus' standard and in the huge difference between its "seventy times seven" and Peter's standard of only "seven times."[27] Both Bonnard and Syreeni opine that Peter asks his question on behalf of the other disciples. If so, blame would be shared. But the text contains no such indication. Therefore Peter stands alone in disgrace.

Matthew 19:27-30 (par. Mark 10:28-31; Luke 18:28-30; 22:28-30)

Talkative as ever, Peter emerges again in Matt 19:27. A rich young man has decided not to sell his possessions, give the proceeds to the poor, and follow Jesus (19:16-22), so that Jesus has told his disciples that it is almost impossible for a rich person to enter God's kingdom (19:23-26). To introduce a statement-cum-question of Peter's, then, Matthew replaces Ἤρξατο λέγειν ὁ Πέτρος αὐτῷ, "Peter began to say to him [Jesus]" (Mark 10:28), with Τότε ἀποκριθεὶς ὁ Πέτρος εἶπεν αὐτῷ, "Then answering, Peter said to him." Τότε attaches the following chronologically to the foregoing, and ἀποκριθείς attaches it topically to the foregoing. To Peter's statement, "Behold, we have left all and followed you," which comes over from Mark (cf. *Acts Pet. 12 Apos.* 10.30), Matthew adds, "What then [ἄρα] will we

---

26. See Wilkins, *Concept of Disciple*, 199.

27. This emphasis undermines Schenk's treatment of the question asked by Peter as favorable to his stature ("Das 'Matthäusevangelium,'" 70), and also Lagrange's psychoanalytic comment that Peter was trying to enter generously into Jesus' spirit (*Matthieu*, 358). Because of the vigor of Jesus' response, "inaccurate" seems too weak a description of Peter's position (against Cassidy, *Four Times Peter,* 79), as do also Bonnard's description, "naturelle et déplacée" (*Matthieu,* 276), and Syreeni's description, "mild" ("Peter as Character and Symbol," 135), though Syreeni later says that "Jesus' answer . . . ridicules the very attitude Peter exemplifies" (p. 141). On target is Nau's saying that Jesus' seventy times seven makes Peter's seven times look ignorant and cheap (*Peter in Matthew,* 119). Likewise, Patte speaks correctly of a "polemical exchange between Peter and Jesus" (*Matthew,* 255).

have?" So Matthew's Peter is angling for present compensation to make up for his and the other disciples' having "left all" to follow Jesus, as though Jesus should have told the rich young man what he would be compensated now, not just eternally, were he to sell his possessions, give the proceeds to the poor, and follow Jesus.[28]

Mark, who does not have Peter angling for present compensation, quotes Jesus as promising "a hundred times as much *now at this time* — houses and brothers and sisters and mothers and children and fields, with persecutions," as well as "eternal life in the coming age" (Mark 10:30 [emphasis added]). Matthew inserts a futuristic reference to "the regeneration," at which time, Jesus promises, the apostles "will sit on twelve thrones judging the twelve tribes of Israel when the Son of Man sits on the throne of his glory" (cf. Luke 22:28-30). (This promise does not ensure salvation, for the false disciple Judas Iscariot is one of the Twelve.) Next, Matthew drops "now at this time," the list of family members and fields, and the reference to persecution (even though persecution figures prominently elsewhere in Matthew[29]), so that "a hundred times as much" looks forward only to what will obtain in "eternal life." Then, after adopting from Mark 10:31 Jesus' statement "But many first ones will be last, and last ones first," Matthew adds by way of explanation (γάρ, "For") a parable unique to his Gospel, i.e., the parable of laborers in a vineyard who all get the same pay though working widely varying amounts of time (Matt 20:1-15). Appended to this parable is an echo of 19:30: "In this way the last ones will be first and the first ones last" (20:16). In Matthew, then, Jesus rebuffs Peter's angling for present compensation and warns against Peter's assumption of discipular entitlement.[30]

---

28. Bonnard notes that Matthew sharpens Peter's question, as compared with Mark 10:28; Luke 18:28 (*Matthieu*, 289), though Wilkins speaks sympathetically of Peter's "anxiety" (*Concept of Disciple*, 204; so too Kingsbury, "Figure of Peter," 79).

29. See below, pp. 90-97.

30. Against Broadus, who avers that Jesus did not regard Peter's inquiry as "self-complacent or mercenary" (*Matthew*, 409). Gnilka regards it as "töricht" (*Matthäusevangelium*, 2:70-71), and France as "both smug . . . and mercenary" (*Matthew*, 741-42). France also recognizes Jesus' parable in 20:1-16 as corrective. Syreeni goes so far as to talk of Jesus' warning Peter as the "first" apostle (10:2) that in the end he may be "last" ("Peter as Character and Symbol," 144). Might one go further by saying that Jesus' use of the future tense makes for a prediction, not just a warning?

Peter from the Mount of Transfiguration through the Garden of Gethsemane

Matthew 26:31-35 (par. Mark 14:27-31; Luke 22:31-34; John 13:36-38)

In Mark 14:27 Jesus is quoted as saying to the disciples, "You will all be snared [σκανδαλισθήσεσθε]." The parallel in Matt 26:31 adds the phrases "in [regard to] me during this night." Though applying to all the disciples present, the added phrase "in [regard to] me" (ἐν ἐμοί [cf. 11:6; 13:57]) will apply most especially to Peter's denying three times that he has any personal acquaintance with Jesus (26:69-74). Though applying again to all the disciples present, the added phrase "during this night" will likewise apply most especially to Peter, because it anticipates the same in v. 34 (so too Mark 14:30), where Jesus predicts that Peter's denials will all occur before the night is over. In advance, then, Matthew adds emphasis on Peter's denials of Jesus (cf. 10:33).[31]

"If even [καί] all will be snared" (Mark 14:29) becomes in Matt 26:33 "If all will be snared in [regard to] you [ἐν σοι]." The omission of "even" by Matthew's Peter self-servingly diminishes the contrast between him and his fellow disciples, but the addition of "in [regard to] you" corresponds to Matthew's addition of "in [regard to] me" in Jesus' foregoing prediction and thereby doubles up on Peter's personal estrangement from Jesus in the coming denials. "Yet not I" (ἀλλ' οὐκ ἐγώ [so Mark]) becomes "I will never be snared" (ἐγὼ οὐδέποτε σκανδαλισθήσομαι). The replacement of Mark's "not" with "never" heightens Peter's contradiction of Jesus and forms the first part of a contrast with Jesus' following prediction that Peter will deny him *three* times": οὐδέποτε versus τρίς (v. 34). The addition of "Will never be snared," which in Mark is left to be inferred, spells out the contradiction explicitly.[32]

In Jesus' emphatic prediction ("Amen I tell you") of the three denials "during this night, before a rooster crows" (v. 34), Matthew omits Mark's σύ, "You" (referring to Peter), and σήμερον, "today" (which is superfluous, given the following), so that all emphasis falls on "during this night, before the rooster crows." Matthew's further omission of "twice" in connection with the rooster's crowing (Mark 14:30) hurries up Peter's predicted denials, as though he will hardly be able to wait to deny Jesus three times — before the rooster crows even once. That Luke 22:34 agrees with Mat-

---

31. See also Syreeni, "Peter as Character and Symbol," 145; against Schweizer, who writes that "Jesus' prediction is so devastating that the Scriptural citation [of Zech 13:7] showing that such things must come may be felt *as a kind of excuse*" (*Matthew*, 492 [emphasis added]).

32. Cf. Grundmann, *Matthäus*, 538; Nolland, *Matthew*, 1090.

thew's omission does not take away its effect (and may reflect Matthean influence on Luke).

Then for an antithetical emphasis Matthew escalates the imperfect tense of ἐλάλει, "he was saying" (Mark 14:31), to the vivid historical present tense of λέγει, "says," and against Mark supplies "Peter" as its subject (26:35), whereas in 26:34 Matthew had de-escalated the emphatic present tense of λέγει in Mark 14:30, "[Jesus] says," to the unemphatic aorist of ἔφη, "[Jesus] said." Thus Peter's foolish contradiction of both Jesus and the Scripture Jesus has just quoted gets more emphasis than what Jesus and the Scripture said. Added to the emphasis on Peter's contradiction is Matthew's omission of Mark's δέ, "But," so that the asyndeton in "Peter tells him" makes the contradiction emphatically abrupt as well as attributable to Peter by name. Both Pesch and Nolland observe that Matthew's mentioning Peter by name a second time in the pericope makes him stand out more — and in a negative light.[33]

In view of these redactionally anti-Petrine moves by Matthew, what is to be made of his omitting Mark's ἐκπερισσῶς, usually translated "vehemently," in describing Peter's speaking? The omission has been interpreted as sparing of Peter.[34] Matthew's other, contrary redactional moves make this interpretation unlikely, however; and Plummer notes that Matthew compensates for omitting "vehemently" by turning Peter's "If [ἐάν] I must die with you" (so Mark) into "*Even* if [κἄν] I must die with you."[35] It should be added that Matthew's present addition of "Even" compensates also for his omission of "even" (καί [so Mark 14:29]) back in v. 33, where the word would have set Peter opposite the other disciples. Here the word stresses his false confidence.

As to the omission of "vehemently," Davies and Allison note that ἐκπερισσῶς occurs nowhere else in the NT and not at all in the LXX, so that Mark may have coined the word and Matthew may therefore have considered it too obscure to adopt.[36] Perhaps so, but more probably the Matthew who distinctively had Peter tell Jesus, "Never, Lord! By no means

---

33. Pesch, *Simon-Petrus*, 40; Nolland, *Matthew*, 1091.

34. Gnilka, *Matthäusevangelium*, 2:405; Bonnard, *Matthieu*, 382; Luz, *Matthew 21–28*, 396 (who apparently uses Matthew's omission to describe Peter's statement as only "somewhat" boastful).

35. Plummer, *Matthew*, 368.

36. Davies and Allison, *Matthew*, 3:487 n. 38. See further Raymond E. Brown, *The Death of the Messiah: From Gethsemane to the Cross: A Commentary on the Passion Narrative in the Four Gospels* (2 vols.; ABRL; New York: Doubleday, 1994), 1:138.

will this happen to you!" (16:22) probably thought that now the Markan Peter "doth protest *too much*" in that the excess in his avowal of loyalty — and ἐκπερισσῶς is better and more literally translated with "excessively" — creates a mistaken suspicion of insincerity.[37] Insincerity would disagree with Peter's "Even if I must die with you, by no means will I deny you," οὐ μή plus the future indicative of ἀπαρνήσομαι (alternatively, an aorist subjunctive) being the strongest way to negate something in Greek.[38] The impression of insincerity on Peter's part would spoil the predictive contest between him and Jesus and blunt the force of his failure to keep the promise not to deny Jesus.[39] And Matthew may make up for his omission of ἐκπερισσῶς here by using the similar-sounding πικρῶς, "bitterly," to describe Peter's weeping in 26:75.

According to Matt 26:35, finally, "all the disciples spoke *similarly* [ὁμοίως]," whereas according to Mark 14:31 "all the disciples were speaking *identically* [ὡσαύτως]." The shift from sameness to similarity makes Peter's coming failure to avoid denying Jesus stand out as distinctive.

Matthew 26:36-46 (par. Mark 14:32-42; Luke 22:39-46; John 18:1)

In 26:37 Matthew replaces the names "James and John" (Mark 14:33) with "the two sons of Zebedee" and retains only the name "Peter." As a result, the weakness of Peter in failing to stay awake with Jesus for one hour stands out even though the other two also failed to stay awake according to 26:40. There, Matthew keeps Mark's "And he [Jesus] says to Peter," but omits Mark's follow-up, "Simon, you are sleeping!" (or as Mark 14:37 is usually translated, "Simon, are you sleeping?"). Matthew's omission of the direct address, "Simon," makes Jesus' following statement abrupt and stern: "In this way you [plural] were not strong enough to stay awake with me for one hour!" (or "In this way were you not strong enough to stay awake with

---

37. Cf. Shakespeare, *Hamlet*, Act III, scene 2.

38. See again Wallace, *Greek Grammar beyond the Basics*, 468. Burnett thinks Matthew's audience will judge Peter favorably for "acknowledg[ing] death as a distinct possibility for both Jesus and for himself" ("Characterization in Matthew," 32). But the more they do make such a favorable judgment, the worse will be their judgment when Peter fails to make good on his promise.

39. Insincerity could characterize false disciples, of course; but Matthew is concerned about those who genuinely think of themselves as Jesus' disciples but in truth are not. For such self-deception see, e.g., 7:21-23.

me for one hour?"). Matthew's insertion of "with me" (not in Mark) adds pathos to abruptness and sternness and marks a contrast with Matthew's Jesus as "'Immanuel,' which is translated, 'God [is] with us'" (Matt 1:23; cf. 28:20 and similar additions in 26:29, 36).

The preceding omission of "you [singular] are sleeping!" (or "are you sleeping?") is due to the even earlier omission of "Simon"; but "In this way" (οὕτως), which means "by way of sleeping," makes up for the omission of "you are sleeping!" and thereby forestalls our thinking that this omission is designed to spare Peter. What might be thought to spare him, though, is Matthew's replacing οὐκ ἴσχυσας, "you [singular, referring to Peter] were not strong enough" (so Mark), with ἰσχύσατε, "you [plural, referring to the two sons of Zebedee as well as to Peter] were not strong enough," so that blame is spread among all three disciples. But Mark has just said that Jesus "comes and finds *them* sleeping," and then quotes him as telling them, not Peter alone, to stay awake and pray lest they enter into temptation, i.e., succumb in trial. So by adding "to the disciples" after "he [Jesus] comes" and by changing the second-person singular to a second-person plural, Matthew is simply making an accommodation to the sleeping of all three and to Jesus' exhorting all three.[40] On the other hand, Matthew's retention of "he [Jesus] says to Peter" shows no loss of attention to Peter's failure.[41]

Matthew's adding "a second [time]" to Jesus' praying (26:42) and shifting "a third [time]" from Jesus' coming (so Mark 14:41) to his praying (26:44) anticipates by way of contrast Peter's three denials — another (though indirect) Matthean denigration of him in particular, since three times has no parallel in connection with the sons of Zebedee. That "a second [time]" is redundant after "again" deepens the denigration.[42] Matthew adopts from Mark 14:40 the disciples' having eyes heavy with sleep, not to ameliorate the failure to stay awake, but to highlight disobedience to Jesus' command not to succumb to sleepiness.[43]

---

40. Brown, *Death of the Messiah*, 1:194-95.

41. Against Pesch, *Simon-Petrus*, 141. See Turner, who correctly relates Jesus' addressing Peter specifically to Peter's having "protested loudly (26:33-35)" and to his future denials of Jesus (*Matthew*, 632).

42. Cf. Hagner, *Matthew 14-28*, 784.

43. Against Cassidy, who describes the reference to eyes heavy with sleep as "slightly exculpatory" (*Four Times Peter*, 80).

CHAPTER 5

Peter's Denials of Jesus along with the Suicide of Judas Iscariot

Matthew 26:57-75 (par. Mark 14:53-72; Luke 22:54-71; John 18:13-27)

Matthew 26:57–27:10, especially 26:69-75, constitutes the heart of Matthew's portrayal of Peter as a false disciple who apostatized. (An argument for including along with 26:57-75 the account of Judas Iscariot's suicide in 27:1-10 will follow in due course.) According to 26:57-58 Peter "was following" Jesus when Jesus was taken to Caiaphas the high priest. To Perkins, Peter thus "shows himself superior to the rest [of the disciples]," at least initially.[1] On the contrary, the additional phrase ἀπὸ μακρόθεν, "from afar, at a distance" (so too Mark 14:54; Luke 22:54), makes a condemnatory contrast with Peter's having promised Jesus, "Even if I must die *with you* [σὺν σοί], by no means will I deny you" (26:35).[2] Despite following Jesus, then, no longer was Peter with him. He had put himself at a distance from Jesus and "was sitting [instead] with [μετά] the servants [of the high priest]" in "the courtyard" rather than in the room where the high priest, scribes, and elders had gathered with

---

1. Perkins, *Peter*, 72; similarly, Pesch, *Simon-Petrus*, 141; Witherington, *Matthew*, 644.
2. Given μακρόθεν, ℵ C L Δ ƒ 33 892 *pm* omit ἀπό as unnecessary. Gnilka thinks ἀπὸ μακρόθεν may echo Ps 37:12 LXX (*Matthäusevangelium*, 2:425). In any case, the phrase shows that Peter was not following in true discipleship. But Patte may go too far in asserting, "Peter *defies* both the prophecy of Scripture and the teaching of Jesus [that all the disciples would be scattered] (26:31)" (*Matthew*, 372 [emphasis added]; cf. Ridderbos, *Matthew*, 500, that "by following his Master, even at a distance, Peter was ignoring Jesus' warning").

Peter — False Disciple and Apostate according to Saint Matthew

Jesus in their midst (N.B.: "as far as [ἕως (so too Mark)] the courtyard," but no farther").[3]

Retention of Mark's emphasis on entry with both ἔσω, "inside," and εἰς, "into" — though in a different word order — will make for a strong contrast with Peter's going progressively outside in v. 71 and, without a Markan parallel, in v. 75. Then Peter's sitting with the servants "to see the end" (ἰδεῖν τὸ τέλος) replaces his warming himself as together they face the firelight (so Mark). The replacement deprives him of a reason, such as being cold, to keep his distance from Jesus; and "to see the end" — i.e., the outcome in regard to Jesus — shows Peter to have reneged on his promise to suffer with Jesus his own end, if necessary (26:35 again).[4] Ironically, Peter will not see the end, which is Jesus' crucifixion. Of the disciples, only women will see it (27:55-56; par. Mark 15:40-41).

In 26:69 Matthew replaces κάτω, "below" (so Mark 14:66), with ἔξω, "outside." This replacement starts an emphasis on Peter's becoming increasingly outside. The emphasis reaches a climax in v. 75, where its theological import will require discussion. For the present, Peter is sitting "outside" from the perspective of the Sanhedrin's assembly room, whereas in v. 58 he was sitting "inside" the high priest's courtyard from the standpoint of having been in Gethsemane.[5]

In his reference to a maid, Matthew designates her as "one maid" (μία παιδίσκη) rather than as "one of the high priest's maids" (μία τῶν παιδισκῶν τοῦ ἀρχιερέως) (so Mark). Thus she stands alone and nondescript so as to stress Peter's weakness when he wilts before her. μία should not be taken as equivalent to the English indefinite article "a."[6] For Matthew habitually uses εἷς, "one," numerically rather than indefinitely in un-

---

3. See Brown, *Death of the Messiah*, 1:593-94, 601-2, on the meaning of αὐλή, "courtyard," and related words.

4. Cf. the fine comment by Garland: "He [Peter] had followed Jesus at a safe distance — no longer as a disciple — and sits with his [Jesus'] captors 'to see the end,' not to die with him as he had promised" (*Matthew*, 234; against the attribution to Peter of a motive to make good on his promise [as in Böttrich, *Petrus*, 124; Davies and Allison, *Matthew*, 3:523; Burnett, "Characterization in Matthew," 34; Gundry, *Commentary on the New Testament*, 122]). On the other hand, Gundry points out that "the distance at which Peter follows avoids a contradiction with his having fled [which fleeing, in view of 26:56 ('Then all the disciples, leaving him, fled'), Bockmuehl wrongly denies (*Simon Peter in Scripture and Memory*, 82)] and thus preserves the fulfillment of Jesus' prediction that 'all' the disciples would be scattered (26:31, 56)."

5. So Luz, *Matthew 21-28*, 424.

6. See Broadus, *Matthew*, 552 n. 1; Brown, *Death of the Messiah*, 1:595 n. 5.

paralleled as well as paralleled material.[7] So "*one* maid" definitely stresses that Peter will wilt before a *lone* maid. That παιδίσκη is diminutive as well as feminine may additionally stress Peter's coming weakness.[8]

As in v. 58, Matthew omits Mark's reference to Peter's warming himself and in this way takes away once again a possible excuse of coldness for sitting with the high priest's servants.[9] When the maid says to Peter, "You too were with Jesus the Galilean" (cf. 21:11), Peter says evasively, "I don't know *what* you're talking about" (v. 70; similarly Mark 14:68, whereas in Luke 22:57 Peter denies knowing *Jesus*), rather than denying that he has been with Jesus.[10] As in Mark, though, Peter's statement counts as a denial: "But he denied" (ὁ δὲ ἠρνήσατο). On the other hand, Matthew damagingly drops Peter's excuse in Mark that he does not understand what the maid has said.[11]

At this point Matthew adds against Mark, Luke, and John the phrase "before all" (ἔμπροσθεν πάντων) — i.e., before all the high priest's servants — and does so despite not having mentioned the high priest's servants since v. 58, prior to the intervening account of Jesus' hearing before the Sanhedrin (vv. 59-68), and despite Peter's now being accosted by only one maid (N.B. the contrast between μία, "one," and πάντων, "all").[12] The addition immediately calls to an audience's mind Jesus' statement in 10:33, "But whoever denies me before human beings [ἔμπροσθεν τῶν ἀνθρώπων] — I will also deny him before my Father in heaven."[13] Matthew might have

---

7. Along with synoptic parallels, see Matt 5:18, 19, 29, 30, 36, 41; 6:27; 8:19; 10:42; 12:11; 18:10, 16; 21:19; 23:8, 9, 10, 15; 24:40, 41; 25:15, 18, 24; 27:14, 48.

8. See France, *Matthew*, 1032-33.

9. Cf. Hagner, *Matthew 14-28*, 804.

10. Matthew's omission of Mark's σύ, "you," in Peter's response to the maid may be designed to leave as much attention as possible on Peter as a denier of Jesus. For σύ in Mark, Luke substitutes γύναι, "woman."

11. Kingsbury notes the dropping of this excuse ("Figure of Peter," 70). Brown seems to think that Mark's "technically ungrammatical" use of οὔτε . . . οὔτε to connect synonyms ("know" and "understand") led to Matthew's omission (*Death of the Messiah*, 1:600).

12. Contrast Peter's denying Jesus "before all" with Jesus' command that the disciples let their light shine "before people" (Matt 5:16), but that passage deals with doing good works rather than with confessing Jesus.

13. Among those who recognize Matthew's addition as an allusion to 10:33 are Ernst Lohmeyer, *Das Evangelium der Matthäus* (ed. Werner Schmauch; 3rd ed.; KEKNT; Göttingen: Vandenhoeck & Ruprecht, 1962), 371; G. W. H. Lampe, "St. Peter's Denial," *BJRL* 55 (1972/1973): 353, 355 (noting that ἀρνέομαι virtually means "apostatize," as often in cited patristic literature); France, *Matthew*, 1033. Inexplicably failing to draw the connection with 10:33 are Broadus, *Matthew*, 552; Zahn, *Matthäus*, 543; Lagrange, *Matthieu*, 610; Klemens

had Peter answer the maid "privately and discretely,"[14] as in his Markan source, or added the less comprehensive phrase "before *them*" (ἔμπροσθεν αὐτῶν). Instead, "before *all*" for the highest possible emphasis.

So the question has to be asked, Why did Matthew add "before all" if not to conform Peter's denial to Jesus' statement and thereby portray Peter as a disciple whom Jesus before his Father in heaven will deny as false? Questions whether in Matthew's view Peter repented and enjoyed restoration remain to be discussed. Meanwhile, it should be noted that Jesus' warning in 10:33 left no room for repentance and restoration. He made a flat-out statement, not that he *might* deny the denier, but that he *would*. No "unless" clause follows (cf. 2 Tim 2:12: "If we'll deny [him], that one ['Christ Jesus'] will also deny us"; contrast "unless you repent" in Luke 13:3, 5).[15]

In v. 71 Matthew highlights Peter's next denial as the second by intro-

---

Stock, "Jesus und seine Jünger nach Markus," in *"Il Verbo di Dio è Vivo": Studi sul Nuovo Testamento in onore del Cardinale Albert Vanhoye, S.I.* (ed. José Enrique Aguilar Chiu et al.; AnBib 165; Rome: Pontifical Biblical Institute, 2007), 152, 162-63; Perkins, *Peter*, 72; Hoffmann, "Der Petrus-Primat im Matthäusevangelium," 107 n. 46; Bockmuehl, *Simon Peter in Scripture and Memory*, 27; Evans, *Matthew*, 444. Worst of all are Syreeni's statements: "Most of the peculiarities in Matthew's version are rather neutral to Peter" and "On the whole, Matthew's account of Peter's denial of Jesus is scarcely less harsh toward Peter than the Markan story" ("Peter as Character and Symbol," 144).

14. This phrase comes from Birger Gerhardsson, "Confession and Denial before Men: Observations on Matt. 26:57–27:2," *JSNT* 13 (1981): 53.

15. Over against both Bonnard's speaking vaguely of the gravity of Peter's denial (*Matthieu*, 382), Nau's saying he is only "tripping dangerously along the precipice of divine rejection" (*Peter in Matthew*, 90), and Gnilka's describing 10:33 generally as a threat (*Matthäusevangelium*, 2:438), see the pointed statement by B. J. Oropeza:

> Jesus affirms that . . . if they ["his disciples"] deny him before others this will be reciprocated with their being denied: at the *parousia* Christ will claim that he does not know them and they will be excluded from his eschatological kingdom (Matt 10:32-33; cf. 7:21-23; Luke 12:8-9; 2 Clem. 3.2). *To deny Christ is to commit apostasy and be eternally condemned. These particular warnings of Jesus speak to persecution and pertain to his disciples. The stakes are eternal rather than temporal, and so the Matthean community should continue to confess Christ openly even though it struggles with hostile outsiders and local synagogues.* (*In the Footsteps of Judas and Other Defectors: The Gospels, Acts, and Johannine Letters* [Apostasy in the New Testament Commentaries 1; Eugene, Ore.: Wipf & Stock, 2011], 70 [italics original]).

Cf. Luz's pithy reference to "all the consequences that involves for the final judgment" (*Matthew 21–28*, 454-55); also Nolland on "the consequence, according to Mt. 10:33" (*Matthew*, 1140).

ducing it a bit more distinctly than in Mark, i.e., with an introductory δέ instead of Mark's (and Luke's) καί. Then instead of saying that Peter "exited outside into the forecourt" (ἐξῆλθεν ἔξω εἰς τὸ προαύλιον) — i.e., from the former courtyard, an inner one, into an outer courtyard — Matthew has him "having gone out into the gateway" (ἐξελθόντα ... εἰς τὸν πυλῶνα) — in other words, away from any courtyard at all and therefore progressively outside. This progression will come to a dreadful climax in v. 75. Stressing Peter's present exit is the forward position of ἐξελθόντα, which modifies αὐτόν later in the clause. (The awkwardness of this position spawned a couple of variant readings.[16]) In other words, Peter is trying to avoid a further confrontation by withdrawing from the firelight that fills a courtyard and into the darkness of a gateway.[17] Mark's ἔξω drops out, because it described the forecourt as outside the inner courtyard, whereas Matthew makes no distinction between courtyards.[18] Besides, Matthew inserted ἔξω back in v. 69, and will insert it again in v. 75.[19]

Next, "another [maid]" replaces "the [same] maid [as before]" in Mark 14:69. Matthew's addition of a second maid relates to his having used μία, "one," for the first maid. The doubling of maids produces a distinct instance, not of Peter's wilting again before the original maid but of his wilting again before another nondescript maid, and may additionally satisfy the law of two or three witnesses, in which law Matthew shows special interest (see esp. the insertions in 18:16; 26:60; plus Num 35:30; Deut 17:6; 19:15).[20] Mark's one and only maid started again to speak "to the bystanders" (τοῖς παρεστῶσιν) in the forecourt. Matthew changes them to "the ones *there*" (τοῖς ἐκεῖ) — i.e., in the gateway — to spotlight the place where Peter was trying to find cover outside the fire-lit courtyard. Instead of saying that Peter is one "of them" (ἐξ αὐτῶν [in reference to Jesus' disciples]; so Mark), the second maid says that Peter was "with Jesus the Nazarene."

---

16. See Lohmeyer, *Matthäus*, 371 n. 5.

17. Lohmeyer, *Matthäus*, 371-72; Grundmann, *Matthäus*, 547.

18. Against Brown, who thinks Matthew omitted ἔξω probably to avoid tautology (*Death of the Messiah*, 1:601).

19. If "and a rooster crowed" is part of Mark's original text in line with 14:30 (see the text-critical apparatus), Matthew omits the statement for correspondence with his omission of "twice" in 26:34 (par. Mark 14:30; see also Luke 22:34; John 13:38 for omission). In commenting on Matt 26:75, Evans inexplicably says that "the cock crowed a second time" (*Matthew*, 444).

20. Zahn, *Matthäus*, 544; Hagner, *Matthew 14-28*, 805. The account in 28:1-10 seems to show that Matthew regarded women as valid witnesses.

This change not only parallels the first maid's statement, "You too were with Jesus the Galilean" (v. 69), and makes up for the replacement in that statement of "the Nazarene" in Mark 14:67; but it also makes Peter's second denial of Jesus directly personal, whereas in his initial denial he had only played ignorant.[21]

Then Matthew adds without parallel that Peter made his second denial "with an oath" (μετὰ ὅρκου). In laying out the elements of superior righteousness necessary for entering the kingdom of heaven (5:20, unique to Matthew), Jesus prohibited oath-taking (5:33-37, also unique to Matthew among the Gospels, though see Jas 5:12). So by denying Jesus with an oath in flagrant disobedience to Jesus' prohibition, Matthew has Peter rule himself out of the kingdom of heaven. *Flagrant* disobedience because this oath did not accompany an ordinary statement. It accompanied a public denial of the very Jesus who had prohibited oaths.

Furthermore, Peter's disobedience stands in stark contrast with Jesus' simultaneously refusing to violate his own prohibition by answering the high priest under oath. For in Matthew's distinctive account (26:63-64) the high priest *adjures* Jesus by the living God — i.e., put him under oath (ἐξορκίζω σε) — that he say whether he is the Christ, the Son of God (contrast Mark 14:61, where the high priest simply "says" [λέγει] to Jesus, "Are you the Christ, the Son of the Blessed One?"). But Jesus tells him, "You yourself have spoken" (σὺ εἶπας). That is to say, "Your words, not mine, because I refuse to answer under oath" (contrast Mark 14:62, according to which Jesus says outright, "I am").[22]

Add to these exacerbations of Peter's second denial the fact that he was not even confronted by the second maid. She merely spoke about him to

---

21. So too Hagner, *Matthew 14–28*, 805; France, *Matthew*, 1033.

22. Against Wiefel, who considers the answer of Matthew's Jesus "ein klar Ja" (*Matthäus*, 462), and Meier, who considers it "a veiled 'yes'" (*Matthew*, 332); similarly, Luz, *Matthew 21–28*, 429, and Gerhardsson, "Confession and Denial before Men," 57. Even in 26:25; 27:11 the same expression throws the interlocutor's words back in his face. The point is not, "If I had to answer, I'd say, 'Yes'"; rather, "Answer your own question." It would have been untruthful for Jesus to have said, "No, I am not the Christ, the Son of God," so that apart from refusing to answer the high priest at all, an avoidance of both falsehood and answering under oath required Jesus to throw the high priest's words back in his face. Failing to relate Peter's oath to 5:33-37 and to Jesus' refusal to answer under oath are Lagrange, *Matthieu*, 510; Hoffmann, *Petrus-Primat im Matthäusevangelium*, 107 n. 46; K. Stock, "Jesus und seine Jünger nach Markus," 152, 162-63; Perkins, *Peter*, 72; Bockmuehl, *Simon Peter in Scripture and Memory*, 27. Somewhat weakly, Nolland says that "Jesus did not *want* his disciples" to use an oath (*Matthew*, 1141 [emphasis added]). But a stated prohibition is stronger than a stated desire.

others, and he overheard. Yet not only does he volunteer his second denial of Jesus — with the oath, no less — but, unlike Mark, Matthew also directly quotes the direct, personal denial: "I do not know the man." "The man" dismissively replaces "Jesus the Nazarene" in the second maid's comment to others and therefore carries the connotation of "I don't know the guy."[23]

To introduce Peter's third denial of Jesus (26:73-74), Matthew substitutes δέ instead of the καί in Mark 14:70b. The substitution sets the denial clearly apart from the first two denials for further evidence of Peter's false discipleship (cf. the δέ in v. 71). Since bystanders have not previously spoken to Peter, Matthew drops πάλιν, "again," and substitutes προσελθόντες, "approaching," whose prefix (προσ-) leads him to drop the prefix παρ- from Mark's παρεστῶτες, "bystanders," the rest of which he adopts (cf. v. 71 again). If they have approached, you can assume a location close by. "Truly" (so too Mark) in their saying to Peter, "Truly you too are [one] of them," makes a contrast with his falsehoods. Matthew's insertion of καὶ σύ, "you too" (not in Mark), brightens the spotlight on Peter as he is about to deny Jesus for the third time.[24] Where Mark has the bystanders say, "you are a Galilean," Matthew has them say, "your speech makes you evident [as one who was with Jesus the Galilean/Nazarene]." This shift makes Peter's third denial the denial of a plain (δῆλον) fact, and therefore worsens the denial.

The replacement of ὁ δέ, "But he [Peter]" (Mark 14:71), with τότε, "Then," welds together chronologically the following denial with the preceding observation on Peter's speech. He wastes no time in denying Jesus again.[25] Naturally, Matthew adopts from Mark Peter's beginning the denial with cursing and the swearing of an oath. "*Started* cursing and swearing" (so too Mark) indicates *extended* cursing and swearing.[26] Possibly, the change of Mark's **ἀνα**θεματίζειν, "to take *up* cursing," to **κατα**θεματίζειν,

---

23. Cf. a contemptuous use of "the man" in Plutarch *Mor.* 870C and Luz, *Matthew 21-28*, 455, who notes that Peter's oath puts him in the bad company of Herod Antipas (14:7, 9) and compares Jesus' "I don't know you" in 25:12; also 7:23 in reference to the Last Judgment. See too France, *Matthew*, 1033; Carter, *Matthew and the Margins*, 520; Grant R. Osborne, *Matthew* (ZECNT; Grand Rapids: Zondervan, 2010), 1001; Jack J. Gibson, *Peter Between Jerusalem and Antioch: Peter, James and the Gentiles* (WUNT 2/345; Tübingen: Mohr Siebeck, 2013), 62-63.

24. So too Nolland, who notes the echo of v. 69 par. Mark 14:67 (*Matthew*, 1141).

25. Cf. Lohmeyer, *Matthäus*, 372; Nolland, *Matthew*, 1142. Nolland speaks of "the sense of climax."

26. Among many examples of ἤρξατο, "started," as introducing extended action, see 4:17 (for Jesus' extended preaching) and 16:21 (for Jesus' passion-and-resurrection predictions, extended by repetition over several occasions).

"to pronounce a curse *against* someone," intensifies the cursing; and certainly in Matthew the self-imposed oath marks yet another flagrant disobedience to Jesus' prohibition of oath-taking (5:33-37), a prohibition the observance of which again forms part of the superior righteousness necessary for entrance into the kingdom of heaven (5:20). The oath also marks yet another contrast with Jesus' refusal to answer under oath (see the comments on v. 72). Matthew's doubling of Peter's oath-taking thus puts Peter in an extremely bad light. Or should we say, in damnable darkness? In either case, he is not put under oath by others, nor is he asked to take an oath. He volunteers the damnable oaths.[27]

Mark quotes Peter as saying, "I don't know this man whom you are talking about." Because those who commented on Peter's speech said nothing about Jesus, Matthew omits "this" and "whom you are talking about." As a result, Mark's ἄνθρωπον, "man," gains in Matthew the connotation of "guy" for a second time: "I don't know the guy" (cf. v. 72). Thus the shortening makes Matthew's version of Peter's denial terse, curt, more dismissive of Jesus, and therefore more guilt-worthy. Instead of denying *himself* so as to follow Jesus and gain eternal life, as Jesus commanded in 16:24-25, Peter has now denied *Jesus* three times.

Naturally, the description in Mark 14:72 of the cockcrow as a "second" drops out in Matthew. Perhaps to forestall any impression that Peter remembered Jesus' prediction a second time, as Mark's ἀνεμνήσθη could be understood in connection with a second cockcrow, Matthew omits the prefix from the verb of remembering (26:75). Except for the omission of "twice" for the cockcrowing, Matthew shares with Mark the re-quotation of Jesus' prediction of Peter's three denials. In both versions of the re-quotation, "during this night" drops out (contrast Matt 26:34; par. Mark 14:30), so that emphasis concentrates on the number of rejections predicted: three, one for each of Peter's failures to pray in Gethsemane. So he has turned into the example par excellence of "the person sown on rocky ground [cf. the meaning of Πέτρος] . . . who hears the word and receives it immediately with joy. But he does not have root in himself, but is temporary. And when pressure [θλίψεως] or persecution comes about because of the word, he is immediately snared" (13:20-21). In place of Mark's difficult phrase καὶ ἐπιβαλών,[28]

---

27. See G. W. H. Lampe, who observes that with his cursing and swearing Peter "exemplifies the most extreme form of apostasy. He is the archetype of the worst class among the *lapsi*" ("St. Peter's Denial," 354).

28. See Robert H. Gundry, *Mark: A Commentary on His Apology for the Cross* (Grand Rapids: Eerdmans, 1993), 891, for a survey of possible meanings and for the suggestion that

Matthew puts ἐξελθὼν ἔξω, "and on going out, outside" (N.B. the twofold emphasis in ἐξ- and ἔξω), changes Mark's imperfect verb ἔκλαιεν, "he was weeping," to the aorist ἔκλαυσεν, "he wept," and adds πικρῶς, "bitterly."

These last changes have almost universally been interpreted as Matthew's intensifying of Peter's repentance, already evident to a certain extent in Mark. But earlier in Matthew the combination of going outside, which Matthew has maximized in the present passage, and weeping has repeatedly gained a connotation radically different from repentance that gains forgiveness — rather, the connotation of bitter despair over salvation lost, over eternal perdition in the outermost darkness. The passages are numerous:

- 8:12: "But the sons of the kingdom will be thrown out into the darkness farther outside.[29] Weeping and gnashing of teeth will be there."
- 13:41-42: "The Son of Man will send his angels, and they will collect out of his kingdom all the snares and those who practice lawlessness, and will throw them into the furnace of fire. Weeping and gnashing of teeth will be there."
- 13:49-50: "Thus it will be in the consummation of the age: the angels will come forth and separate the evil [false disciples] from the midst of the righteous [true disciples] and throw them [the false] into the furnace of fire. Weeping and gnashing of teeth will be there."
- 22:13: "After binding his feet and hands, throw him [the man at the wedding feast without a wedding garment] into the darkness farther outside. Weeping and gnashing of teeth will be there."
- 24:51: "And he [the master] will slice him [the 'wicked slave'] in two and put his portion with the hypocrites. Weeping and gnashing of teeth will be there."
- 25:30: "And throw the useless slave into the darkness farther outside. Weeping and gnashing of teeth will be there."

The statements in 22:13; 24:51; 25:30 appear by way of Matthew's insertion into otherwise paralleled material. The statements in 13:41-42, 49-50 appear in Matthew's unparalleled material (cf. 5:13; 13:48). Only 8:12 has

---

ἐπιβαλών means "proceeding." Further discussion is to be found in Brown, *Death of the Messiah*, 1:609-10; Nolland, *Matthew*, 1143.

29. Here and elsewhere, ἐξώτερον is comparative and therefore can be translated as such ("farther outside") or as elative ("outermost").

a parallel (in Luke 13:28). All the other, distinctively Matthean statements have to do with the fate of false disciples who help populate "the kingdom of heaven" till the final separation of the false out from among the true. And throughout his account of Peter's denials, Matthew has Peter going farther and farther outside — from the courtyard "outside" the room where Jesus was standing before the Sanhedrin "out" into the gateway and then completely and doubly "out, outside," or as we might say, "altogether outside" — and finally has him weeping at that outermost point (vv. 69, 71, 75). The bitterness of his weeping corresponds to the gnashing of teeth by the damned.[30]

After repeating time after time after time that false disciples would be thrown outside, where there is weeping and gnashing of teeth, Matthew must have intended his audience, with that statement ringing in their ears, to have understood Peter's denials of Jesus farther and farther away from him as evidence of false discipleship, and his bitter weeping outside as an omen of eternal damnation in the outermost darkness.

Here it becomes necessary to take up the nearly universal attempt to read into Matthew a rehabilitation of Peter. The attempt takes various forms. One consists in mere assertion, which merits no reply — e.g., "Kein Fall und Abfall muss so endgültig sein, dass eine Einkehr und Umkehr nicht mehr möglich."[31] The attempt also takes many other, reasoned forms, however, which do merit replies:

- The resurrected Jesus' appearance to Peter according to Luke 24:34; 1 Cor 15:5 implies rehabilitation.[32] (But we want to know Matthew's view, not Luke's or Paul's — or John's, for that matter.)

---

30. The statement "And on going outside, he wept bitterly" has an exact parallel in Luke 22:62. It is debatable whether both Matthew and Luke drew on a common tradition, or whether Luke drew at least somewhat on Matthew (or even vice versa). For argument that Luke drew throughout on Matthew, see again the bibliography above in n. 10 on p. 4. Text-critical evidence for the omission of Luke 22:62 (*vs* 0171 it) is so weak as to have been omitted in NA[28], but see Burnett Hillman Streeter, *The Four Gospels: A Study of Origins* (London: Macmillan, 1964), 323. If inclusion is to be accepted in Luke, the obvious restoration of Peter in Luke-Acts (see Luke 22:31-32; 24:12, 34; et passim in Acts), plus the fact that Luke 13:28 does not have to do with professing disciples who try unsuccessfully to repent, favors that in contrast with Matt 26:75, Peter repents successfully in Luke 22:62 (see Meier, *A Marginal Jew*, 3:240).

31. Zahn, *Matthäus*, 545. Cf. the statement of Bockmuehl that Peter becomes "a prototype of the fallen and restored believer" (*The Remembered Peter*, 8).

32. Gnilka, *Matthäusevangelium*, 2:438.

Peter's Denials of Jesus along with the Suicide of Judas Iscariot

- Jesus' having kept Peter from drowning back in 14:30-31 symbolized Peter's future rehabilitation after denying Jesus, and also assured Peter-like deniers of Jesus that he will save them despite their denials because of little faith and doubt, like Peter's.[33] (But little faith and doubt do not rise to the level of denial.)
- Peter's denials marked "a temporary lapse under pressure" rather than "a settled course of dissociation," as in 10:33, so that he "did not ultimately come under the threat of 10:33."[34] (On what ground is 10:33 limited to *settled* dissociation, though; and if given, would not *three* denials of increasing intensity count as settled?)
- "By 'going outside' of the high priest's courtyard, Peter . . . dissociates himself from those 'inside' the place where Jesus has been judged deserving of death,"[35] so as to be able to repent.[36] (But going outside the high priest's courtyard runs counter to Peter's promise to die with Jesus, if necessary.)
- That bystanders identify Peter as a disciple of Jesus shows that he remains a true one despite denying him.[37] (In the *bystanders'* estimation, yes. But what of *Matthew's* estimation?)
- "Strictly speaking," Peter's denials are not unique to him, because 26:35 "implicates all the disciples in this."[38] (But 26:35 implicates all the disciples in a promise not to deny Jesus, not in the denials themselves, of which only Peter is guilty.)
- Jesus' statement-cum-quotation of Zech 13:7 in Matt 26:31 "indicates restoration."[39] (How? The verse speaks of the disciples' being snared and scattered, not of restoration.)
- The cockcrow heralds a new day and therefore symbolizes a new beginning for Peter.[40] (According to the scriptural text the cockcrow reminds him, rather, of Jesus' prediction of the denials.)

---

33. Dschulnigg, "Gestalt und Funktion," 178; Dschulnigg, *Petrus im Neuen Testament*, 54-55; France, *Matthew*, 1032.

34. France, *Matthew*, 999-1000, also 406.

35. John Paul Heil, *The Death and Resurrection of Jesus: A Narrative-Critical Reading of Matthew 26–28* (Minneapolis: Fortress, 1991), 66.

36. So the Venerable Bede. For the text, see Robert W. Herron Jr., *Mark's Account of Peter's Denial of Jesus* (Lanham, Md.: University Press of America, 1991), 46, 157.

37. Patte, *Matthew*, 375.

38. Kingsbury, "Figure of Peter," 74; cf. Osborne, *Matthew*, 807.

39. Carter, *Matthew and the Margins*, 519.

40. Böttrich, *Petrus*, 9-15.

Peter — False Disciple and Apostate according to Saint Matthew

- Matthew's audience "recognize the potentially transforming nature of his [Peter's] self-recognition as a culpable and abject failure."[41] (But self-recognition of culpable and abject failure just as easily breeds despair.)
- The bitterness of Peter's weeping shows him to be repentant.[42] (Bitter weeping just as easily shows remorseful despair, however, as in Gen 37:34; Isa 15:3b; 22:4 LXX; 33:7 LXX.)
- The immediacy of Peter's weeping shows repentance.[43] (Yet it can equally well show immediate remorse and despair.)
- "While Peter's weakness contrasts unfavorably with Jesus' courage, it contrasts favorably with Judas's despair (27:3-10)."[44] (Who is to say, though, that Peter's tears do not *match* Judas's despair?)
- Though Peter's failure was great, his repentance was greater.[45] (This argument assumes repentance rather than despair, and without justification rates the assumed repentance as greater than the failure.)
- In Matt 26:74-75 Peter "repents" bitterly.[46] (No, he "wept" bitterly.)
- He underwent an "Umkehr."[47] (Why not a downturn instead of a turnaround?)
- In contrast with Mark 14:72, Matthew deepens Peter's repentance with "bitterly."[48] (But "bitterly" modifies weeping, which can indicate despairing remorse rather than contrite repentance.)
- Though Peter's bitter weeping "is left uninterpreted for the moment," "the careful reader may remember that a word spoken against the Son of Man is forgivable (12:32)."[49] (Denying *knowledge* of Jesus so as to

---

41. Richard Bauckham, *Jesus and the Eyewitnesses: The Gospels as Eyewitness Testimony* (Grand Rapids: Eerdmans, 2006), 177; cf. Burnett, "Characterization in Matthew," 36.

42. Grappe, *Images de Pierre*, 84-91; Brown et al., *Peter in the New Testament*, 166.

43. Plummer, *Matthew*, 383; Meier, *Matthew*, 335; cf. Jerome's comment: "With bitter tears he [Peter] immediately washes away the sin of denial that sprang up from fear" (*Commentary on Matthew* 2.14.28 according to the translation in Manlio Simonetti, ed., *Matthew 14-28* (Ancient Christian Commentary on Scripture, New Testament Ib [Downers Grove, Ill.: InterVarsity Press, 2002], 13).

44. Meier, *Matthew*, 335.

45. Laurentin, *Petite vie de saint Pierre*, 63.

46. Bockmuehl, *Simon Peter in Scripture and Memory*, 27.

47. Pesch, *Simon-Petrus*, 45.

48. Pesch, *Simon-Petrus*, 141; Osborne, *Matthew*, 1002.

49. France, *Matthew*, 1032. Cf. the view that speaking against the Son of Man before his exaltation, but not afterward, is forgivable; also the view that an Aramaic original meant "a son of man," i.e., any human being (Evans, *Matthew*, 257-58). This latter view does not

hide one's discipleship does not equate with speaking *against* him, however.⁵⁰)
- "The careful specification that it was *eleven* disciples who met Jesus in Galilee (28:16 [cf. *Acts Pet. 12 Apos.* 9.17]) ensures that Peter is included in the 'disciples' of 28:7 and the 'brothers' of 28:10."⁵¹ (But should we not expect a false disciple to be included?)
- The tares will not be extracted from among the wheat until harvest-time at the end of the age, when there will be weeping and gnashing of teeth (13:36-43).
- The foul fish will not be divided from among the good till the end of the age, when there will be weeping and gnashing of teeth (13:47-50).
- The "called" man without a wedding garment will not be thrown into the outer darkness, where there will be weeping and gnashing of teeth, until the king arrives (22:11-14).
- The wicked slave will not be sliced in two and put with the hypocrites,

---

mesh with Matthew's meaning, however. N.B. the definite articles in κατὰ τοῦ υἱοῦ τοῦ ἀνθρώπου.

50. Against G. W. H. Lampe, "St. Peter's Denial," 357; Brown, *Death of the Messiah*, 1:608. Luz notes that "neither the text, which reveals no similarity to the language of 12:32, nor the progression of the narrative encourages that association" (*Matthew 21–28*, 456-57). On the other hand, it has become popular to say that since elsewhere ἀναθεματίζω/καταθεματίζω always takes a direct object, Peter must have cursed Jesus; but out of reverence for Jesus, Matthew omitted naming him as the object of Peter's cursing (Günther Bornkamm, *Jesus of Nazareth* [trans. Irene McLuskey and Fraser McLuskey with James M. Robinson; New York: Harper & Brothers, 1960], 211-12 n. 13; Helmut Merkel, "Peter's Curse," in *The Trial of Jesus: Cambridge Studies in honour of C. F. D. Moule* [ed. Ernst Bammel; SBT 2/13; London: SCM, 1970], 66-71; G. W. H. Lampe, "Saint Peter's Denial," 354; Lampe, "Church Discipline and the Interpretation of the Epistles to the Corinthians," in *Christian History and Interpretation: Studies Presented to John Knox* [ed. W. R. Farmer et al.; Cambridge: Cambridge University Press, 1967], 357). If so, the cursing of Jesus could count as the forgivable sin of speaking against him. In the first place, however, the verb has no direct object in our text. In the second place, the verb could imply a reflexive direct object (Peter put himself under a curse) just as easily as it could imply Jesus as the direct object — probably more easily, in fact, since Peter is also putting himself under an oath (ὀμνύει; cf. "with an oath" in v. 72; see Acts 23:14, 21 for ἀναθεματίζω with an expressed reflexive direct object). Third, it is even possible, though unlikely, that by implication Peter cursed the bystanders who had accosted him. In Matthew, finally, the forgivable sin of speaking against Jesus "is committed by someone who has never professed to follow Jesus, whereas [according to 10:33] he'll unforgivingly disown a professing disciple who has disowned him" (Gundry, *Commentary on the New Testament*, 52; see the context of 12:32). So the argument that, with his cursing, Peter forgivably spoke against Jesus lacks conviction.

51. France, *Matthew*, 1032; also Brown, *Death of the Messiah*, 1:608, and many others.

where there will be weeping and gnashing of teeth, until the master arrives (24:48-51).
- The foolish virgins will not be shut out until the bridegroom arrives (25:1-13).
- The useless slave will not be thrown into the outermost darkness, where there will be weeping and gnashing of teeth, until his master returns after being away a long time (25:14-30).

Almost all these passages are unique to Matthew. So we should expect Peter to have been among Jesus' "disciples," "brothers," and "the Eleven" despite a Matthean portrayal of him as false — a tare, a foul fish(erman), and so on. (See further the comments below on the omission in Matt 28:7 of "and Peter" in Mark 16:7.)

Notably, none of the foregoing defenders of a Petrine rehabilitation in Matthew take note of the emphatically Matthean combination of weeping outside by the damned as an interpretive background for Peter's weeping outside. Yet Dschulnigg does admit that Peter's denials are not "gemildert" by any comparable acts of the other disciples.[52] And Ben Witherington III says, "Our Evangelist portrays Peter doing a pilgrim's regress, both physically and morally."[53] Perhaps, then, the best commentary on Peter's bitter weeping outside is to be found in a parallel with Esau, who "when wanting to inherit the blessing, he was rejected; for he did not find a place of repentance even though having sought it earnestly with tears" (Heb 12:17).[54] To the parallel with Esau should be added the declarations in Heb 6:4-6:

> For in the case of those who have once been enlightened and tasted the heavenly gift and become partakers of the Holy Spirit and tasted God's word as good and the miracles of the coming age and have fallen by the

---

52. Dschulnigg, *Petrus im Neuen Testament*, 53. Dschulnigg is reduced to suggesting that Matthew attacks a false idealization of Peter and making him, instead, typical of disciples in their vices as well as their virtues.

53. Witherington, *Matthew*, 500. Contrast the erroneous statement of Bauckham, "A remarkable feature of this [Markan sympathetic] characterization of Peter is that it remains constant through all four canonical Gospels" (*Jesus and the Eyewitnesses*, 177). Not in Matthew!

54. See Gundry, *Commentary on the New Testament*, 912. For histories of the interpretation of Peter's denials, see Luz, *Matthew 21-28*, 459; Herron, *Mark's Account*, 22-25, 52, 149-52, 162-63.

Peter's Denials of Jesus along with the Suicide of Judas Iscariot

wayside, *it is impossible to renew [them] again to repentance*, since they are re-crucifying God's Son for their own sakes and making a spectacle of him.

And also 10:26-31:

> For if we sin willfully after having received the knowledge of the truth, a sin-offering no longer remains. But something [does remain]: *a fearsome expectation of judgment*, even of a fervor of fire that is going to devour the opponents. On disregarding the law of Moses someone dies without pity [by execution] on the basis of two or three witnesses. Of how much worse punishment do you suppose he will be deemed deserving who has trampled God's Son and regarded as defiled the covenantal blood by which he was consecrated and [who has] insulted the Spirit of grace? For we know the one who said, "Retribution belongs to me; I will give back in return," and again, "The Lord will judge *his people*." Falling into the hands of the living God is fearsome.

(See also Heb 3:7–4:11 with Num 14:1-45, esp. 39-45, in regard to Israel's wilderness generation that reproached themselves too late.)

Matthew 27:1-10 (par. Mark 15:1; Luke 23:1; John 18:28; Acts 1:15-20)

According to France, "the Christian reader . . . is prepared [by Peter's subsequent role in church history] to read a more positive repentance into Peter's weeping than into the unavailing remorse of Judas (27:3-5)."[55] This comparison — or contrast, as France would have it — with Judas Iscariot's remorse calls for a consideration of the relation between 26:69-75 and 27:1-10. To forge that relation, Matthew first moves Jesus off stage temporarily: the chief priests and the elders of the people take Jesus to Pilate (27:1-2). Next, and without parallel in the other Gospels, Matthew interjects the story of Judas Iscariot's suicide (27:3-10). Matthew's "Then" (Τότε) brings Judas's returning to the chief priests and elders the reward for betrayal into chronological contact with their having condemned Jesus. But therein lies

---

55. France, *Matthew*, 1032. Cf. the statement of Evans: "Peter's reaction to his betrayal [sic, denials] stands in contrast to the tragic reaction of Judas the following day (Matt 27:3-10)" (*Matthew*, 445).

an inconcinnity. For at the time, the chief priests and elders were not at the temple, where they and Judas are said to confront each other and into which he hurls the reward money. According to 27:1-2, 11-14, they were busy elsewhere, taking Jesus to Pilate and accusing him before Pilate.[56] So Matthew has misplaced the story of Judas's suicide both chronologically and topographically in order to bring the suicide into relation with Peter's bitter weeping outside. But what kind of relation? One of contrast, or one of similarity?

To answer that question, the differences between Matthew's account of Judas's death and the parallel account in Acts 1:15-20 need noting. In Acts, Judas shows no remorse. In Matthew, he does show remorse. In Acts, he retains the price of betrayal, which in Luke 22:5, par. Mark 14:11, was promised him prior to the betrayal but apparently not delivered to him till after he had carried out the bargain. In Matthew, he returns the price of betrayal, which according to Matt 26:15 he got prior to betraying Jesus. In Acts, he purchases a field with the money. In Matthew, the chief priests do. In Acts, naturally, he makes the purchase prior to his death. In Matthew, the chief priests make the purchase after his death. In Acts, he dies accidentally, by falling headlong, bursting, and spilling his guts on the field he has purchased. In Matthew, he dies deliberately, by hanging himself, in an unidentified location. In Acts, the field where he suffered his fatal accident is subsequently named "Field [χωρίον] of Blood," in reference to *his* blood spilled out on the field. In Matthew, the field is named "The Field [ὁ ἀγρός] of Blood," in reference to *Jesus'* blood, which Judas had remorsefully called "innocent." Acts does not tell the future use of the field where Judas died. Matthew says that the field where Judas did *not* die (for it had yet to be purchased by the chief priests) was used for the burial of aliens. Neither Acts nor Matthew identifies his burial place.[57]

What stands out in bold relief among these differences is Matthew's emphasizing the remorse of Judas, evident in his confession of sin, in his description of Jesus' blood as innocent, in his attempt to give back the reward money, in his throwing it into the sanctuary upon refusal of the

---

56. See, e.g., Francis Wright Beare, *The Gospel according to Matthew: Translation, Introduction and Commentary* (New York: Harper & Row, 1981), 525; France, *Matthew*, 1038; Witherington, *Matthew*, 506; Brown, *Death of the Messiah*, 1:637-38; Audrey Conard, "The Fate of Judas: Matthew 27:3-10," *Toronto Journal of Theology* 7 (1991): 158.

57. On efforts to harmonize the accounts in Matthew and Acts, see Keener, *Acts: An Exegetical Commentary*, vol. 1: *Introduction and 1:1–2:47* (Grand Rapids: Baker Academic, 2012), 761-65.

attempt, and in his committing suicide. If Matthew redacted material similar to that in Acts 1:15-20, this emphasis on Judas's remorse looks all the more significant. Therefore does the remorse following betrayal count as a repentance leading to salvation in the hereafter, so that the relation of this episode to Peter's bitter weeping after the denials implies final salvation for Peter, too? No, for such a conclusion would contradict Jesus' statements in Matt 26:24, "Woe to that man through whom the Son of Man is being betrayed! It would have been better for him if he — that man — had not been born!" (par. Mark 14:21; Luke 22:22). Jesus distances the betrayer soteriologically by twice calling him "*that* man."

To the contrary, some social-scientific and cross-cultural analyses have portrayed Judas's suicide as noble and atoning in that he had confessed his sin and rid himself of the blood money.[58] But ancient attitudes toward suicide spanned the spectrum from considering it noble to considering it ignoble. So to consider Judas's suicide noble and atoning is to invalidate the horrifying woe that Jesus pronounced on his betrayer and thus make Jesus what literary critics call "an unreliable character," not at all the image of Jesus that Matthew wants to project. It has been retorted that just as the omni-ethnic Great Commission in Matt 28:19-20 cancels the earlier limitation to Israel in 10:5b-6, so too may Judas's remorse-cum-suicide nullify Jesus' earlier woe against Judas.[59] To say so, however, is on the one hand to overlook the difference between one and the same person (Jesus) changing his instructions from one circumstance to another and, on the other hand, a prediction by one person, elsewhere portrayed as a reliable character, and an action by a completely different person, elsewhere portrayed as unreliable.

Furthermore, for Judas's remorse Matthew uses the verb μεταμέλομαι, not μετανοέω, the verb ordinarily used for salvific repentance, as in the preaching of John the Baptist and Jesus (3:2; 4:17; 11:20, 21; 12:41).[60] For nonsalvific uses of μεταμέλομαι in the NT, see 2 Cor 7:8 (bis); Heb 7:21. Blomberg cites 2 Cor 7:8-10 as evidence that remorse (μεταμέλομαι) precedes repentance.[61] But in that passage sorrow (λύπη and its verbal cog-

---

58. See, e.g., David A. Reed, "'Saving Judas' — A Social Scientific Approach to Judas's Suicide in Matthew 27:3-10," *BTB* 35 (2005): 51-59; Conard, "Fate of Judas," 158-68; see also Davies and Allison, *Matthew*, 3:561-63, all with references to other literature.

59. Davies and Allison, *Matthew*, 3:562.

60. Böttrich describes μεταμέλομαι as an "Allerweltswort" in distinction from μετανοέω as "theologisch gefüllten" (*Petrus*, 128).

61. Blomberg, *Matthew*, 407.

nate), not remorse, precedes repentance (μετάνοιαν). The verb of remorse has to do with *Paul's* changing and not changing his mind, moreover, and therefore does not run parallel to the *Corinthians'* repentance. And wishing that something could be undone does not equate with repentance. In Heb 7:21 the Lord's not changing his mind obviously has nothing to do with nonrepentance in a moral sense.

True, in Matt 21:32 μεταμέλομαι occurs for a remorse — i.e., a change of mind — that should have but did not characterize the unbelieving chief priests and elders after (ὕστερον) they had seen the tax collectors and prostitutes believe John the Baptist. In this respect the chief priests and elders contrast with the initially disobedient boy who later (ὕστερον) did change his mind according to Jesus' preceding parable (21:28-31). The whole parable is unique to Matthew, but it provides only questionable support for the evangelist's equation of μεταμέλομαι with μετανοέω. For it is a stretch to say that the boy's change of mind carries the theologically moral freight characteristic of μετανοέω. And Jesus' application of the parable does not have to do with a change of behavior, as the parable would lead one to expect and as μετανοέω would have connoted — rather, with only the mental activity of believing. N.B. the three forms of πιστεύω in v. 32: "For John came to you in the way of righteousness, and you did not believe him [οὐκ ἐπιστεύσατε αὐτῷ]. But the tax collectors and the prostitutes did believe him [ἐπίστευσαν αὐτῷ]. But you, on seeing [that they believed him], did not even suffer remorse later on so as to believe him [πιστεῦσαι αὐτῷ]."[62] On the other hand, Judas addresses his remorse, his change of mind, to the chief priests and elders, who by no means have authority to forgive him.[63] Instead, they say to him, "What [is your betraying innocent blood] to us? You shall see [to it] yourself!" (27:4, exhibiting an imperatival future). In other words, Judas is on his own. He gets no absolution from the chief priests and elders, and he does not even seek forgiveness from God (or from Jesus, since Jesus was unavailable).

Boxall tries to turn Judas's remorse into repentance by suggesting that "Matthew's Judas acknowledges the value of Jesus' life (30 shekels of silver

---

62. Against Davies and Allison, *Matthew*, 3:561-63.

63. As Garland writes, "Judas ... makes a fatal mistake by returning to the temple to seek absolution through his co-conspirators when the temple is no longer the place of God's presence or the seat of forgiveness" (*Matthew*, 255). Unfortunately, Garland takes Peter's presence among "the Eleven" in 28:16 as implying he had repented and obtained forgiveness rather than as indicative of the presence of false disciples among the true until the consummation (see above).

being the wages of the shepherd: Zech. 11.12)."[64] The *wages* of a shepherd do not equate with the value of his *life,* though; and, more decisively, it was the chief priests, not Judas, who according to Matt 26:14-16 set the sum of thirty shekels.

In Matt 27:24 Pilate will declare his innocence of the righteous Jesus' blood, perform the hand-washing rite prescribed in Deut 21:1-9 as evidence of genuine innocence, and tell the crowd, "You shall see [to it] yourselves!" All the people accept the responsibility by saying, "His [Jesus'] blood [be] on us and on our children" (cf. 23:35).[65] Judas, too, accepts responsibility — by throwing the silver coins into the sanctuary, going off, and hanging himself.

According to Deut 21:22-23, the corpses of those executed for a capital offense were to be hung on a tree. But Judas hanged himself, so that the hanging was causative of his death rather than consequent on it. The standard harmonization with his falling, according to Acts 1:18 (πρηνὴς γενόμενος, literally, "becoming headlong"), that the rope with which he hung himself broke or was cut, does not pass muster. For if the rope broke or was cut, he would have fallen feet first, not headfirst (the meaning of πρηνής as "headlong").[66]

Because of the Aramaic "Hakeldama" in Acts 1:19 and because of Matthew's distinctively strong emphasis on Son of David Christology,[67] it looks as though Luke presents earlier tradition concerning the way Judas died (cf. Luke 1:1-4)[68] and Matthew conforms the way this traitor died to the way Ahithophel, the traitor of King David, died, i.e., by hanging himself (2 Sam 17:23).[69] Helping this connection with David's traitor Ahithophel is the echo of Jonathan's words to King Saul, "Why then will you sin against innocent blood by killing David?" (1 Sam 19:5) in Judas's words, "I have sinned by betraying innocent blood." Ahithophel correctly despaired of reconciliation with David.[70] Judas correctly despaired of reconciliation

---

64. Boxall, *Discovering Matthew,* 160.

65. For further commentary, see Gundry, *Matthew,* 564-65.

66. See the discussion of πρηνής by Brown, *Death of the Messiah,* 2:1405-6.

67. See Matt 1:1, 6, 17, 20; 9:27; 12:3, 23; 15:22; 20:30, 31; 21:9, 15 in comparison with their synoptic parallels.

68. See Keener, *Acts,* 1:760-65.

69. Against Osborne, *Matthew,* 842, and others cited by him.

70. Cf. the statement in *m. Sanh.* 10:2 that Ahithophel will "have no share in the world to come." Luz says, "Judas feels remorse and Ahithophel does not" (*Matthew 21–28,* 472). One wonders, however, whether Ahithophel's suicide was not itself evidence of remorse,

with Jesus. The parallel between Peter and Judas then favors that like Judas, Peter correctly despaired of reconciliation with Jesus.

This verdict, as regards Judas, agrees with Deut 27:25, which levels a curse on anyone who takes a bribe, as he did, to shed innocent blood. In killing himself, moreover, Judas violated the sixth commandment (Exod 20:13; Deut 5:17; Matt 5:21). "His suicide indicates hopeless despair, not repentance," because he "never seeks Jesus' forgiveness."[71] Only by misinterpreting as repentance Peter's going outside and weeping bitterly — i.e., by overlooking multiple Matthean instances of false disciples' weeping and teeth-gnashing far outside the kingdom of heaven — can a contrast be drawn between forgiveness for Peter and nonforgiveness for Judas.[72] Syreeni perceptively asks, "Did Peter's recognition (26:75) lead to a more positive outcome [than Judas Iscariot's]? Nothing to that effect is suggested. There is no narrative of Peter's presence at the empty tomb (cf. John [21:1-14; contrast also 1 Cor 15:5; Luke 24:34])," and "Why first worry the readers so thoroughly about Peter and then simply *imply* that all ended well for him?"[73] We could ask further, Why does Matthew introduce after Peter's going outside and weeping bitterly a chronologically and topographically disjointed account of Judas Iscariot's suicide if not to draw a parallel of similarity between Peter's final state and that of the man who would have been better off if he had not been born?

---

a remorse triggered by shame in that Absalom had not taken his advice. Shame is likely to have triggered the remorse of Peter and Judas, too. See Craig S. Keener, *A Commentary on the Gospel of Matthew* (Grand Rapids: Eerdmans, 1999), 658-59, against Judas's suicide as evidence of true repentance and as a means of atonement.

71. Turner, *Matthew*, 650; against Heil, *Death and Resurrection of Jesus*, 67-68; France, *Matthew*, 1153.

72. Against Meier, *Matthew*, 338; Blomberg, *Matthew*, 393; Osborne, *Matthew*, 1002; Oropeza, *In the Footsteps of Judas*, 75, among others.

73. Syreeni, "Peter as Character and Symbol," 146 (emphasis original). Disregarding the presence of false disciples among the true until the consummation, Syreeni disappointingly goes on to suggest that "brothers" in Matt 28:10 may imply a restoration of Peter's good relationship to Jesus (so too Garland, *Matthew*, 264).

CHAPTER 6

Matthew's Omissions of Peter

Matthew 28:7 (par. Mark 16:7)

An apparent confirmation of Peter's Judas-like false discipleship comes in Matt 28:7, whose parallel in Mark 16:7 quotes the young man at Jesus' empty tomb as saying to the women who have come there, "But go tell his disciples and Peter, 'He [Jesus] is going ahead of you into Galilee. There you will see him, as he told you.'" Matthew omits "and Peter." So deafening is the resultant silence that Lagrange cites it as proof positive that Matthew did not borrow from Mark.[1] It is generally though not universally agreed, however, that overwhelming counter-evidence for Matthew's borrowing from Mark throughout his Gospel makes Lagrange's position untenable. Others simply leave Matthew's silence unexplained, even when noting the portrayal of Peter elsewhere in the NT as the primary witness of the risen Jesus.[2]

---

1. Lagrange, *Matthieu*, 540.
2. Schnelle, *Theology of the New Testament*, 452; Bockmuehl, *Simon Peter in Scripture and Memory*, 5, 27, 29; Bockmuehl, *The Remembered Peter*, 6; Helyer, *The Life and Witness of Peter*, 62; Gerald O'Collins, "Peter as Easter Witness," *TS* 73 (2012): 251-74; Evans, *Matthew*, 478 (cf. William Thomas Kessler, *Peter as the First Witness of the Risen Lord: A Historical and Theological Investigation* [Tesi Gregoriana, Serie Teologia 37; Rome: Gregorian University Press, 1998], 63-67). Schnackenburg writes that Matthew's Peter enjoys so much favor as "the normative apostolic authority" that "at *most* we might wonder that he is not, as he is in Mark 16:7, singled out as the addressee of the Easter proclamation (the first appearance)" (*Matthew*, 8 [emphasis added]). In Luke 24:5-7 the women at Jesus' empty tomb are not *ordered* to tell anything to the disciples and Peter, as in Mark. But they *do* tell "all these things to the Eleven." Hence, Peter is included (cf. Luke 24:34).

Peter — False Disciple and Apostate according to Saint Matthew

If Herron is correct in treating καί as ascensive in Mark 16:7, so that the phrase "*even* Peter" offers hope for other repentant apostates,[3] then Matthew's omission looms more significant than ever. For he amplified Peter's denials of Jesus. The omission looms still more significant if Cullmann is correct in suggesting that Mark's lost ending carried a reference to the risen Jesus' appearance to Peter.[4] For if favorable, Matthew's fascination with Peter would likely have caused him to retain "and Peter" as preparation for the appearance and the appearance itself.

But if Matthew did not know a lost ending of Mark, it is argued that he omitted "and Peter" because those words lacked a fulfillment in Mark's following narrative, which, containing only 16:8, recounts no unique appearance of the risen Jesus to Peter.[5] But the instruction that the women at Jesus' empty tomb should go tell the disciples and Peter that Jesus is preceding them to Galilee, "There you [*plural*, for *all* the disciples] will see him [ἐκεῖ αὐτὸν ὄψεσθε]," does *not* herald a unique appearance to Peter.

After describing the omission of "and Peter" as "strange" and "difficult," McNeile resorts to saying that the words "and Peter" were "perhaps a later addition in Mark, by one who knew of an appearance to Peter (cf. I Cor. xv. 5, and perhaps Lk. xxiv. 34)," so that Matthew's text of Mark did not contain those words.[6] But no manuscript evidence supports an original lack of those words in Mark's text.

It is more often explained that Matthew omits "and Peter" because in 16:17-19 he has already secured Peter's special position.[7] But this explana-

---

3. Herron, *Mark's Account*, 143. See the foregoing against Herron's assumption of Peter's repentance.

4. Cullmann, *Peter*, 60-61. Cullmann's assumption of a lost ending is, of course, debatable, though in favor of it see Gundry, *Mark*, 1009-21; N. Clayton Croy, *The Mutilation of Mark's Gospel* (Nashville: Abingdon, 2003), all pages except 113-36; Robert H. Stein, "The Ending of Mark," *BBR* 18 (2008): 79-98. For a survey of views, see David Alan Black, ed., *Perspectives on the Ending of Mark: Four Views* (Nashville: Broadman & Holman, 2008), though this volume is remarkably weak on literary-critical arguments for a lost ending.

5. So, apparently, Meier, *Matthew*, 362: "Perhaps Matthew feels that Mark's special mention of Peter heralds a unique appearance to Peter (as in 1 Cor 15:5)." Cf. Schweizer, *Matthew*, 525.

6. McNeile, *Matthew*, 432. So too Sabourin, *Matthew*, 2:928.

7. Claudel, *La Confession de Pierre*, 81-82 n. 174, 375; Kähler, "Zur Form- und Traditionsgeschichte," 40-43 n. 5; Van Cangh, *Les sources judaïques*, 617. So too Meier, who adds the oft-repeated suggestion that Matt 16:16-19 may have derived from "the traditions about Jesus' resurrection" (*Matthew*, 362).

tion suffers from lack of attention to Peter's intervening denials of Jesus, which Matthew (as already noted) amplified — and did so in ways that indicate false discipleship. Only through neglect of such denials, plus a wrong identification of Peter as the church's foundation, can 16:17-19 make up for Matthew's omission of Mark's "and Peter."

Mark Goodacre thinks Matthew made the omission because it is nonsensical for Mark to have the women told, "Go tell the disciples and Peter," only to portray them as saying nothing to anybody (Mark 16:8).[8] Apart from the question of a lost ending for Mark, however, Matthew has the women go to tell the disciples (28:8), so that *Matthew* had no reason to omit "and Peter" out of embarrassment over the women's silence. They are *not* silent in his Gospel. Becker thinks Matthew omitted "and Peter" to keep his audience from thinking of Peter as superior to the other disciples.[9] That explanation could incline toward a portrayal of him as a false disciple, and it certainly disagrees with the usual view that Matthew highlights Peter as the apostolic first among equals and the church's foundation. Luz reasons that "since Peter is their [the disciples'] representative, he need not be mentioned separately [in Matt 28:7]."[10] But one could reason oppositely that Peter's representation of the others called for him to be mentioned.

Pesch says that in 28:7 Matthew omits "and Peter" because Jesus' discourse in 28:16-20 is directed to all the disciples.[11] But Mark's "and Peter" has to do with the women's discourse to the disciples, not with Jesus' later discourse to the disciples. Nevertheless, Pesch's view introduces the most popular of all the varied explanations of the omission, viz., that Matthew merges Peter into "the eleven disciples" of 28:16. Van Cangh presents this explanation dogmatically: the omission proves nothing ("ne prouve rien"), in that Peter is included among the Eleven.[12] Others present the explanation cautiously. The authors of *Peter in the New Testament* state that Jesus' appearance to the Eleven "may *partially* explain" Matthew's omission of

---

8. Goodacre, "The Rock on Rocky Ground," 72-73.
9. Becker, *Simon Petrus im Urchristentum*, 19.
10. Luz, *Matthew 21-28*, 597.
11. Pesch, *Simon-Petrus*, 141.
12. Van Cangh, *Les sources judaïques*, 513. Cf. Zahn's statement that for Matthew "der eigentliche Platz des Petrus" is "innerhalb des Jüngerkreises" (*Matthäus*, 331). Davies and Allison say "the deletion corresponds to 28:16-20, where Peter is just one of a group" (*Matthew*, 3:667). For P. Lampe, Matthew's Peter "fades anonymously into the group of disciples" ("Peter [the Disciple]," 3).

Peter — False Disciple and Apostate according to Saint Matthew

"and Peter."[13] According to Nolland, Matthew "*probably* drops 'and to Peter' in light of his focus in v. 16 on the eleven disciples as a body, *but possibly the shadow of Peter's denial is also involved.*"[14] Osborne thinks "Peter's forgiveness is taken for granted," because "he is among the eleven at 28:16," yet the omission is *"very surprising."*[15] "The specific reference to the eleven disciples meeting the risen Jesus . . . shows the reader that Peter's denial is followed by restoration," writes Wiarda, who then has to admit that the restoration "is *not* explicitly narrated."[16]

This appeal to "the Eleven" needs more than caution. It needs negation. For Matthew's singling out Peter time after time up through Jesus' trial and amplifying Peter's denials of Jesus make the omission of "and Peter" inexplicable — unless by means of Matthew's downgrading him as a false disciple because of Jesus' coming denial of Peter before the Father in heaven on account of Peter's having denied Jesus the first time "before all" (10:33; 26:70); a second time "with an oath" in violation of Jesus' having prohibited oaths in his laying out behavioral conditions for entering the kingdom of heaven (5:20, 33-37; 26:72); and the third time "with cursing and swearing," so that he went outside even farther than he had before and "wept bitterly" (26:74-75), like the false disciples whom Jesus earlier said would be thrown into the darkness "farther outside," where there is "weeping and gnashing of teeth" (see again 13:42, 50; 22:13; 24:51; 25:30), though in the meantime they intermingle with true disciples like tares among wheat (13:24-30, 36-43) and like foul fish among good fish (13:47-50).

The rock on which Jesus said he would build his church was identified above with Jesus' words.[17] As noted there, this identification fits into the theme of Jesus' teachings, which pervades Matthew's Gospel and thereby supports the identification. In the foregoing paragraph here, the element of false discipleship was mentioned in connection with Jesus' parables of the tares and foul fish, and received passing mention earlier, too. But this element remains to be elaborated more fully, so that the portrayal of Peter as a false disciple will be seen as fitting into, and con-

---

13. Brown et al., *Peter in the New Testament*, 77 (emphasis added).
14. Nolland, *Matthew*, 1250 (emphasis added).
15. Osborne, *Matthew*, 868 (emphasis added). Cf. France, who also thinks the omission surprising both in view of Peter's prominence elsewhere in Matthew and in view of Peter's "spectacular failure" (*Matthew*, 1101 n. 28).
16. Wiarda, *Peter in the Gospels*, 96, 98 (emphasis added).
17. See pp. 20-26.

tributing to, a theme — false discipleship — that pervades Matthew's Gospel also outside that portrayal. This wide-ranging theme will be seen, in turn, to confirm the individual portrayal of Peter as a false disciple. Meanwhile, the omission in 28:7 of "and Peter" (Mark 16:7) leads to a consideration of several other Matthean omissions of Markan references to Simon Peter.

Mark 1:35-38 (par. Luke 4:42-43)

Mark 1:35-38 has "Simon and the ones with him" hunting down Jesus, who has gotten up early and left Capernaum for a deserted place to pray. They find him and say to him, "All are seeking you," and he replies, "Let us be going elsewhere . . . in order that I may preach there as well." The mention of Simon as leader of the otherwise anonymous search party, whom Jesus then invites to accompany him on a wider mission, puts Simon in a good light. Though Luke 4:42-43 contains a parallel passage (in which, incidentally, crowds act as the search party), Matthew omits the Markan passage altogether.

Matthew 9:23-25 (par. Mark 5:35-43; Luke 8:49-56)

In Mark 5:35-43 and Luke 8:49-56 Jesus does not allow anyone, "except for Peter and James and John the brother of James," to enter Jairus's house and the room within it where the daughter lies dead and where Jesus raises her to their and her parents' great astonishment. Though James and John share the privilege of seeing Jesus' largely private miracle, Peter stands again in a good light, especially because he heads the list of exceptions to all those whom Jesus "threw out" (ἐκβαλὼν πάντας [v. 40]). The parallel in Matt 9:23-25 makes no mention of the exceptions, and therefore of the privilege Peter enjoys with James and John.

Matthew 21:18-22 (par. Mark 11:12-14, 20-24)

According to Mark 11:12-14, 20-24 (for which Luke has no parallel), Jesus curses a barren fig tree in the presence of the Twelve on the Monday right after Palm Sunday. The next morning (Tuesday) Peter, "on remembering

[Jesus' curse]," says to him, "Rabbi, look! The fig tree that you cursed is withered." As emphasized in the vivid present tense of λέγει, "says," Peter honors Jesus by addressing him with "Rabbi" and noting the fulfillment of Jesus' curse. On the other hand, Mark honors Peter by highlighting his memory of Jesus' curse and observation of its fulfillment. The parallel in Matt 21:18-22 advances the withering of the fig tree from Tuesday to Monday, so that "it withered at once [παραχρῆμα]," while all the Twelve are watching. Thus Matthew denies Peter the distinctions of remembering Jesus' curse and noting its fulfillment.

Matthew 24:3 (par. Mark 13:3-4; Luke 21:7)

In Mark 13:3-4, Peter heads a quartet that includes also James, John, and Andrew. "Privately" (κατ' ἰδίαν) they ask Jesus a question; and they constitute his private audience for the answer, the Olivet Discourse, which takes up the rest of Mark 13. N.B. the distinction between them and the other disciples in v. 37: "And what I [Jesus] am saying to you [Peter, James, John, and Andrew according to vv. 3-5] I am saying to all [my disciples]." Matthew erases this distinction by having Jesus address all the disciples in private (24:3) and by omitting entirely the statement in Mark 13:37. Thus Peter, along with James, John, and Andrew, loses the privilege of a specially private instruction.

Arguments from silence are weak unless strong reasons exist to expect the opposite, as there are especially for Matt 28:7. Reasons other than the denigration of Peter can be offered for some of Matthew's other omissions of him. Perhaps Matthew omitted the search for Jesus by Peter and the ones with him simply by way of abbreviating Markan material. The omission of Jesus' taking Peter, James, and John into Jairus's house may have had the purpose of concentrating on the figure of Jesus alone. Advancing by a day the withering of a cursed fig tree, so that Peter is deprived of displaying his superior powers of memory and observation, may arise out of a Matthean desire to stress the effectiveness of Jesus' curse. And Matthew's widening the audience of Jesus' Olivet Discourse may have the purpose of making the discourse apply more apparently to the whole church, not just to a select few within it. But given Matthew's habit of incorporating distinctively Petrine materials, often into otherwise paralleled material, we have at least some reason to believe that these earlier Matthean omissions of Peter in addition to the striking omission in 28:7 may contribute to his overall denigration in the First Gospel. Nau has noted "the surprising fact that in none of the original MARCAN passages involved is Peter viewed negatively. He is never corrected or rebuked. Rather, he is given modest prominence."[18]

---

18. Nau, *Peter in Matthew*, 61 (caps original). Against Nau, see Boxall, *Discovering Matthew*, 140-41. Lutz Doering rightly questions whether there was, as Nau thinks, a category of "encomiastic dispraise" ("Schwerpunkte und Tendenzen der neueren Petrus-Forschung," *BTZ* 19 [2002]: 212).

CHAPTER 7

False Discipleship in Matthew

Matthew 5:13 (par. Mark 9:49-50; Luke 14:34-35)

Matthew introduces the theme of false discipleship already in 5:13. Differently from Mark 9:49-50 and Luke 14:34-35, where salt represents a quality of discipleship, Matthew makes salt represent disciples themselves. For in addressing his disciples (5:1-2: "his [Jesus'] disciples came to him; and on opening his mouth, he began teaching them"[1]), Jesus says emphatically, "You *yourselves* [ὑμεῖς] are the salt of the earth." There follows the possibility that the salt "becomes foolish" (μωρανθῇ; so too Luke against Mark's ἄναλον γένηται, "becomes unsalty"), in which case, "With what will it be made salty?" Implied answer: With nothing. There is no remedy. "It is no longer strong for anything" (εἰς οὐδὲν ἰσχύει ἔτι) in the sense that it is forever incapable of doing its job, "except on being thrown outside [βληθὲν ἔξω] to be trampled by people." Since the salt represents disciples themselves, their loss of saltiness represents loss of salvation because of their falsity as disciples. The use of a verbal form of foolishness anticipates the distinctively Matthean use of μωρός, "foolish," for false disciples in 5:22; 7:26; 25:2, 3, 8.[2] The impossibility of regaining saltiness then represents the impossibility of regaining salvation (see again Heb 6:4-8; 10:26-31; 12:15-17). The throwing of the salt outside anticipates, and will

---

1. ἐδίδασκεν is an inceptive imperfect.
2. In particular, see Gundry, *Matthew*, 85-86, on 5:22; and cf. the likewise distinctively Matthean use of "fools" for the hypocritical scribes and Pharisees in 23:17 in relation to 24:51.

get its interpretation from, the throwing of false disciples outside where there is weeping and gnashing of teeth (8:12; 13:42, 47-50; 22:13; 25:30; cf. 5:29-30; 7:19; 18:8-9). And being trampled by people corresponds to other figures of speech for the fate of false disciples, viz., being dichotomized, entering the black hole of outermost darkness, and suffering the fire of gehenna (see Matt 24:51; par. Luke 12:46; and, again, the immediately foregoing citations).[3]

Matthew 5:20-22

There follows a series of warnings. If the disciples' righteousness does not exceed that of the scribes and Pharisees, the disciples will by no means enter the kingdom of heaven (Matt 5:20: οὐ μή plus an aorist subjunctive in εἰσέλθητε for emphatic negation). If a disciple calls his fellow disciple a "fool" — i.e., takes on himself as an individual the prerogative of calling his fellow's profession of discipleship false — he will be subject to the gehenna of fire (5:22). These two warnings are unique to Matthew.

Matthew 5:27-30; 6:14-15 (par. Mark 9:47, 43)

In Matt 5:29 and 5:30 a professing disciple's failure to exercise moral self-discipline will eventuate in his or her whole body being thrown into gehenna/going away into gehenna. Matthew's omission of entering into life/the kingdom of God (so Mark 9:47, 43) leaves the stress on damnation. In 6:15 Jesus warns that God the Father will not forgive the trespasses of disciples who do not forgive others' trespasses. If, as seems likely, Mark 11:26 is due to parallel influence from Matthew,[4] this warning is again unique to Matthew. Jesus' addressing these warnings to disciples, plus the element of damnation in the warnings, points up the danger — indeed, the reality — of false discipleship as exemplified by Peter alongside Judas Iscariot.

---

3. On questions of the use of salt in relation to the earth, or soil, the way in which salt can lose its saltiness, etc., see Gundry, *Matthew*, 75-76, and other standard commentaries.

4. See the text-critical evidence.

Matthew 7:15-23 (par. Luke 6:43-46; 13:25-27)

False prophets make an appearance in Matt 7:15-23. They are numbered among Jesus' disciples; for they wear the clothing of sheep, an animal that stands for Jesus' disciples especially in 25:31-46. Furthermore, they address him with "Lord, Lord," prophesy in his name, cast out demons in his name, and perform many miracles in his name (7:21-22). (We might compare Peter's using the keys of the kingdom and binding and loosening things according to 16:19.) But despite the prophesying, the exorcisms, and the miracle-working, at the Last Judgment Jesus will pronounce their profession of discipleship false and condemn them.[5]

Matthew 7:26-27 (par. Luke 6:49)

Finally in the Sermon on the Mount, Jesus speaks of a man who is "foolish" (μωρῷ) because he hears "these words" of Jesus but does not practice them (7:26-27). Since Jesus has been addressing the words to his disciples,[6] and since "foolish" has been and will yet be used of false disciples (see above), this man qualifies as one of them. "Everyone" (πᾶς) implies multiple such fools among Jesus' disciples. The total collapse of the house that the foolish man had built on sand then represents false disciples' destruction at the end under divine judgment, represented in turn by the rainstorm, flooding streams, and blowing winds.

Matthew 8:18-22; 10:4 (par. Mark 3:19; Luke 6:16; 9:57-60)

In Matt 8:18-22 a false disciple is characterized by avoidance of Jesus' rigorous demands — in contrast with a true disciple, who volunteers to fol-

---

[5]. See Evans's statement that these false prophets "never really were true members of the church (as their fruits give evidence); in the day of judgment they will be cast out" (*Matthew*, 177).

[6]. See 5:1-2 again. To be sure, 7:28-29 will say that Jesus had been teaching "the crowds." But whether or not they are to be equated with Jesus' disciples, as possibly in 4:25–5:2 (so Gundry, *Matthew*, 64-65, 136-37; Gundry, *Commentary on the New Testament*, 15, 29), or as bystanders who simply listened in, the fact remains that in 5:1-2 Matthew specifies the disciples of Jesus as the addressees of the Sermon on the Mount. See further J. R. C. Cousland, *The Crowds in the Gospel of Matthew* (NovTSup 102; Leiden: Brill, 2002).

low Jesus wherever he goes.[7] In 10:4 (par. Mark 3:19; Luke 6:16) Matthew identifies Judas Iscariot as the one "who also betrayed him [Jesus]" despite Jesus' having "summoned" him along with the rest of "the twelve disciples" — i.e., "the twelve apostles" — and given him (and them) "authority over unclean spirits so as to cast them out and [authority] to heal every kind of disease and every kind of ailment," and despite Jesus' proceeding to send him along with the rest "like sheep in the midst of wolves" (10:16) on a mission of preaching, healing, and exorcism. Jesus even says, "The one who welcomes you [ὑμᾶς, plural, including Judas the betrayer] welcomes me" (v. 40). (More along this line below.) If one false disciple among the twelve apostles, in principle why not another? And in fact why not another if given damaging evidence, as in regard to Peter?

Matthew 10:22, 33 (par. Mark 13:13; Luke 12:9)

In Matt 10:22 Jesus says that "the one enduring to an end — this one will be saved." Whatever the kind of end Jesus had in mind, the apostle Peter sat down later in the priest's courtyard with the high priest's servants "to see the end" (26:58) — i.e., the outcome in Jesus' crucifixion (as so it happened) — but never saw it, because he did not endure.[8] No salvation for him, therefore? Not a strong argument, but perhaps a hint. As already argued, though, Peter's denying Jesus "before all" (ἔμπροσθεν πάντων), and doing so despite having been accosted by only a single maidservant (26:69-70), provides strong evidence of false discipleship. For Jesus says in 10:33, "But whoever denies [= disowns] me before people [ἔμπροσθεν τῶν ἀνθρώπων] — I will also deny [= disown] him before my Father in heaven." That "whoever" (ὅστις . . . ἄν) includes Peter.

Matthew 13:20-21 (par. Mark 4:16-17; Luke 8:13)

In the parable of the sower, the seeds that fall on rocky ground represent "the person who hears the word ['about the kingdom'] and receives it im-

---

7. For brief expositions, see Gundry, *Commentary on the New Testament*, 32-33; Gundry, *Matthew*, 150-54; and for thorough argumentation, see Gundry, "On True and False Disciples in Matthew 8.18-22," *NTS* 40 (1994): 433-41.

8. According to Evans, "endures to an end" means "endures the suffering 'to the end' of the period of persecution and tribulation, a period that will end when the Son of Man comes," i.e., "not quitting or abandoning the faith" (*Matthew*, 223, 404).

mediately with joy" (13:20). So that person counts as a professing disciple. "But he does not have a root in himself, but is temporary" (13:21a). So his professed discipleship proves false. "And when pressure [θλῖψις, as in the case of Peter during Jesus' trial] or persecution comes about because of the word, he is immediately snared [σκανδαλίζεται]" (13:21b), i.e., led to apostatize. For in 18:8-9, being snared contrasts with "enter[ing] into life" and equates with being "thrown into eternal fire/the gehenna of fire." Again, then, false discipleship that encounters the pressure of persecution issues finally in damnation.

Matthew 13:24-30, 36-43

Because many commentators have misinterpreted the parable of the tares as portraying the whole of humanity as a mixed body of nondisciples and disciples (tares and wheat, respectively) rather than the church as a mixed body of false and true disciples, this parable requires more extensive discussion. It needs denying, first of all, that Jesus' equating "the field" with "the world" (13:38) supports a jejune portrayal. *Of course* the human race consists of nondisciples and disciples! Not as in Johannine literature, where "the world" (ὁ κόσμος) refers predominantly to human society, Matthew uses "the world" spatially.[9] So to equate the field with the world is not to say that the parable deals with the whole of humanity as a mixed body rather than limitedly with the church as a mixed body of false and true disciples. It is only to say that the mixed church extends throughout the world: "Just as the crop exists within the field, so the believing community exists within the world."[10] Distinctive of Matthew is not only his description of the kingdom as belonging to the Son of Man (16:28; 20:21; both against synoptic parallels, in addition to 13:41) but also his similar description of the church as belonging to Jesus (16:18: "my church"). This similarity of description favors that presently the Son of Man's kingdom consists in Jesus' reigning over the church. Since Matthew emphasizes the worldwide extent of Christian evangelism (5:13-16; 24:14; 26:13; 28:19), the

---

9. See 4:8; 5:14; 13:35 (text-critically questionable); 16:26; 18:7; 24:21; 25:34; 26:13.

10. R. K. McIver, "The Parable of the Weeds among the Wheat (Matt 13:24-30, 36-43) and the Relation between the Kingdom and the Church as Portrayed in the Gospel of Matthew," *JBL* 114 (1995): 652. See also Daniel Marguerat, "L'église et le monde en Matthieu 13,36-43," *RTP* 110 (1978): 116: "il ['the world'] représente bien plutôt l'espace dans lequel se déploie la mission, le lieu géographique de l'Eglise."

tares and the wheat growing in the field represent the evil and the good, the false and the true, coexisting in the churchly kingdom that has spread throughout the world as leaven permeates a large batch of dough (13:33; cf. 13:31-32).

Undergirding this view is Matthew's earlier use of "the ones working lawlessness" for false disciples (they have prophesied, exorcised demons, and performed miracles in Jesus' name [7:22]), just as here the tares are identified as "the ones doing lawlessness" (13:41). They are also identified with "the snares," i.e., τὰ σκάνδαλα (13:41). Elsewhere in Matthew this noun and its verbal cognate σκανδαλίζω occur by far most often as causes of sin in and among professing disciples of Jesus (5:29-30; 13:21; 16:23; 17:27; 18:6-9; 24:10; 26:31, 33 for a total of fifteen occurrences, over against 11:6; 13:57; 15:12 for a total of only three nondiscipular occurrences). A third to one-half of the occurrences for snares in and among Jesus' professing disciples are unique to Matthew, almost always by way of insertion into paralleled material. We have good reason, then, to think of snares in the church who make for a mixed body of false and true disciples. The omission of wheat from the title "The Parable of the Tares of the Field" (13:36) combines with the uniqueness to Matthew of this parable and its interpretation to spotlight a high level of concern over the presence of tares in the church, those who cause sin and practice lawlessness.[11]

Jesus' description of the tares as "the sons of the evil one" and as sown by "the devil" also suits the presence of false disciples in the church. For the devil's sowing them *after* the Son of Man has sown the wheat (ἐπέσπειρεν [13:25]) fits an infiltration of false disciples into the church. Otherwise, the Son of Man would be sowing wheat (his disciples, who constitute the church that he has yet to build [N.B. the future tense in 16:18: "I will build my church"]) among the already-sown tares (nondisciples, who make up the rest of humanity). Furthermore, the presence of tares did not become apparent till the grass-like blades of wheat had not only sprouted but also produced ears of grain (13:26). Similarly, it takes time and circumstance for false disciples to become apparent, just as in the parable of the sower the rocky ground represents "the person who hears the word and receives it immediately with joy but does not have a root in himself — rather, is temporary — and when pressure or persecution comes about because of

---

11. In denying that this parable portrays the church as a *corpus mixtum*, Kraus neglects the theme of false discipleship that runs throughout the Gospel of Matthew ("Zur Ekklesiologie des Matthäusevangeliums," 216-18, 231-34).

the word, he is immediately snared" (13:20-21). Peter is the rocky ground, the tare, the snared snare (16:23).[12]

In the parable the master prohibits his "slaves" from uprooting the tares prior to harvest time and says that then, but only then, will he have "the reapers," who differ from his slaves, collect, bind, and burn the tares. Therefore it remains only to note that false disciples will continue to crop up in the church until the harvesting angels of the Son of Man, not his true disciples, collect them out of his kingdom at "the consummation of the age" and "throw them into the furnace of fire," where there is "weeping and gnashing of teeth." Such will be the fate of false disciples such as Peter, whose bitter weeping anticipates weeping on doomsday.

Matthew 13:47-50

The parable of the dragnet in 13:47-50 carries the same message. The sea represents the nations of the world, as often in the OT. The casting of a dragnet into the sea and its gathering all kinds of fish represents successful evangelism, as in fishing for human beings (4:19). Throwing the foul fish "outside" (ἔξω) after beaching the dragnet represents angels' "separat[ing] the evil ones [cf. 'the sons of the evil one' in 13:38] from the midst [ἐκ μέσου] of the righteous ones" "at the consummation of the age." "From the midst" forms an antithetic parallel to "in the midst" (ἀνὰ μέσον) in 13:25; and like the phrase with which it contrasts, this phrase shows that the evil ones are to be understood as false disciples within the Son of Man's churchly kingdom rather than as evil people in general. Otherwise, "the righteous ones" would have been located in *their* midst and separated from *them* rather than vice versa. The final fate of the evil, false disciples is to be "throw[n] into the furnace of fire," the location outside of "weeping and gnashing of teeth." Heikki Räisänen observes, "Strikingly, the promise given to the righteous in v. 43 is much shorter than the fate of the wicked and in v. 50 the reward of the righteous is not mentioned at all; all emphasis is placed on the warning."[13] Anticipating such a fate is the bitter weeping "outside" (ἔξω) of Peter, a fisherman turned foul fish (26:75).

---

12. The foregoing has drawn heavily on Robert H. Gundry, "In Defense of the Church in Matthew as a *Corpus Mixtum*," *ZNW* 91 (2000): 160-63. See also Marguerat, "L'église et le monde," 111-29, where older bibliography can be found.

13. Heikki Räisänen, "Jesus and Hell," in *Jesus in Continuum* (ed. Tom Holmén; WUNT 289; Tübingen: Mohr Siebeck, 2012), 376.

False Discipleship in Matthew

Matthew 18:1-3 (par. Mark 9:33-36; Luke 9:46-47)

Appearing in Matthew's next collection of Jesus' sayings (ch. 18) are several indications of false discipleship that will end in damnation. *To his disciples* (v. 1) Jesus says, "Amen I tell you, if *you* are not converted [ἐὰν μὴ στραφῆτε] and become like little children, by no means will *you* enter [οὐ μὴ εἰσέλθητε] into the kingdom of heaven" (v. 3; cf. 5:20). Stressing the possibility of exclusion are the introduction, "*Amen* I tell you," and οὐ μή plus the aorist subjunctive in εἰσέλθητε, the strongest way to express negation in Greek. Mark 10:15 and Luke 18:17 bear some similarity to this saying, but only in Matthew does Jesus tell the disciples *they* must be converted and become like little children to avoid nonentry into heaven's kingdom ("you" and being "converted" as opposed to "whoever" and "accept[ing] this kingdom" in the other Synoptics). However conversion by becoming like little children is to be understood, the threat of nonentry on the part of disciples highlights Matthew's concern over false profession.

Matthew 18:8-9 (par. Mark 9:43-48)

After a series of "whoever"-statements in 18:4-6 and another third-person statement in 18:7, Matthew has Jesus address the disciples directly again in 18:8-9 (par. 5:29-30 as well as Mark 9:43-48):

> But if your hand or your foot ensnares you, cut it off and throw [it] away from you. It is good for you to enter into life maimed or lame rather than that having two hands or two feet you be thrown into eternal fire. And if your eye is ensnaring you, gouge it out and throw [it] away from you. It is good for you to enter into life one-eyed rather than that having two eyes you be thrown into the gehenna of fire.

As in 5:29-30, these sayings indicate that a professing disciple's failure to exercise moral self-discipline will eventuate in the throwing of his or her whole body into eternal fire/the gehenna of fire. The very repetition in 18:8-9 of the sayings in 5:29-30 exhibits Matthew's deep concern over the presence and fate of false disciples in the church. The addition of an ensnaring foot, unmentioned in 5:29-30, magnifies that concern.

Peter — False Disciple and Apostate according to Saint Matthew

Matthew 18:15-18, 23-35 (par. Luke 17:3)

In Matt 18:15-18 the treatment of "your [sinning] brother" (i.e., fellow disciple) who has refused churchly correction as though he were a Gentile and a tax collector — such treatment implies a provisional, collective recognition of evidently false discipleship, much as prior to harvest time the slaves recognized the presence of tares among wheat in the parable of the tares of the field (13:26-27).[14] In the parable that concludes chapter 18, a forgiven but unforgiving slave incurs the wrath of his master, who "gave him over to the torturers till he [the slave] would pay back all [the debt] that was owed [by him]" (v. 34) — an impossible repayment, given his debt of ten thousand talents and his status as a slave.[15] Then Jesus issues a warning to his disciples: "In this way will my heavenly Father, too, treat you if you each do not forgive from your hearts his brother" (v. 35; cf. 6:15). That is to say, unforgiveness of a fellow disciple draws irreversible damnation for falsity of profession. The uniqueness of this parable to Matthew's Gospel exhibits the importance to him of the theme of false discipleship, a theme into which the example of Peter fits.

Matthew 22:1-14 (par. Luke 14:15-24)

Distinctively Matthean features in the parable of the wedding feast (22:1-14), which has a Lukan parallel, further the theme of false discipleship. Luke speaks of "a certain man" who put on "a big banquet" (δεῖπνον μέγα) into which many are brought (in agreement with the theme of evangelistic success throughout Luke-Acts). Matthew speaks of "a king" (cf. 18:23) who makes "a wedding feast for his son." The king represents God the Father (cf. 21:31). As in 21:37-39, but here only implicitly, the son represents Jesus. The wedding feast represents the eschatological celebration of God's people with their Messiah.[16]

---

14. There remains, of course, something of a tension between the said disciplinary treatment and the prohibition in 13:28b-29 of uprooting the tares. Matthew does not resolve the tension, though one might hypothesize a distinction between disciplinary shunning and outright condemnation. See 5:46-47; 6:7; 9:10-11; 11:19; 21:31-32 for "Gentiles" and "tax collectors" as nondisciples, though they enter kingdom fellowship upon repentance and faith.

15. According to Josephus, one year's tax revenue from Judea came to a total of six hundred talents during the reign of Archelaus (*Ant.* 17.320).

16. See Rev. 19:6-10; cf. Matt 8:11-12; 26:29; Mark 14:25; Luke 13:28-29; 22:18, 29-30;

False Discipleship in Matthew

For Matthew, the church constitutes God's people, "a nation" according to 21:43.[17] But according to 22:10, this nation consists of "evil people" as well as "good people," i.e., of false as well as true disciples of Jesus. The placement of the evil before the good is a telltale example of Matthew's emphasis on, and concern over, false disciples in the church (cf. again the sole mention of tares in the title, "The Parable of the Tares of the Field" [13:36]). Only Matthew mentions the mixture of evil people and good people, just as in his distinctive parables of the tares and the dragnet (13:24-30, 36-43, 47-50; see 7:17, 18; 12:34; 20:15 for other distinctively Matthean pairings of "evil" [πονηρός] and "good" [ἀγαθός], such a paralleled pairing appearing only in 12:35; par. Luke 6:45); and in the present parable only Matthew presents the episode of the man at the feast who is not wearing a wedding garment (22:11-14).

That the man is attending the wedding feast marks him as a professing disciple. That he is not wearing a wedding garment marks his profession as false. So he serves as an example of the evil people who along with good people were brought into the wedding feast. The vivid historical present tense in καὶ λέγει αὐτῷ, "And he ['the king'] says to him [the 'man not garbed with a wedding garment']," underscores the following, stern question: "Comrade, how is it that you came in here not having a wedding garment?" The address ἑταῖρε, "Comrade," is unique to Matthew and recalls 20:13-16, where the complainer of injustice who, though he was first will be last, is addressed the same way, and anticipates 26:50, where Jesus will address Judas Iscariot, a false disciple if ever there was one, with ἑταῖρε.

As Jesus will "muzzle" the Sadducees (so 22:34 against the wording in Mark 12:28; Luke 10:25), the man not wearing a wedding garment is "muzzled" by the king's question. Worse yet, the king tells his servants to "bind" the man, as the reapers were told to "bind" the tares, i.e., false disciples (so Matthew alone in 13:30). The servants are to bind his "feet and hands," which phrase recalls "having two hands or two feet" to be "thrown into eternal fire" (18:8). The rest of the command, viz., to "throw him out

---

Rev. 2:17; Isa 25:6; 1QSa; 4QpPs 37; *1 Enoch* 62:14; *2 Apoc. Bar.* 29:4-8; and see Gundry, "In Defense," 154-56, against the attempt of Petri Luomanen to make the wedding feast a description of the general judgment of all humanity ("*Corpus Mixtum* — An Appropriate Description of Matthew's Community?" *JBL* 117 [1998]: 469-80).

17. Evans denies that "a nation" in 21:43 consists in "the Christian church"; it consists, rather, in "true believers ... includ[ing] Jews and Gentiles" (*Matthew*, 375). Except for the noninclusion of false believers, this latter identification looks remarkably like the Christian church!

[ἐκβάλετε αὐτόν] into the darkness farther outside [i.e., the outermost darkness] [εἰς τὸ σκότος τὸ ἐξώτερον]," matches Matthew's distinctive phraseology in 8:12; 25:30. "Weeping and gnashing of teeth will be there" is likewise distinctive of Matthew, with the sole exception of Luke 13:28 (perhaps an example of Matthean influence), in 8:12; 13:42, 50; 24:51; 25:30. Taken together, these details resemble Peter's going farther and farther outside and weeping bitterly in 26:69-75.

The parable of the wedding feast concludes with Jesus' comment, "For many are called [= invited], but few are chosen [= selected]." This comment distinguishes between the many of the mixed church and its true disciples, the "chosen," among the many, so that the rest are unchosen and false. Moreover, the description of the chosen as "few" implies a preponderance of the evil and false over the good and true (cf. the "many" who take the broad road "that leads to destruction" and the "few" who take the narrow road "that leads to life" in 7:13-14).[18] Matthew's portrayal of Peter puts him among the unchosen.[19]

Matthew 24:10-12

The large number of false disciples comes up again in Matt 24:10-12, which consists of a Matthean insertion into paralleled material and therefore displays a special emphasis in Matthew's Gospel. After the paralleled statement in 24:9b that "you [disciples] will be hated by all nations on account of my name" (only "nations" being a Matthean addition; cf. 10:22), Matthew writes, "And then *many* will be snared," i.e., will be led by the aforementioned hatred to apostatize, as in the case of "the person sown on rocky ground . . . who hears the word and receives it immediately with joy" but

---

18. In view of 7:13-14; 24:10-12, the attempts of some commentators to dull 22:14, so that it means merely, "Everyone is called, but not everyone is chosen," falls short and seems to stem, not from candid exegesis, but from a visceral reaction against the thought that Matthew teaches the falsity and final damnation of most professing Christians (cf. the apparent implication of Luke 13:23-24 that most human beings will be condemned; also David C. Sim's description of judgment in Matthew as a "rather unpleasant theme" ["Matthew's Use of Mark: Did Matthew Intend to Supplement or to Replace His Primary Source?" *NTS* 57 (2011): 181]). Considered *alone*, to be sure, those who will come from the east and the west to eat with Abraham, Isaac, and Jacob in the kingdom of heaven will be "many" (Matt 8:11). But *compared* with the many who take the broad road, those who take the narrow road are "few."

19. See Gundry, *Matthew*, 432-41, 669 nn. 166-69, for interpretation of elements in the parable not germane to the topic of false discipleship.

because of "not hav[ing] a root in himself... is temporary," so that "when pressure or persecution comes about because of the word, he is immediately snared [the same verb as occurs in 24:10]" (13:20-21).

Matthew's insertion continues: "and [the 'many' who were 'snared'] will betray one another [i.e., give their fellow disciples over to the hate-filled persecutors, much as Judas Iscariot, the quintessential false disciple, gave Jesus over to his enemies, in order to save their own necks] and will hate one another [in disobedience to Jesus' command to love even your enemies rather than hating them (5:43-44; par. Luke 6:27-28), obedience to which command constitutes part of the superior righteousness necessary for entrance into the kingdom of heaven (5:20, unique to Matthew)]." Matthew's insertion keeps on going: "And *many* false prophets [cf. 7:15, 22; 24:24] will arise and deceive *many*; and because lawlessness [in the church] will be multiplied [πληθυνθῆναι, cognate to the repeated πολλοί/-ῶν/-ούς — hence, to coin a term, 'manyfied'; cf. Dan 12:4 LXX], the love of the *many* will grow cold [cf. 7:13-14, 21-23; 13:41; 22:14, where false prophets, along with other false disciples, are described as 'workers of lawlessness' and as 'many' in contrast to the 'few' who are 'chosen' and find the narrow gateway into 'life']." Their lawlessness will make cold — i.e., extinguish — their love of enemies, God, and neighbor, especially here of fellow disciples. See the comments above on 10:22 for "enduring to an end" to be "saved" (24:13).

Matthew 24:45-51 (par. Luke 12:41-46)

In Matt 24:45-51 Jesus contrasts "that wicked slave" (ὁ κακὸς δοῦλος ἐκεῖνος) with "the faithful and prudent slave" (ὁ πιστὸς δοῦλος καὶ φρόνιμος). Though ἐκεῖνος, "that," will refer in v. 46 back to the faithful and prudent slave in v. 45, the ἐκεῖνος that in v. 48 refers to the wicked slave makes narratival nonsense for lack of a preceding referent — hence the variant reading which omits this second occurrence of ἐκεῖνος (ℵ* Γ Θ 0204 sy^s sa mae). Making up for the narratival nonsense is a conceptual emphasis on the slave's wickedness: "the *wicked* slave, *that* one," who represents false disciples in contrast with "the faithful and prudent slave," who represents true disciples. That the wicked slave represents false *disciples* is evident from his being called a slave in relation to "the master/Lord" (ὁ κύριος) — this in connection with Jesus' (second) coming as the Son of Man (Matt 24-25) — and also from the reference to this slave's fellow slaves, i.e., the Christian community. Using the master's delay to start beating his fellow slaves exposes the falsity of his discipleship. "Starts" (ἄρξηται) indicates extended beating, so that the falsity is left in no doubt. Confirming falsity further is this slave's "eat[ing] and drink[ing] with drunkards," activities that imply the presence of other false disciples in the Christian community.

The master's return represents Jesus' second coming, of course. Its unexpectedness for the wicked slave makes another indication of false discipleship, for true disciples obey Jesus' commands to stay awake and ready for his coming (24:32-33, 42-44; 25:13). The master's "slicing" the wicked slave "in two" (διχοτομήσει) warns of a horrible fate for false disciples. "Put[ting] his portion with the hypocrites" spells the same fate for false disciples as for the scribes and Pharisees, repeatedly called "hypocrites" in chapter 23. What is that fate? Answer: "the judgment [consisting] of gehenna" according to 23:33. So "weeping and gnashing of teeth will be *there* (ἐκεῖ)," the statement that caps this parable, describes what goes on in gehenna as a result, according to the parable, of false discipleship. The weeping arises out of sorrow and regret for having proved false. In other contexts gnashing — i.e., gritting — of teeth connotes anger, as in Acts 7:54. But because of association here with being sliced in two, with being put with the hypocrites in the fire of gehenna, and with weeping, the teeth-gnashing probably connotes pain.[20] That such a fate befalls this wicked slave despite his master's having "put [him] in charge over his household to give them [their] food on schedule" shows Peter's similar position of leadership to be no guarantee of salvation. Notably, most of Jesus' harshest warnings of eternal punishment are reserved for the in-group of disciples.[21]

Matthew 25:1-13

The parable of ten virgins in Matt 25:1-13 carries forward the themes of false disciples' presence in the church and their final exclusion from the kingdom of heaven. The uniqueness to Matthew of this parable under-

---

20. Cf. Guillaume Migbisiegbe, "Entering into the Joy of the Master or Being Cast Out into the Outer Darkness: Re-Imagining the Eschatological Judgement in Matthew 25,30," in *The Gospel of Matthew at the Crossroads of Early Christianity* (ed. Donald Senior; BETL 243; Leuven: Peeters, 2011), 609-10, 613-14. Against a softening of διχοτομήσει and for an interpretation of the slaves as ecclesiastical leaders in particular, see Gundry, *Matthew*, 495-97.

21. Räisänen emphasizes this phenomenon ("Jesus and Hell," 381-82).

lines the importance of these themes. As in 7:24, 26, the future tense of ὁμοιωθήσεται in the introduction, "Then the kingdom of heaven will be like," looks forward to what will happen at the consummation of the age. The first word of the introduction, Τότε, "Then," points to the time of the Son of Man's coming that was portrayed in the immediately preceding parable (24:45-51) as the coming of a master, i.e., the Lord (ὁ κύριος [cf. 25:11]). "Who *as such*" (αἵ**τινες**) stresses the virginity of the ten as qualifying them provisionally to play a particular role in the upcoming wedding celebration.

"Having taken lamps [λαμπάδας]" recalls Matt 5:15-16: "Neither do people light a lamp [λύχνον] and place it under a basket, but on a lampstand [λυχνίαν]; and it gives lamplight [λάμπει] to all in the house. In this way your light [φῶς] is to give lamplight [λαμψάτω] in people's presence, so that they may see your good deeds and glorify your Father in heaven." (Only Matthew identifies the lamplight with good deeds [contrast Mark 4:21; Luke 8:16; 11:33].) Which is to say that in the present parable, taking enough oil to keep the lamps burning stands for doing enough good deeds to demonstrate true discipleship (cf. Jesus' statement in the uniquely Matthean 5:20: "For I tell you that unless your righteousness abounds more than [that] of the scribes and Pharisees, by no means will you enter the kingdom of heaven"). Contrariwise, failure to take enough oil stands for having done so few good deeds as to prove oneself a false disciple. "Their *own* [ἑαυτῶν] lamps" stresses personal responsibility for taking enough oil/doing enough good deeds.

"Went out to meet the bridegroom" looks forward to his arrival, which represents the coming of Jesus, whom the parable of the wedding feast in 22:1-14 also portrayed as a bridegroom. As there, the distinctively Matthean wedding feast represents the eschatological celebration of God's people with their Messiah.[22] The description of five virgins as "foolish" and of the other five as "prudent" recalls the contrast in 7:24-27 between a "prudent" builder, in that he obeys Jesus' words, and a "foolish" builder, in that he does not obey Jesus' words.[23] But just as in 22:10 the placement of "evil people" before "good people" is a telltale example of Matthew's emphasis on, and concern over, false disciples in the church (cf. once more the sole mention of tares in the title, "The Parable of the Tares of the Field" [13:36]), so too the placement of "foolish [virgins]" before "prudent [virgins]" is a

---

22. See p. 78 with n. 16.
23. See also the comments above on salt becoming "foolish" in 5:13.

telltale example again of that emphasis and concern. The contrastive pairing of foolish virgins and prudent ones falls in line with Matthew's other contrastive pairings which have to do with false and true disciples, but most especially with false ones: not only prudent versus foolish builders and evil people versus good people, but also tares versus wheat (13:24-30, 36-43), good versus foul fish (13:47-48), a faithful and prudent slave versus a wicked one (24:45-51), and good and faithful slaves versus an evil and lazy slave (25:14-30).[24] Verse 10 describes the prudent virgins as "prepared" for the bridegroom's arrival (cf. Jesus' telling the disciples to get "prepared" for the Son of Man's coming [24:44]). Preparation for it will distinguish true disciples from the false.

Shutting the door into the wedding hall represents for the foolish virgins their nonentrance into the kingdom of heaven, as in 23:13 (unique to Matthew in this respect). The reference to them as "the rest" (αἱ λοιπαί) sounds a doleful warning note of being left out. Their futile plea for entrance resembles the lawless false prophets' equally futile plea for entrance in 7:21-23. The doubled address κύριε, κύριε, "L/lord, L/lord," characterizes both pleas; and his answer here in 25:12, "I don't know you," was previewed in 7:23: "I never knew you." But now this rejection of foolishly false disciples is reinforced with the introduction, "Amen I tell you." There is no second chance once Jesus the bridegroom has come.

Matthew 25:14-30 (par. Mark 13:34; Luke 19:11-27)

Another parable follows immediately in Matt 25:14-30. (As usual, comments will concentrate on the element of false discipleship and leave other elements of the parable largely unaddressed.) The parable starts with an ellipsis: "For . . . just as a man, going on a journey, called his own slaves and gave his possessions over to them." The ellipsis is to be filled futuristically from v. 1 of this chapter with "the kingdom of heaven will be like"; for as the preceding parable ended with a futuristically symbolic reference to the Last Judgment (vv. 11-12), so too will the present parable (cf. the future tenses in v. 29: "For [further talents] will be given to everyone who [already] has [additional talents], and his talents will be made to abound [so as to be more than enough]. But the one who does not have [an additional

---

24. See Gundry, "In Defense," 160, that the pairing of sheep and goats in 25:31-46 does not have to do with true versus false disciples.

talent] — even what he has [the original talent] will be taken away from him." And like the preceding parable, the present parable features a false disciple, but one who according to vv. 26-27 is "evil" (πονηρέ) because he is "lazy" (ὀκνηρέ) and "useless" (ἀχρεῖον). He failed to invest the talent given him by his "master" (κύριος, with overtones of Jesus' lordship, as recently in v. 11). This third of three slaves is included in the phrase "his [the master's] very own [ἰδίους] slaves" (v. 14), where Matthew might have written an unemphatic "his [αὐτοῦ] slaves." The emphasis guarantees that the third slave is meant to represent a disciple of Jesus just as the first two slaves are also meant to represent disciples of Jesus.

The verb for investing, ἐργάζομαι (see v. 16), is cognate to ἔργον, the noun used in 5:16 for the public "good deeds" required for entrance into the kingdom of heaven (5:20). Highlighting this requirement is the master's describing the work of investment as "necessary" (v. 27). So it should come as no surprise that this evil, lazy, useless slave represents false disciples, who hide their supposed discipleship to avoid persecution just as the slave hid in the ground the talent entrusted to him. In the taking from him of the talent with which he failed to work, falsity of discipleship is symbolically exposed. His and false disciples' fate is then projected in the master's command to "throw [him] into the darkness farther outside," the location of "weeping and gnashing of teeth." Here we see shades of Peter's going from the firelight of the high priest's courtyard out into the gateway, then farther outside into the darkness, and weeping there bitterly (26:69-75).[25]

Matthew 26:14-16 with 10:2-4
(par. Mark 14:10-11 with 3:16-19; Luke 22:3-6 with 6:13d-16)

The Matthean theme of false discipleship includes the story of Judas Iscariot, of course, just as it includes the story of Peter. The conjunction of Judas's suicide with Peter's bitter weeping has received attention above.[26] But back to Judas's appearance as one of the twelve apostles (10:2-4): In concert with the other Gospels, Matthew includes the notation that Judas

---

25. For a more detailed interpretation of this parable as a whole, see Gundry, *Commentary on the New Testament*, 111-13; and esp. for comparisons with Mark 13:34; Luke 19:11-27, Gundry, *Matthew*, 502-10.

26. See pp. 57-62.

was the one who betrayed Jesus. So from the start Judas is announced as a false disciple. In Matthew he does not come up by name again till 26:14-16.

In this subsequent passage Matthew advances the phrase, "one of the Twelve," ahead of Judas's name (contrast Mark 14:10; Luke 22:3) and introduces the name with "the one called" (ὁ λεγόμενος), which does not appear in the synoptic parallels (Mark 14:10-11; Luke 22:3-6). The advancement lays stress on Judas's discipleship — indeed, close discipleship — and the introduction, particularly given its definite article, distinguishes him emphatically from the rest of the Twelve, among whom he has just been numbered — just as in 4:18 and 10:2 "the one called Peter" distinguished Peter emphatically from Andrew his brother, in 26:3 "the one called Caiaphas" distinguished Caiaphas emphatically from other, anonymously mentioned chief priests, and in 27:17 "the one called Christ" will distinguish Jesus emphatically from Jesus Barabbas (contrast the unemphatic anarthrous λεγόμενος in 2:23; 9:9; 26:36; 27:16, 33). Distinctive of Matthew is also Judas's asking the chief priests, "What are you willing to give me, and I will betray him to you?" How brazenly voluntary and mercenary! But what do you expect of a false disciple?

Matthew 26:20-25
(par. Mark 14:17-21; Luke 22:14, 21-23; John 13:21-30)

At the Last Supper in Matt 26:20-25 Jesus announces that one of the Twelve will betray him, identifies the betrayer as "the one who has dipped [his] hand with me in the bowl," and says, "But woe to that man through whom the Son of Man is being betrayed. It would have been good for him if he — that man — had not been born." "*That* man" puts the betrayer at a moral distance from "the Son of Man," and repetition of "*that* man" magnifies the distance. Its being "good for him if he . . . had not been born" exposes the enormity of his treachery by headlining the horror of his fate.

Differently from Mark and Luke, Matthew has Judas answer Jesus (v. 25). But to underscore Judas's falsity Matthew first describes him again as "the one betraying him [Jesus]" (see 10:4, which has the aorist participle παραδούς, whereas 26:25 features the present participle παραδιδούς to enliven a betrayal in process now that Judas has gotten his money and "started seeking a favorable opportunity to betray him [Jesus]" [26:15-16]). Judas addresses Jesus with "Rabbi," not necessarily a wrong address in view of Jesus' having implied in 23:8 (distinctive of Matthew) that as the disciples' one teacher he was their rabbi.[27] But Judas's addressing Jesus presently with "Rabbi" anticipates his addressing Jesus with "Rabbi" in the very act of betraying him to the chief priests and elders (26:49). Judas's question, "Surely I am not [the betrayer], am I, Rabbi?" exudes hypocrisy. He knows very well that he is the betrayer. He has already been paid to betray Jesus. Thirty silver coins, the payment, are jingling in Judas's pocket. So his question, worded like that of the other apostles in a way that expects a negative answer, lacks sincerity. The abruptness of asyndeton and the present tense in "He [Jesus] tells him" (λέγει αὐτῷ) highlight Jesus' answer, "You yourself have spoken" (σὺ εἶπας). The answer amounts to a refusal to answer, as if to say, "Your words, not mine." This abruptness and refusal put Judas in a bad light because of the falsity of his discipleship.

Matthew 26:47-50
(par. Mark 14:43-46; Luke 22:47-48; John 18:2-5)

The actual betrayal takes place in Matt 26:47-50. In concert with Mark 14:43 and Luke 22:47 (cf. John 18:2), Matthew again identifies Judas as "one of the Twelve." And again the identification calls attention to Judas's perfidy as one of Jesus' inner circle. The same goes for "the one betraying him," which for emphasis (26:48) and in contrast with the parallel Mark 14:44, comes to the head of its sentence. This perfidy foreshadows the perfidy of other false disciples who will betray their fellow disciples (so Matthew alone in 24:10).

Judas's kissing Jesus as a signal to seize him deepens the perfidy with a show of affectionate homage. "Seize him" exposes the show as a charade, which is exactly the nature of false discipleship, whether or not self-conscious. The immediacy of Judas's approaching Jesus portrays Judas as hell-bent on the betrayal. The address "Rabbi" echoes v. 25, where Judas pretended not to know whether he was going to be the betrayer, though he had gotten advance payment and was seeking a favorable opportunity (vv. 14-16). His greeting Jesus with "Hail" (χαῖρε [so Matthew alone]) anticipates the same in 27:29, where soldiers will mock Jesus with this greeting. As a false disciple, then, Judas stands on the side of mockers. So the

---

27. Byrskog disagrees with this implication (*Jesus the Only Teacher*, 284-87). He may be right.

mockingly cheerful greeting, the respectful address, and the affectionate kiss characterize hypocrisy at its height.

Irony too. The greeting is ironic in that it literally means "Rejoice" or, as we might say, "Have a nice day," whereas Jesus is going to be crucified this very day. The address is likewise ironic in that "Rabbi" means "my great one," yet Judas has gotten only the price of a slave for betraying Jesus (Exod 21:32). And the kiss is ironic in that the verb for it (κατεφίλησεν) either intensifies the connotation of affection (if κατ- is perfective) or denotes kissing the hand or feet rather than the face (if κατ- is spatial, "down" [cf. Xenophon *Mem.* 2.6.33]). So Judas was feigning affection or humility. Jesus then addresses Judas with "Comrade" (ἑταῖρε [so Matthew alone]), which occurred for a false disciple in 22:12-13 (cf. 20:13), so that Jesus' addressing Judas with this term, itself ironic in that Judas is proving himself a betrayer rather than a true comrade, designates him a false disciple. Nor does the irony stop even here. For Matthew's Jesus, unlike Jesus in the other Gospels, goes on to issue Judas an ironic command to proceed with what he has come to do (ἐφ' ὃ πάρει, "do what you are here for"). All this irony undergirds the portrayal of Judas as a false disciple, like Peter, and contributes mightily to the theme of false discipleship that in other respects, too, runs throughout Matthew.

It is worth contemplating, moreover, that like Peter as well as the other apostles, the quintessential false disciple and apostate, viz., Judas Iscariot

- received from Jesus "authority over unclean spirits so as to cast them out and [authority] to heal every kind of disease and every kind of ailment" (10:1);
- was commissioned to "preach, saying, 'The kingdom of heaven has drawn near,'" and to "heal sick people, raise dead people, cleanse lepers, [and] cast out demons" (10:7-8);
- was "sent off" by Jesus "like [a] sheep in the midst of wolves" (10:16);
- was assured that the Spirit of his and the others' Father would be "the one speaking in [him]" (10:20);
- was told that the person who welcomed him welcomed both Jesus and the Father, who sent Jesus (10:40);
- became the object of Jesus' beatitude for having seen and heard things that many prophets and righteous people had "longed to see and hear," but did not (13:16-17);
- along with the other disciples, but not Peter, had "worshiped" Jesus, saying, "Truly, you are God's Son" (14:33);

- was given the authority of binding and loosening (18:18);
- was promised he would sit on one of twelve thrones in judgment over Israel's tribes (19:28);
- received assurance that with faith he could remove a mountain and "receive all things" that he "might ask for" (21:21-22); and
- was promised to drink "this produce of the vine" with Jesus in the "Father's kingdom" (26:29).

So if after all these positive notes Judas Iscariot would have been better off if he had not been born, what is to keep us, given the textual evidence surveyed above, from accepting that Matthew has portrayed Peter too as a false disciple, one who went so far as to apostatize in speech just as Judas apostatized in deed?

CHAPTER 8

Persecution in Matthew

As the story of Peter's apostasy, alongside that of Judas Iscariot, fits and supplements the Matthean theme of false discipleship, so the additional theme of persecution also fits and supplements the theme of false discipleship. For it is especially persecution that exposes falsity when, to protect themselves, erstwhile disciples hide their profession of discipleship and, in the worst cases, apostatize outright. To the Matthean theme of persecution, then, is added not only persecution as such, but also flight from persecution and precautionary avoidance of persecution.

Matthew 1–4

We see precautionary avoidance "on being warned in a dream" in the magi's "withdrawing [from Bethlehem] to their country by another way [than via Jerusalem, where the murderous Herod awaited them]" (2:12). An example of flight from persecution appears in Joseph's fleeing, at the behest of the angel of the Lord in another dream, from Herod's "seek[ing] the little child [Jesus] to destroy him" (2:13-15). Another example of precautionary avoidance comes in Joseph's being "warned in a dream," so that "he withdrew [from Egypt with 'the little child and his mother'] to the parts of Galilee" rather than going to Judea, where Herod's successor Archelaus was ruling (2:19-23). Jesus himself becomes an example, indeed an exemplar, of precautionary avoidance of persecution when "on hearing that John [the Baptist] had been delivered over [into prison], he withdrew into Galilee [from Judea]" (4:12). That these examples are unique to Matthew signals that the theme of persecution will continue prominently in this Gospel.[1]

Matthew 5–7

Persecution takes up the first part of the Sermon on the Mount, most prominently in 5:10-12:

> Blessed [are] those who have been persecuted on account of righteousness, because theirs is the kingdom of heaven. Blessed are you whenever people vilify you and persecute [you] and on account of me say every kind of evil thing against you, lying [when they do]. Rejoice and be glad, because your reward in heaven [is] much. For in this way they persecuted the prophets before you.

The first of these two beatitudes is unique to Matthew. Together, they cast a persecutory light on the preceding beatitudes, so that "the poor in spirit" are seen to be the inwardly dependent on God who because of persecution have no outward means of support (5:3); so that "those who are mourning" are seen to be the ones grieving over their and other disciples' persecutions (5:4); so that "the meek" are seen to be those who suffer persecution without retaliating (5:5); so that "those who hunger and thirst for righteousness" are those who long for God to rescue and vindicate them (5:6);[2] so that "the merciful" are seen to be those who treat mercifully the ones who treat them mercilessly (5:7); so that "the pure in heart" are seen to be those whose internal purity fortifies them against external temptations to recant under persecution (5:8); and so that "the peacemakers" are seen to be those who make peace with

---

1. Matthew 4:12 has parallels in Mark 1:14a and Luke 4:14a, but Jesus' "hearing" of John's imprisonment and the verb of withdrawal are unique to Matthew.

2. Against the view that they long to be righteous themselves. According to 5:10 they are already righteous and consequently persecuted (cf. "your [plural, referring to the disciples] righteousness" in 5:20; 6:1). See too Roland Deines, *Die Gerechtigkeit der Tora im Reich des Messias: Mt 5,13-20 als Schlüsseltext der matthäischen Theologie* (WUNT 177; Tübingen: Mohr Siebeck, 2004), 137-52; Donald A. Hagner, "Righteousness in Matthew's Theology," in *Worship, Theology and Ministry in the Early Church* (ed. Michael J. Wilkins and Terence Paige; JSNTSup 87; Sheffield: JSOT Press, 1992), 112-15, though Deines and Hagner underplay the context of persecution.

their persecutors (5:9). Of these seven beatitudes, five are distinctive of Matthew.

The matter of persecution comes up again in the Sermon on the Mount at 5:43-48, where Jesus tells his disciples, "Love your enemies, and pray for the ones persecuting you" so as "to be perfect as your heavenly Father is perfect." "His kingdom and his righteousness" (6:33) consist in the coming to pass of his will "on earth as also [it does] in heaven" (6:10), so that "the kingdom of heaven" belongs to "those who have been persecuted on account of [their] righteousness" (5:10; cf. "your [plural] righteousness" in 5:20; 6:1). So to seek the Father's righteousness is again to seek from him a rescue from persecution and a vindication before one's persecutors, for that is the right thing for him to do. It is also for the persecuted to seek his righteousness by persevering under persecution, which brings economic deprivation that might easily lead to anxiety over food, drink, and clothing. Hence, the prohibition of anxiety throughout 6:25-34 rests on the context of persecution.[3]

Finally for the Sermon on the Mount, "the constricted road that leads to life" according to 7:14 represents the way of persecution suffered by Jesus' true disciples. For the Greek word underlying "constricted" — i.e., τεθλιμμένη — is the verbal cognate of the noun θλῖψις, "pressure, tribulation, affliction," which refers to persecution (13:21; 24:9, 21, 29). Contrastively, the broad way that leads to destruction (7:13) represents the course of least resistance: that is to say, avoiding persecution through loose and lawless living so far as the superior righteousness demanded by Jesus (5:20) is concerned.

Matthew 10

It is questionable, even doubtful, that the storm on the Sea of Galilee (8:23-27) symbolizes persecution of the church.[4] But Jesus' commissional speech in chapter 10 contains a number of references to persecution. The rapacity of wolves makes his statement, "Behold, I am sending you like sheep in the midst of wolves" (v. 16), a prediction of persecution, even of possi-

---

3. See further Gundry, *Commentary on the New Testament*, 25; against Deines, *Die Gerechtigkeit*, 441-46; Hagner, "Righteousness in Matthew's Theology," 112-15, who underplay the context of persecution here more seriously than they do in the case of 5:6.

4. See Gundry, *Matthew*, 154-57, against Günther Bornkamm, *Tradition and Interpretation in Matthew* (Philadelphia: Westminster, 1963), 52-57.

ble martyrdom. Hence the command to "become shrewd," so as to avoid martyrdom — not by way of hiding the light of discipleship, much less by way of apostasy, but by way of withdrawal for the purpose of ministry elsewhere: "But whenever they persecute you in this city [where you have gone], flee into another [city]" (v. 23). In vv. 17-18 Jesus urges precaution: "For they will give you over to sanhedrins [Jewish local courts]; and in their synagogues they will flog you; and you will be led before both governors and kings on account of me for a testimony to them and the nations." Next, Jesus urges his disciples not to grow anxious over how or what they should say when given over to the authorities: "For what you should say will be given to you in that hour. For you are not the ones speaking; rather, the Spirit of your Father [is] the one speaking in you" (vv. 19-20).

After a warning of betrayal to death among members of the same family, and of being "hated by all [kinds of people as well as by members of one's own family]" because of Jesus' "name," there comes the assurance that "the one enduring to an end — this one will be saved" (vv. 21-22). Then Jesus makes himself archetypical of the persecuted: "If people have nicknamed the house owner 'Beelzebul,' how much more [will they stigmatize] the members of his household" (vv. 24-25). A follow-up consists in three prohibitions of fear: First, Jesus tells his disciples not to fear those who stigmatize him and them, because the truth will out (v. 26). Second, he tells them not to fear those who can kill the body, because they cannot kill the soul (v. 28a). Third, he tells them not to fear, because they are more valuable than many sparrows, not one of which falls unless the Father wills it to (vv. 29-31).

The first two prohibitions lead to commands to proclaim Jesus' teachings publicly despite persecution (v. 27) and to fear God rather than persecutors, because unlike them he can destroy both soul and body in gehenna (v. 28b). The third prohibition leads to a declaration that before his heavenly Father, Jesus will confess those who confess him in public but deny those who deny him in public (vv. 32-33). Emphasizing the publicity of confession is the command to speak "in the light" and make proclamation "on the housetops."

Under the figure of a sword, Jesus declares his coming to have a purpose of sowing deadly discord among members of the same household (vv. 34-36), and declares further that a professing disciple's failure to risk betrayal by members of his own family will show him to be false and therefore unworthy of Jesus (v. 37). Likewise showing him to be false and unworthy of Jesus will be the professing disciple's failure to take his own cross and follow behind Jesus, i.e., failure to expose himself through public discipleship to the possibility of martyrdom (v. 38). "The one who has found his life" is the false disciple who has preserved his present life by drawing back from public discipleship. But he will lose the eternal life that would otherwise be his. "The one who has lost his life" is the true disciple who has suffered martyrdom for public discipleship. But he will find eternal life. Not that eternal life *requires* martyrdom; rather, Jesus is encouraging his disciples not to draw back from *risking* martyrdom (vv. 38-39).

Finally, Jesus states a reward for those who demonstrate true discipleship by harboring fellow disciples who are fleeing persecution in accordance with v. 23 (vv. 40-42). So the whole of chapter 10 is shot through with the theme of persecution, and this in relation to the theme of false versus true discipleship, of which Matthew's Peter is a case in point. A glance at synopses of the Gospels will show that a great deal of the content in this chapter and of its organization around these themes is distinctive of Matthew.

Matthew 11-12

Matthew 11:12 records Jesus' saying, "But from the days of John the Baptist till now the kingdom of heaven suffers violence, and violent [men] plunder it." The interpretation of this saying is disputed.[5] The immediate context of John's imprisonment, however, joins the larger Matthean theme of persecution to favor another reference to the sort of persecution that will distinguish between false and true disciples. Like John, Jesus becomes an exemplary target of persecution in 12:14: "the Pharisees took counsel against him, as to how they might destroy him."

The text goes on to read, "And Jesus, on coming to know [about the plot], withdrew from there" (12:15). This withdrawal from the location of danger to his life and limb results in a continuation and extension of his ministry and thus sets again an example for the disciples to follow in accordance with 10:23 (see 4:12 for his first such example; cf. 2:12, 13, 14, 22). He will set another such example in 14:13a: "And on hearing [the report of John's death], Jesus withdrew from there in a boat to a deserted place by himself."[6] And he will set yet another such example in 15:21: "And going out from there [Gennesaret in view of 14:34], Jesus withdrew [because of

---

5. See Nolland, *Matthew*, 457-58, for a brief but representative discussion.
6. See Gundry, *Commentary on the New Testament*, 64, for the location of "there."

the antagonism of the Pharisees and scribes in 15:1-2] into the districts of Tyre and Sidon." Back in 13:20-21, meanwhile, Jesus interprets "the person sown on rocky ground" as one who after hearing the word and receiving it immediately with joy "is immediately snared" "when pressure and persecution come about because of the word," which bring out his rootlessness and temporariness as a false disciple. Jesus' interpretation of the person sown on rocky ground (τὰ πετρώδη) fits to a T Matthew's portrayal of Peter (Πέτρος).[7]

Matthew 16

In 16:18 "the gates of hades" echoes Isa 38:10, where the expression stands for death (cf. "the gates of death" in Job 38:17; Pss 9:13; 107:18). So Jesus' saying that the gates of hades will not "prevail *against*" (**κατ**ισχύσουσιν) his church likely means that not even persecution to the point of martyrdoms will obliterate the church. But martyrdoms become so much a possibility that in 16:24-26 Jesus says, "If anyone wants to come behind me, he has to deny himself [contrast Peter's denying Jesus instead of himself] and pick up his cross [i.e., expose himself to shame, ridicule, and persecution] and follow me." The further statements that "whoever wants to save his life [i.e., avoid martyrdom] will lose it [so far as eternity is concerned]," and that "whoever loses his life on account of me [by way of martyrdom for open discipleship] will save it [for eternity]," prove that persecution, sometimes to the point of martyrdom, even martyrdom by crucifixion, is in view.

Matthew 17, 23

According to 17:11-13, John the Baptist's fate was a preliminary example of persecution to the death. Prediction of such persecution yet to come appears also in Jesus' telling the scribes and Pharisees, "I am sending to you prophets and sages and scribes [see 13:51-52 for a uniquely Matthean reference to Jesus' disciples as scribes]. [Some] of them you will kill and crucify, and [some] of them you will flog in your synagogues and persecute from city to city" (23:34).

---

7. See again Goodacre, "The Rock on Rocky Ground," 61-73; Bubar, "Killing Two Birds," 147-50.

Peter — False Disciple and Apostate according to Saint Matthew

Matthew 24-25

Further predictions of persecution appear in the Olivet Discourse (chs. 24-25), much of which has no parallels in the other Gospels. In 24:9-12 Jesus predicts that people in general will give his disciples over to tribulation and kill them, that all nations will hate them on account of his name, that many of them will be snared (i.e., will apostatize) and betray others of their number and hate one another. "And because lawlessness will be multiplied, the love of the many will grow cold [so as to betray and hate each other and thus give evidence of their own falsity]."[8] The command that Judean disciples should flee on seeing the abomination of desolation arises out of the prediction of a tribulation — i.e., persecution — unequaled in the past or future (24:20-22). And the feeding or nonfeeding, the giving or nongiving of drink, the granting or nongranting of hospitality, the clothing or nonclothing, and the visitation or nonvisitation of Jesus' "littlest brothers" (25:34-45) implies their persecution, so that they go hungry and thirsty, need hospitality during flight, lack sufficient clothing, and suffer sickness and imprisonment.

Matthew 26-27

Finally, Jesus becomes the chief exemplar not only of precautionary avoidance of persecution and of flight from it, as already noted, but also of actually suffering it. The passion predictions in 16:21; 17:22-23; 20:17-19; 26:1-2 present him as the coming object of persecution to the death. A parabolic such prediction appears in the killing of the son of a vineyard owner (21:37-39). The Pharisees were "seeking to seize him [Jesus]" according to 21:45-46, and tried to "trap him" in regard to a politically sensitive issue according to 22:15-17. In 26:3-5 the chief priests and elders of the people "plotted together in order that they might seize Jesus with cunning and kill [him]." His Words of Institution (26:26-29) declare his imminent death by violence. (N.B. the separation of his body and blood.) The remainder of chapters 26-27 narrates in detail his arrest, trials, mockery, and crucifixion.

Two uniquely Matthean passages underline that Jesus was "persecuted on account of righteousness" (5:10): (1) Pilate's wife is said to have sent him a message, saying, "Have nothing to do with that righteous [man], for

---

8. Cf. the wicked slave's "beating his fellow slaves" in the parable of 24:45-51, esp. v. 49.

I have suffered severely today in a dream because of him" (27:19). (2) By washing his hands with water, Pilate follows the rite prescribed in Deut 21:1-9, a rite indicating true innocence of murder, so that "all the people" take on themselves bloodguiltiness for Jesus' murder (27:24-25). In the context of persecution, murder produces martyrdom.

All in all, as the case of Peter merges with the Matthean theme of false discipleship and apostasy, so that theme merges with the further Matthean theme of persecution, which exposes false disciples for who they really are, especially when they apostatize by denying Jesus publicly, as Peter did.[9]

---

9. Because the themes of false discipleship and persecution are so self-evident in Matthew, the foregoing discussions have not required extensive documentation in secondary scholarly literature; but for a brief summary, see Gundry, *Matthew*, 5-10. Commentators who neglect these themes do not argue against their presence so much as they overlook them (see, e.g., Nolland, *Matthew* [throughout]). The discussions here do not consist in mirror readings that argue for Matthew's addressing actual situations of persecution and of a mixture of the true and the false in the church(es). As in the case of Peter himself, only Matthew's literary portrayals have formed the subject matter. For the same reason the historical critical arguments in Douglas R. A. Hare's *The Theme of Jewish Persecution of Christians in the Gospel according to St Matthew* (SNTSMS 6; Cambridge: Cambridge University Press, 1967) need no treatment here. Mirror readings would require further discussion.

CHAPTER 9

A Recapitulation and Some Possible Implications

The time has come to recapitulate the main ways in which Matthew portrays Peter as a false disciple of Jesus and as one who publicly apostatized, so that this portrayal fits other main themes in Matthew's Gospel. Peter appears in Matt 4:18-20 as one of Jesus' first disciples and as somewhat prominent, but the nature of his prominence is not spelled out. Though mentioned in 8:14-15, he plays no role there. Even his presence remains unattested. The description of him as "first" in 10:2 awaits definition as "last" in 19:29–20:16 and therefore as destined not to "inherit eternal life" with the "last" who will be "first." In contrast with the parallel Mark 3:16, moreover, Matthew omits Jesus' having given him the nickname "Peter."

In 14:22-33 Peter starts and ends with little faith and doubt. Between them, disobedient fear (when he was walking on the waters) characterizes him; and Jesus rebukes him, whereas the other disciples confess Jesus as truly God's Son. In 15:12-20 Matthew makes Peter representative of blameworthy ignorance — this in contrast with Matthew's often portraying the disciples as more knowledgeable than they appear to be in Mark.

Whereas the other disciples had earlier and on their own confessed Jesus as truly God's Son, in 16:13-20 Peter belatedly confesses him as such only by virtue of God the Father's revelation to him. Rather than saying, "You are Peter, and on you I will build my church" or "You are Cephas, which translated means bedrock, and on you I will build my church," Jesus shifts from the second-person address, "You are Peter," to a third-person reference, "and on this bedrock." The shift recalls 7:24, where "the bedrock" represents "these my words" of Jesus, so that in line with Matthew's highlighting Jesus' words by gathering them into five long discourses and

A Recapitulation and Some Possible Implications

elsewhere reducing narratival material in favor of Jesus' words, they form the bedrock on which he will build his church. They likewise form the keys to be used for opening and closing the door to the kingdom of heaven in accordance with the behaviors they prohibit ("bind") and require ("loosen").

In 16:21-23 Matthew inserts into Peter's objection to Jesus' first passion-and-resurrection prediction both the rebuke, "Never, Lord!" and the contradiction, "By no means will this happen to you!" Though shared with Mark's parallel, the command addressed by Jesus to Peter, "Go behind me, Satan!" recalls "Go, Satan!" in Matthew's but not Mark's account of Jesus' temptation (4:10; contrast Mark 1:12-13). Furthermore, Matthew adds a third insertion by way of Jesus' statement to Peter, "You are my snare," the designation "snare" being used elsewhere in this Gospel for false or nondisciples.

In his account of Jesus' transfiguration (17:1-8) Matthew exacerbates Peter's foolishness by having him say, "*I* will make here three tents," rather than "Let *us* make three tents" (so the Markan and Lukan parallels). In the distinctively Matthean passage 17:24-27, Jesus brusquely corrects Peter by citing a voluntary rather than legal reason for paying the temple tax; and Matthew omits saying that Peter caught a fish with a coin in its mouth. Likewise in 18:21-22 and against the Lukan parallel, Matthew has Peter ask Jesus how many times one should forgive his brother (up to seven times?), and has Jesus abruptly correct Peter (with seventy times seven). Unlike Mark's Jesus, in 19:27-30 Matthew's Jesus omits present compensation for discipleship, limits the compensation to eternal life in the future, and thus faults Peter's self-aggrandizing question, "What then shall we have?" which to Peter's discredit Matthew has inserted into largely paralleled material.

By inserting "never," Matthew strengthens Peter's promise not to be "snared" in regard to Jesus (26:31-35), a promise Peter will disgracefully fail to keep. By omitting the names of James and John and retaining in 26:36-46 only Peter's name, Matthew concentrates on Peter's failure to stay awake and pray with Jesus in Gethsemane. In 26:57-75 the insertion "before all" in Matthew's account of Peter's first denial of Jesus makes Peter the object of Jesus' denial before the heavenly Father according to 10:33. The insertion of "with an oath" in Matthew's account of Peter's second denial of Jesus makes Peter rule himself out of the kingdom of heaven through flagrant disregard of the prohibition of oaths in 5:33-37 (so Matthew alone among the Gospels) and in stark contrast with Jesus' distinctively simultaneous refusal to answer under oath. In other words, Peter fails to exhibit the superior righteousness required for entrance into that kingdom (5:20).

Peter — False Disciple and Apostate according to Saint Matthew

By going outside and weeping bitterly after his third denial of Jesus, Peter falls in line with the damned, who are repeatedly and distinctively (with only one exception) said in Matthew to weep and gnash their teeth "farther outside" the kingdom. Underlining this point is Matthew's carefully noting Peter's regress farther and farther outside the judgment hall where Jesus is standing trial.

To cement the connotation of damnation in Peter's bitter weeping outside, Matthew adds his topographically and chronologically disjointed and distinctive account of Judas Iscariot's remorseful, hopeless suicide (contrast Acts 1:15-20, and see Jesus' woe on Judas in Matt 26:24). No wonder, then, that in 28:7 Matthew omits "and Peter" from the instruction to the women at Jesus' empty tomb that they should go tell the disciples the good news of his resurrection and that he is going ahead of them into Galilee. Peter will be among the Eleven who see him there according to 28:16-17, but as a tare among wheat he remains as a false disciple and apostate among true and enduring disciples until separation occurs at the consummation of the age.[1]

The recency of detail concerning the related and intertwined Matthean themes of false discipleship and persecution makes unnecessary their recapitulation here. It remains then to explore some possible implications, both higher-critical and theological, of Matthew's portrayal of Peter as a false disciple who apostatized and is consequently bound for eternal damnation.

As to the higher-critical question of Matthew's date of writing, it seems unlikely that he would have portrayed Peter as a false disciple who apostatized if Peter had already died in the mid-60s as a martyr for the cause of Christ.[2] One might suppose that Matthew, though writing afterward, may not have known of Peter's martyrdom. But given the prominence of Peter and the widespread lines of communication in the Roman Empire and among Christians therein, that possibility too seems unlikely. Though not an airtight argument, then, the likelihood that Matthew's ultimately negative portrayal of Peter antedates Peter's martyrdom joins other con-

---

1. It is common coin in the NT that apostates mingle with the true and faithful. See not only Jude 4, 12–13; 2 Pet 2:1, 13; 1 Tim 1:18-20; 4:1-3; 6:3-5, 20-21; 2 Tim 2:16-18, 20-21 (with Gundry, *Commentary on the New Testament*, 854); 3:1-9; but also Rom 16:17-18; 2 Cor 11:3-4, 12-15, 21b-23; Phil 3:2; Gal 1:6-9; 2:4; 5:7-8. By saying that in Galatians Paul is writing of discipline rather than salvation, of impermanent rather than permanent deviation from grace, and of only a suggestion of permanent such deviation, N. T. Wright does not take seriously enough Paul's double anathema in Gal 1:8-9 (*Paul and the Faithfulness of God* [2 vols.; Christian Origins and the Question of God 4; Minneapolis: Fortress, 2013], 2:1140-41).

2. For the martyrdom of Peter, see esp. John 21:18-19; 2 Pet 1:14; *1 Clem.* 5.2-4.

A Recapitulation and Some Possible Implications

siderations favoring a date prior to the mid-60s for Matthew's writing. These other considerations include the following:

- The irrelevance after the demise of the Sadducees in A.D. 70 of Matthew's inserting them half a dozen times (against only one additional, paralleled occurrence and no further mentions in Mark and Luke).
- The irrelevance after the destruction of the temple in A.D. 70 of Jesus' exemplary payment of the temple tax in the uniquely Matthean passage 17:24-27.
- The irrelevance of offering "a gift at the altar" (5:23-24, almost entirely peculiar to Matthew) if the altar was no longer standing as a result of its destruction in A.D. 70.
- The irrelevance after Jerusalem's destruction in A.D. 70 of Matthew's preoccupation with Jerusalem as the center of Jewish leaders' antagonism.
- The disagreement between a post-destruction date of writing and Matthew's using the present tense instead of Mark's and Luke's past tenses in Jesus' reference to corrupt trafficking in the temple (21:13; contrast Mark 11:17; Luke 19:46).
- The similar disagreement of a post-destruction date of writing with Matthew's completely unparalleled paragraph on swearing by the temple and items associated with it (23:16-22).
- The disagreement of Christians' having fled from Jerusalem to Pella on the edge of the Jordan Valley and before seeing the abomination of desolation (Eusebius *Hist. eccl.* 3.5.3) with Jesus' command in 24:15-16 to flee into the Judean mountains only after seeing that abomination — also the irrelevance of Matthew's inserting the Sabbath as an undesirable time for flight (24:20; contrast Mark 13:18) if after A.D. 70 the flight had already taken place.
- The disagreement of Matthew's highly unusual insertion of εὐθέως, "immediately," into Jesus' statement that celestial portents and the Son of Man's coming will take place after the great tribulation (24:29) — the disagreement of this insertion of immediacy with the need after A.D. 70 to create instead a gap between the events of A.D. 66-70 and the Son of Man's not-yet-visible but yet-to-be very visible coming in the future.

These and other considerations have convinced a number of recent commentators that Matthew wrote early, i.e., before A.D. 70, as would allow

Peter — False Disciple and Apostate according to Saint Matthew

him to portray Peter more easily as a false disciple who apostatized though staying within the mixed church.[3]

As to the higher-critical questions of provenance and impulse, it has often been thought that Matthew's Gospel emanated from Antioch, Syria. For in 4:24 "Syria" replaces "Tyre and Sidon" (Mark 3:8; Luke 6:17) and thereby suggests a place of writing in Syria, such as Antioch, apart from Tyre and Sidon; and according to Acts 11:19-21 et passim (cf. Gal 2:11-13) Jewish Christians from Palestine emigrated to Syrian Antioch, started the church there, and evangelized a large number of Gentiles. The Jewish-cum-Gentile character of Matthew fits perfectly Luke's description of the church in Antioch, and Matthew's twenty-one unparalleled uses of πόλις, "city," suit Antioch as the third-largest city in the Roman Empire. Furthermore, the early church father Ignatius appears in his letter *To the Smyrnaeans* 1.1 to have been the first to allude to the Gospel of Matthew; and he was bishop of the church in that very city. An Antiochene provenance for Matthew's Gospel also facilitates the hypothesis of Matthean influence on Luke (see Eusebius *Hist. eccl.* 3.4.6; Acts 11:26 D for Luke's association with Syrian Antioch).[4]

According to Gal 2:11-14 the apostle Paul opposed Peter face-to-face, calling him Cephas, in Antioch, Syria. Might Matthew's portrayal of Peter have received its impulse at least in part from that opposition so as to effect in Matthew an anti-Petrine stance rather than the often-favored pro-Petrine stance, and even favor against much recent opinion to the contrary that Paul won his argument with Peter?[5] Despite Paul's more or less

---

3. For fuller discussion of Matthew's date of writing, see Gundry, *Matthew*, 602-9, 672-73 nn. 216-23. This discussion includes an argument that the burning of a city in Matt 22:7 reflects Isa 5:24-25, the same chapter in Isaiah that was reflected a little earlier in Matt 21:33ff., rather than the burning of Jerusalem in A.D. 70. Donald A. Hagner lists additionally the following scholars, almost all of them recent, as advocating an early date: Allen, Moule, Reicke, Nolland, France, Blomberg, Wilkins, Carson, Gibbs, and Turner (*The New Testament: A Historical and Theological Introduction* [Grand Rapids: Baker Academic, 2012], 215 n. 56). To Hagner's list may now be added the name of Craig Evans.

4. Revisit p. 4 n. 10 for bibliography favoring at least subsidiary influence of Matthew on Luke.

5. See Schäfer, *Paulus bis zum Apostelkonzil*, 234-43, 480-81, for Paul as the winner in Antioch, though the likelihood of her conative interpretation of the imperfect verbs ὑπέστελλεν and ἀφώριζεν in Gal 2:12b is subject to some doubt, as is also the necessity of that interpretation for Paul's victory. One could ask why Paul would have argumentatively brought up the incident at Antioch if he had lost and was known to have lost, as he surely would have been.

A Recapitulation and Some Possible Implications

favorable references to Peter/Cephas in Gal 1:18; 2:7-9; 1 Cor 1:12; 3:22; 9:5; 15:5, might Matthew's portrayal of Peter as a false disciple and apostate also represent an intensification of Paul's attack on Peter in Antioch? Echoes, then, of the old Tübingen hypothesis, but with Matthew replacing Paul? These possibilities are intriguing and may call for further investigation.

Theologically, Luke and John contradict Matthew's portrayal of Peter as a false disciple and apostate destined for damnation by portraying him instead as rehabilitated after his denials of Jesus (see Luke 22:31-32; 24:34; John 21:15-22; Acts 1–12; 15:7-11; cf. Mark 16:7; 1-2 Peter and the above-cited Petrine passages in Paul's letters). Or is it the other way around, that Matthew contradicts Luke and John?[6] Either way, the contradiction raises a theological as well as historical question concerning the unity of Scripture.

Historical contradictions between the accounts of Judas Iscariot's death in Matt 27:3-10 and Acts 1:15-20 have been canvassed above.[7] Other historical contradictions abound, as in Matthew's placing Jesus' cleansing of the temple on Palm Sunday (21:1-17), to take a minor example, over against Mark's placing the cleansing on the next day (11:1-17). Nor are such contradictions limited to the Gospels or to the NT as a whole. In the OT, for example, the Israelites' conquest of Canaan looks complete in Josh 1–12 (see esp. 10:40-43; 11:16-23) but only partial in Judges (see esp. 1:1–2:5).

Examples of theological contradictions are more relevant, however, to the theologically contradictory portrayals of Peter as an apostate whom Jesus will deny and as a true disciple whom Jesus rehabilitated. According to 2 Sam 24:1, for example, Yahweh incites David to take a census of the people of Israel and Judah; but in 1 Chron 21:1 an adversary incites David to do so. Whether that adversary was Satan (as in many English translations) or a human, national, or angelic opponent (as according to some interpreters), the contradiction remains, especially since it looks as though the Chronicler is trying to get rid of the theological scandal in 2 Sam 24:1, viz., the scandal that Yahweh himself incited David to do something so wrong that even Joab, chief of the army, and his staff objected to it, and so wrong that Israel suffered the judgmental, plague-caused deaths of 70,000

---

6. Because of identical referents, what philosophers of language call extensional statements — e.g., "Simon denied Jesus" and "Peter denied Jesus" — can be substituted for each other. But because of contextual differences, intensional (≠ intentional) statements — e.g., "Peter's denials of Jesus ended in apostasy" and "Peter's denials of Jesus ended in rehabilitation" — cannot be substituted for each other. So a contradiction between Matthew's portrayal and Luke's and John's portrayals stands firm.

7. See pp. 58-59.

(2 Sam 24:15; 1 Chron 21:14). Though according to 2 Sam 24:1 it was out of anger against Israel that Yahweh incited David to do the wrong, it remains that the incitement led David to do a wrong about which he later said to Yahweh, "Behold, I have sinned; and behold, I have acted wickedly" (2 Sam 24:17). Perhaps most relevant as an analogy to the theologically contradictory portrayals of Peter are the likewise theologically contradictory portrayals of King Solomon in the OT. To warn against idolatry, 1 Kings 11 portrays him as an apostate. To stress the importance of worship at the temple, 2 Chron 1–9 portrays him as the temple-builder in a wholly favorable light.

Switching back to the NT, an example of theological contradiction arises in God's "not willing" (μὴ βουλόμενος) that any perish but that all come to repentance, on the one hand (2 Pet 3:9), and God's choice of only some for salvation, "For many are called, but few are chosen" (Matt 22:14), on the other hand. According to Rev. 22:17 the human being "who wills" (ὁ θέλων) is to drink the water of life for salvation, but Rom 9:16 denies that election to salvation has to do with the human being "who wills" (τοῦ θέλοντος). In his discussion of divine election of some but not others, moreover, the apostle Paul asks, "For who has resisted his [God's] will [τῷ βουλήματι αὐτοῦ]?" (Rom 9:19), and avers by way of contrast with the above-cited statement in 2 Pet 3:9 that God is "willing" (θέλων) some to be "prepared for destruction" (Rom 9:22). And against the irresistibility of God's will in Rom 9:19, Luke 7:30 declares that "the Pharisees and the lawyers rejected the will of God [τὴν βουλὴν τοῦ θεοῦ ἠθέτησαν] for themselves." The asseveration of God's will that everybody repent has the purpose of highlighting both the patience of God and the universality of his invitation to salvation. The contrary asseveration of God's electing for salvation some, but not all, has the purpose of highlighting the nonelects' obstinacy and God's justice (cf. the interplay between divine sovereignty and human responsibility in the Fourth Gospel).

Yes, then, scriptural diversity does go so far as to exhibit theological as well as historical contradictions. Though Matthew does not say so explicitly, in his Gospel Peter appears to be headed for hell, whereas in Luke-Acts and John 21 Peter appears on the contrary to be rehabilitated. Is it right to gloss over Matthew's portrayal in favor of Luke's and John's, or vice versa? No, for a choice of one portrayal over the other undermines the canonical authority of all Scripture; and systematization in the form of harmonization damages one or another, or both, of the portrayals and in the process makes one or both of them mean less than they naturally and even obviously mean.[8] Pastoral concerns seem to be at play, both minatory so as to warn against eternal damnation (take Matthew's portrayal of Peter, for instance, as though to say, "If even Peter, prince of the apostles, could forfeit his salvation by denying Jesus publicly, don't think you can escape the same fate despite denying Jesus similarly") and heartening so as to encourage repentance (take Luke's and John's portrayals, for instance, as though they are saying, "Don't despair; for if even so cowardly a denier of Jesus as Peter was restored, you can be too"). May such pastoral concerns override theological unity as well as historical accuracy? Out of respect for the texts one is tempted, or forced, to think so.

Francis Watson discusses contradictions in Scripture in regard to Jesus as a historical and theological figure or, better, as a historical-theological figure. Many of Watson's observations can be applied also to scriptural contradictions concerning Peter as a historical-theological figure:

> The possibility of contradictions only arises on the assumption that correspondence with factual occurrence [or that theological unity, we might add] is the appropriate criterion for assessing gospel truth.... The problem of alleged contradictions can only be resolved by recognizing that the criterion of correspondence to factual occurrence [or that the criterion of theological unity] is already rejected in the canonical form itself.... The apparent contradiction ... compels the reader to seek the truth on a different plane to that of sheer factuality [or of theological unity].[9]

On what plane? In the present case, apparently, on the plane of different paraenetic needs and purposes.[10] But more discussion, especially of systematic theological and philosophical sorts, is surely needed.

---

8. Cf. the church fathers' attempted refutation of the Novationists' and, later, the Donatists' rigorism in relation to *lapsi*. The rigorists argued for keeping *lapsi* under lifelong discipline so as to let God decide their eternal fate in the end. See G. W. H. Lampe, "St. Peter's Denial," 355-68.

9. Francis Watson, *Gospel Writing: A Canonical Perspective* (Grand Rapids: Eerdmans, 2013), 14. See pertinent observations also on pp. 605, 615-16.

10. Compare the following statements of Aristotle: "The political and the poetic do not share the same [standard] of correctness [ὀρθύτης]"; "They [ἀδύνατα, 'impossibilities'] are correct [ὀρθῶς ἔχει] if they achieve the purpose of [poetry] itself" (*Poet.* 25.1460b.13-14, 23-24). Aristotle defends the right of a poet like Sophocles to portray people as they ought to be rather than as they are in fact (*Poet.* 25.1460b.32-34). Might we say that writers of Scripture enjoyed similar liberties?

Peter — False Disciple and Apostate according to Saint Matthew

Perhaps a way forward is to be found in Kevin J. Vanhoozer's "major thesis" that "theology in postmodernity must orient itself to wisdom rather than knowledge"; that "a virtue-based epistemology" based on "practical reason" is needed; that "epistemic humility means being tolerant, not in the sense of embracing plurality and difference, as would a postmodern relativist, but rather in the sense of enduring it"; and that "questions about the truth of our theology are thus tied up with questions about the effectiveness of our discipleship and martyrdom."[11]

---

11. Kevin J. Vanhoozer, *First Theology: God, Scripture and Hermeneutics* (Downers Grove, Ill.: InterVarsity Press, 2002), 348, 351, 367, 373. The suggestion of an application to the question of scriptural contradictions is mine, not Vanhoozer's.

Afterword

Noted above is the possibility that Luke saw Matthew's portrayal of Peter, recognized its severity, and set about softening the portrayal to encourage repentance and restoration.[1] There is the further possibility that John the evangelist knew Luke's Gospel and followed suit in regard to a rehabilitation of Peter.[2] Apart from these possibilities, why the failure of most people throughout subsequent church history to have understood Matthew's portrayal as unnervingly severe despite its being hard to overlook that severity? An answer to this question is likely severalfold:

- Apologetic harmonizing of the Gospels started already in the second century with Tatian's *Diatessaron* and has continued ever since. As a result, the distinctively severe features in Matthew's portrayal of Peter have been softened in the light of Peter's rehabilitation elsewhere in the NT.
- The tradition of Peter's martyrdom lent support to that softening.
- What we might also call the airbrushing of Matthew's Peter has proved irresistibly attractive, because it offers comfort to the many who see in themselves a Peter-like mixture of good and bad behavior, of success

---

1. For Luke's subsidiary use of Matthew's Gospel, see yet again p. 4 n. 10; and for the possible substitution of Matthew's Gospel for Q, so that Luke used Matthew rather than a Q, see esp. the works of Austin Farrer, Michael Goulder, and Mark Goodacre listed in Hagner, *New Testament,* 150, plus Watson, *Gospel Writing,* 117-216.

2. For John's use of one or more of the Synoptics, see esp. the articles by Frans Neirynck that are listed in Hagner, *New Testament,* 300.

and failure, and who at the same time see in Peter outside Matthew a promise of their own ultimate redemption.[3]
- Enthronement of Peter as the first pope, though tardy, bathed him in an aura of glory. Protestant Reformers dethroned him, but there remains even apart from Roman Catholic circles a certain glow in his being at least (and supposedly) *primus inter pares*.
- Widespread aversion to a doctrine of divine judgment makes for resistance (whether conscious or unconscious) to Peter's being portrayed as a condemned apostate.

It remains to be seen whether an unblinking exegesis of the Petrine passages in Matthew will overcome interpretive and ecclesiastical traditions and the attractiveness of a Peter who offers us a mirror image of our flawed but redeemable selves. Not that the portrayal in Matthew should eviscerate other portrayals in the NT. But neither should they eviscerate the one in Matthew.

---

3. Cf. Demacopoulos's statement, "Remarkably, [Pope] Leo [the Great] is able to transform a passage about Peter's denial [of Jesus] into an encomium on the apostle's devotion.... Peter is 'permitted to hesitate,' Leo reckons, so that we might all learn the power of repentance" (*Invention of Peter*, 47-48).

Index of Modern Authors

Albright, W. F., 9n9, 29n44
Allen, Willoughby C., 29n44
Allison, Dale C., Jr., 6n2, 8n7, 9n9, 11n14, 14n24, 15n2, 17n6, 18n9, 20n17, 21n21, 25n31, 32nn2-3, 40, 40n36, 44n4, 59nn58-59, 60n62, 65n12

Barber, Michael Patrick, 21n17
Bauckham, Richard, 54n41, 56n53
Beare, Francis Wright, 58n56
Becker, Jürgen, 1n2, 8n6, 17n6, 19n13, 65n9
Bigane, John E., III, 22, 22n24
Bird, Michael F., 4n10
Biven, David, 20n16
Black, David Alan, 64n4
Blomberg, Craig L., 36n22, 59, 59n61, 62n72
Bockmuehl, Markus, 1n2, 6n2, 16n3, 20n15, 21n21, 44n4, 46n13, 48n22, 52n31, 54n46, 63n2
Bonnard, Pierre, 29n4, 33, 33n7, 37, 37n27, 38n28, 40n34, 46n15
Bornkamm, Günther, 55n50, 92n4
Böttrich, Christfried, 1n2, 44n4, 53n40, 59n60
Boxall, Ian, 5n12, 10n10, 16n5, 22n23, 22n25, 24n28, 27, 27nn35-36, 60, 61n64, 69n18

Broadus, John A., 19n12, 38n30, 44n6, 45n13
Brown, Raymond E., 1n2, 2n3, 4n10, 9n9, 17n7, 19n13, 23n26, 29n44, 40n36, 42n40, 44n3, 44n6, 45n11, 47n18, 51n28, 54n42, 55nn50-51, 58n56, 61n66, 66n13
Bubar, Wallace W., 21n21, 23n26, 95n7
Bultmann, Rudolf, 19n12
Burgess, Joseph A., 20n17
Burnett, Fred W., 4n11, 6n2, 8n4, 8n7, 9n7, 22n23, 23n26, 35, 35nn19-20, 36n21, 44n4, 54n41
Byrskog, Samuel, 3n6, 9n9, 18n11, 23n26, 24n28, 25n30, 87n27

Calvin, John, 10n10, 36, 36n24
Caragounis, Chrys C., 18n11, 19n13, 20nn15-16, 21n21
Carson, D. A., 12n16, 25n32, 28n41, 32n5, 34n15
Carter, Warren, 11n12, 49n23, 53n39
Cassidy, Richard J., 1n2, 8n7, 10n10, 12n15, 20n16, 26, 26n34, 30, 30n46, 31n1, 34n15, 37n27, 42n43
Claudel, Gérard, 18n8, 27n37, 28n44, 29n45, 65n7
Conard, Audrey, 58n56, 59n58
Cousland, J. R. C., 72n6

Index of Modern Authors

Croy, N. Clayton, 64n4
Cullmann, Oscar, 1, 1n1, 15n2, 16n3, 19n12, 64n4

Davies, W. D., 6n2, 8n7, 9n9, 11n14, 14n24, 15n2, 17n6, 18n9, 20n17, 21n21, 25n31, 32nn2-3, 40, 40n36, 44n4, 59nn58-59, 60n62, 65n12
Deines, Roland, 91n2, 92n3
Demacopoulos, George E., 3n5, 18n9, 22n24, 108n3
Doering, Lutz, 69n18
Dschulnigg, Peter, 1n2, 2n4, 8n4, 19n13, 22n25, 27n37, 53n33, 56, 56n52

Ehrman, Bart D., 16n3
Elliott, Mark Adam, 15n2
Evans, Craig A., 18n9, 23n27, 46n13, 47n19, 54n49, 57n55, 63n2, 72n5, 73n8, 79n17

Finley, Thomas, 20n15
Fitzmyer, Joseph A., 20n15
Fornberg, Tord, 15n2
France, R. T., 9n9, 11n11, 12n14, 13n19, 17n6, 21n21, 25n32, 32n4, 33n8, 35n17, 36, 36n23, 38n30, 45n8, 45n13, 48n21, 49n23, 53nn33-34, 54n49, 55n51, 57, 57n55, 58n56, 62n71, 66n15
Frankemölle, Hubert, 8n7, 16n5, 28n44, 30, 30n48

Gaechter, Paul, 8n7, 15n2, 33n9
Garland, David E., 33, 33n10, 44n4, 60n63, 62n73
Gerhardsson, Birger, 46n14, 48n22
Gibbs, Jeffrey A., 10n10, 12n17, 25nn31-32, 27n37, 28n40, 32n5, 34n13
Gibson, Jack J., 49n23
Gnilka, Joachim, 19n12, 32n4, 38n30, 40n34, 43n2, 46n15, 52n32
Goodacre, Mark, 23n26, 29n44, 30nn46-47, 65, 65n8, 95n7
Goulder, Michael, 2n3, 27n37, 28n43
Grappe, Christian, 1n2, 54n42

Grundmann, Walter, 9n9, 13n18, 19n12, 39n32
Gundry, Robert H., 3n8, 4n10, 11n13, 12nn15-16, 14n20, 14nn22-23, 15n2, 16n3, 17n8, 22n22, 27n38, 28n40, 44n4, 50n28, 55n50, 56n54, 61n65, 64n4, 70n2, 71n3, 72n6, 73n7, 76n12, 79n16, 80nn19-20, 84n24, 85n25, 92nn3-4, 94n6, 97n9, 100n1, 102n3

Hagner, Donald A., 32nn2-3, 32n5, 33n8, 42n42, 45n9, 47n20, 48n21, 91n2, 92n3, 102n3, 107nn1-2
Hare, Douglas R. A., 97n9
Heil, John Paul, 12n17, 53n35, 62n71
Helyer, Larry R., 17n6, 63n2
Hengel, Martin, 1n2
Herron, Robert W., Jr., 53n36, 56n54, 64, 64n3
Hoffmann, P., 8n7, 28n44, 46n13, 48n22
Hummel, Reinhart, 3n5

Kähler, Christoph, 2n3, 15n2, 64n7
Keener, Craig S., 58n57, 61n68, 62n70
Kessler, William Thomas, 63n2
Kingsbury, Jack Dean, 9n7, 32n4, 38n28, 45n11, 53n38
Kraus, Wolfgang, 8n7, 24n30, 75n11
Kvalbein, Hans, 3n6, 8n7, 16n3, 17n6

Lagrange, M.-J., 9n8, 11n14, 28n40, 33n9, 37n27, 45n13, 48n22, 63, 63n1
Lampe, G. W. H., 45n13, 50n27, 55n50, 105n8
Lampe, Peter, 19n13, 20nn15-16, 65n12
Lapham, F., 1n2
Laurentin, René, 1n2, 28n40, 35, 35n17, 54n45
Lohmeyer, Ernst, 45n13, 47nn16-17, 49n25
Luomanen, Petri, 79n16
Luz, Ulrich, 2n5, 8n7, 11n14, 19n13, 21n20, 22nn24-25, 24n28, 25n31, 32n3, 33n8, 40n34, 44n5, 46n15, 48n22, 49n23, 55n50, 56n54, 61n70, 65, 65n10

Index of Modern Authors

Maier, Gerhard, 15n1
Mann, C. S., 9n9, 29n44
Marguerat, Daniel, 75n10, 76n12
Markley, John R., 3n5, 29n44, 35n20
McIver, R. K., 74n10
McNeile, Alan Hugh, 9n8, 18n10, 29n44, 64, 64n6
Meier, John P., 8n7, 9n9, 11n14, 19n12, 30n46, 34, 34n12, 34n14, 48n22, 52n30, 54nn43-44, 62n72, 64n5, 64n7
Merkel, Helmut, 55n50
Merkle, Benjamin L., 15n2
Migbisiegbe, Guillaume, 82n2

Nau, Arlo J., 1n2, 33n8, 37n27, 46n15, 69, 69n18
Neirynck, Frans, 27n37
Nicholls, Rachel, 10n10
Nolland, John, 24n28, 36n25, 39n32, 40, 40n33, 48n22, 49nn24-25, 51n28, 66, 66n14, 94n5, 97n9

O'Collins, Gerald, 63n2
Oropeza, B. J., 46n15, 62n72
Osborne, Grant R., 49n23, 53n38, 54n48, 61n69, 62n72, 66, 66n15
Overman, J. Andrew, 12n17, 25n33, 26

Patte, Daniel, 14n24, 32n5, 37n27, 43n2, 53n37
Perkins, Pheme, 1n2, 4n9, 8n7, 14n24, 29n44, 35n18, 43, 43n1, 46n13, 48n22
Pesch, Rudolf, 2n2, 8n7, 12n15, 12n17, 14n24, 32n3, 33n6, 33n8, 35n17, 40, 40n33, 42n41, 43n1, 54nn47-48, 65, 65n11
Plummer, Alfred, 9n9, 20n16, 28n44, 40n35, 54n43

Räisänen, Heikki, 76, 76n13, 82n21
Reed, David A., 59n58
Ridderbos, H. N., 30n47, 33n6, 43n2
Rigaux, Béda, 15n1, 21n2
Robinson, Bernard P., 15n2, 17n8

Sabourin, Leopold, 16n5, 21n18, 64n6

Schäfer, Ruth, 19n13, 102n5
Schenk, Wolfgang, 2n3, 14n24, 37n27
Schnackenburg, Rudolf, 33, 33n11, 63n2
Schnelle, Udo, 11n14, 63n2
Schweizer, Eduard, 13n18, 14n21, 39n31, 64n5
Shakespeare, William, 41n37
Sim, David C., 80n18
Simonetti, Manlio, 54n43
Smith, Barry D., 19n12
Stein, Robert H., 64n4
Stock, Augustine, 8n5, 23n26
Stock, Klemens, 45n13, 48n22
Strecker, George, 3n5
Streeter, Burnett Hillman, 52n30
Syreeni, Kari, 2n5, 4n11, 6n1, 7n3, 8n7, 9n9, 10n10, 11n11, 12n17, 14n24, 28n40, 29n44, 32nn2-3, 33n8, 34nn15-16, 37, 37n27, 38n30, 39n31, 46n13, 62n73

Thiede, Carsten Peter, 10n10
Turner, David L., 21n19, 42n41, 62n71

Van Cangh, J.-M., 19n12, 64n7, 65, 65n12
Van Esbroeck, M., 19n12
Vanhoozer, Kevin J., 106, 106n11
Van Iersel, B., 8n5, 23n26
Verheyden, Joseph, 2n2, 3n5, 22n24
Volkmar, Gustav, 2n4

Wallace, Daniel B., 28n42, 41n38
Watson, Francis, 105, 105n9
Wiarda, Timothy, 2n2, 10n10, 11n14, 66, 66n16
Wiefel, Wolfgang, 9n7, 12n17, 48n22
Wilkins, Michael J., 9nn8-9, 14n24, 15n2, 21n19, 23n26, 37n26, 38n28
Witherington, Ben, III, 21n19, 33n8, 43n1, 56, 56n53, 58n56
Wright, N. T., 100n1

Zahn, Theodor, 8n7, 11n14, 21n21, 29n44, 34n15, 45n13, 47n20, 52n31, 65n12

Index of Ancient Texts

OLD TESTAMENT

Genesis
4:24	39
17:1-8	18n9
32:22-32	18n9
37:34	54

Exodus
20:13	62
21:32	88

Numbers
14:1-45	57
35:30	47

Deuteronomy
5:17	62
5:26	16
17:6	47
19:15	47
21:1-9	61, 97
21:22-23	61
27:25	62

Joshua
1–12	103
3:10	16
10:40-43	103
11:16-23	103

Judges
1:1–2:5	103

1 Samuel
17:26	16
19:5	61

2 Samuel
17:23	61
24:1	103, 104
24:15	104
24:17	104

1 Kings
11	104

2 Kingdoms LXX
23:17 LXX	28n41

1 Chronicles
11:19	28n41
21:1	103
21:14	104

2 Chronicles
1–9	104

Job
38:17	95

Psalms
9:13	95
37:12 LXX	43n2
42:2	16
107:18	95

Isaiah
5:24-25	102
15:3b	54
22:4 LXX	54
22:22	25
25:6	79n16
33:7 LXX	54
38:10	95
51:1-2	18n9

Jeremiah
10:10	16

Daniel
12:4 LXX	81

Hosea
1:10	16

Index of Ancient Texts

Zechariah
11:12	61
13:7	39n31, 53

NEW TESTAMENT

Matthew
1–4	90
1:1	17n6, 61n67
1:6	61n67
1:16	17n6
1:17	17n6, 61n67
1:20	61n67
1:23	4, 22, 23, 42
2:4	17n6
2:12	90, 94
2:13	94
2:13-15	90
2:14	94
2:19-23	90
2:22	94
2:23	86
3:2	59
4:3	10, 17n6
4:5-6	10
4:6	10, 17n6
4:8	74n9
4:10	22, 28, 99
4:12	90, 90n1, 94
4:12-13	34
4:12-16	26
4:17	26, 27, 49n26, 59
4:17–16:20	26
4:18	6n2, 7, 8, 16, 86
4:18-20	6, 16, 98
4:19	29, 76
4:24	102
4:25–5:2	72n6
5–7	23, 91
5:1-2	70, 72
5:3	91
5:4	91
5:5	91
5:6	91, 92n3
5:7	91
5:8	91
5:9	92
5:10	91n2, 92, 96
5:10-12	91
5:13	51, 70, 83n21
5:13-16	74
5:14	74n9
5:15-16	83
5:16	45n12, 85
5:18	45n7
5:19	45n7
5:19-20	25
5:20	48, 50, 66, 71, 77, 81, 83, 85, 91n2, 92, 99
5:20-22	71
5:21	62
5:22	3, 5n12, 70, 71
5:23-24	101
5:27-30	71
5:29	30n47, 45n7, 71
5:29-30	71, 75, 77
5:30	30n47, 45n7, 71
5:33-37	48, 48n22, 50, 66, 99
5:36	45n7
5:41	45n7
5:43-44	81
5:43-48	92
5:46-47	78n14
6:1	91n2, 92
6:7	78n14
6:10	92
6:14-15	71
6:15	71, 78
6:24	5n12
6:25-34	92
6:27	45n7
6:30	11n14
6:33	92
7:1-2	3
7:13	92
7:13-14	80, 80n18, 81
7:14	92
7:15	81
7:15-23	72
7:17	79
7:18	79
7:19	71
7:21-22	10, 36n21, 72
7:21-23	41n39, 46n15, 81, 84
7:22	75, 81
7:23	49n23, 84
7:24	20, 20n17, 21, 21n17, 21n19, 21n21, 22n21, 23, 23n26, 24, 83, 98
7:24-25	22, 23n26, 25, 26
7:24-27	22, 22n25, 25, 83
7:25	23
7:26	21, 23n26, 24, 70, 83
7:26-27	72
7:28	24
7:28-29	72n6
8:2	10
8:4	27n37
8:5-13	8n4
8:6	10
8:7	8n4
8:8	10
8:11	80n18
8:11-12	78n16
8:12	51, 71, 80
8:14	6n2, 34
8:14-15	7, 7n3, 8, 98
8:18-22	72
8:19	45n7
8:23-27	92
8:26	11n14
8:29	17n6, 29
9:9	86
9:10-11	78n14
9:23-25	67
9:25	5n12
9:27	61n67
9:30	27n37

113

Index of Ancient Texts

9:31	27n37	12:15	94	14:9	49n23
10	23, 92, 94	12:23	61n67	14:13a	94
10:1	88	12:32	54, 55n50	14:22-27	10
10:2	6n2, 9, 16, 38n30, 86, 98	12:34	79	14:22-33	10, 28, 98
		12:35	79	14:26	11
10:2-4	8, 85	12:41	59	14:26-28	10
10:4	72, 73, 86	13	23	14:27	10, 11
10:5b-6	59	13:5-6	23n26	14:28	6n2, 10, 32
10:7-8	88	13:16	17	14:28-33	10
10:16	73, 92	13:16-17	88	14:29	6n2
10:17-18	93	13:20	74	14:30	10, 47n19
10:19-20	93	13:20-21	23n26, 50, 73, 76, 81, 95	14:30-31	10, 53
10:20	88			14:33	10, 13n18, 16, 16n4, 17, 17n6, 88
10:21-22	93	13:21	30n47, 75, 92		
10:22	12, 73, 80	13:21a	74		
10:23	93, 94	13:21b	74	14:34	94
10:24-25	93	13:24-30	3, 14, 66, 74, 79, 84	15:1-2	95
10:26	93			15:2	13
10:26-31	9	13:25	75, 76	15:3	13
10:27	93	13:26	75	15:5	5n12
10:28a	93	13:26-27	78	15:6	13
10:28b	93	13:28b-29	78n14	15:12	13, 14, 30n47, 75
10:29-31	93	13:30	79	15:12-20	13, 98
10:32-33	22n25, 46n15, 93	13:31-32	75	15:13-14	13, 14
		13:33	75	15:15	6n2, 13, 14
10:33	39, 45, 46, 53, 66, 73, 99	13:35	74n9	15:16	13
		13:36	75, 79, 83	15:21	94
10:34-36	93	13:36-43	14, 55, 66, 74, 79, 84	15:22	10, 61n67
10:37	93			15:25	10
10:38	93	13:37-43	55	15:27	10
10:38-39	93	13:38	74, 76	15:29-31	5n12
10:40	73, 88	13:41	74, 75, 81	16	95
10:40-42	93	13:41-42	30, 51	16:5-12	25
10:42	45n7	13:42	66, 71, 80	16:8	11n14
11–12	94	13:43	76	16:12	14
11:2	17n6	13:47-48	84	16:13-20	15, 26, 27, 27n35, 27n37, 98
11:6	30n47, 39, 75	13:47-50	55, 66, 71, 76, 79	16:13-23	6, 15, 24, 29n44
11:12	94			16:16	6n2, 13n18, 16, 17n6, 27, 29, 32
11:19	78n14	13:48	51		
11:20	59	13:49-50	51		
11:21	59	13:50	66, 76, 80	16:16-17	13
11:25-27	16n5	13:51	14	16:16-18	2n4
12:3	61n67	13:51-52	95	16:16-19	15n1, 64n7
12:9-14	8n4	13:53-58	8n4	16:17	7n2, 16, 17, 27, 34
12:11	45n7	13:57	30n47, 39, 75		
12:14	94	14:7	49n23	16:17-19	2n2, 6, 9, 10,

Index of Ancient Texts

	16n2, 19, 23n26,	18:7-9	30	21:33ff.	102
	26, 29n44, 65	18:8	30n47, 79	21:37-39	78, 96
16:18	6n2, 16, 17,	18:8-9	71, 74, 77	21:43	79
	19, 21, 21n17,	18:9	30n47	21:45-46	96
	21n19, 21n21,	18:10	45n7	22:1-14	78
	22, 22n23, 23,	18:15-17	36	22:7	102
	23n26, 24, 26,	18:15-18	25, 78	22:10	78, 83
	74, 75, 95	18:16	45n7, 47	22:11-14	55, 79
16:18-19	16	18:18	24, 89	22:12-13	88
16:19	25, 72	18:21-22	36, 99	22:13	9, 51, 66, 71
16:20	27, 27n37, 29	18:23	78	22:14	9, 80n18, 81,
16:21	26, 27, 49n26,	18:23-35	78		104
	96	18:34	78	22:15-17	96
16:21-23	26, 27, 27n35,	18:35	78	22:34	79
	27n37, 99	19:1	24, 27	22:36	9
16:21–28:20	26	19:16-22	37	22:38	9
16:22	36n21, 41	19:23-26	37	23–25	23
16:22-23	11n11	19:27	37	23	95
16:23	22, 27, 29n44,	19:27-30	37, 99	23:2-3	25
	30n47, 31, 32,	19:28	89	23:8	24, 35n20,
	75, 76	19:29-30	9		45n7, 86
16:24-26	95	19:29–20:16	98	23:8-12	24
16:26	74n9	19:30	38	23:9	45n7
16:28	74	20:1-15	38	23:10	45n7
17	95	20:1-16	9, 38n30	23:13	25, 84
17:1	31n1	20:13	88	23:15	45n7
17:1-8	31, 99	20:13-16	79	23:16-22	101
17:3	33	20:15	79	23:17	70n2
17:4	33n6	20:16	9, 38	23:33	82
17:5	34	20:17-19	96	23:34	95
17:11-13	95	20:21	74	23:35	61
17:13	14	20:30	10, 61n67	24–25	23, 24, 81, 96
17:15	10	20:31	10, 61n67	24:3	68
17:20	11n14	20:33	10	24:9	92
17:22-23	96	21:1-17	103	24:9-12	96
17:23	14	21:9	5n12, 61n67	24:9b	80
17:24-27	33, 99, 101	21:11	45	24:10	30n47, 75, 81,
17:27	33n47, 75	21:13	101		87
18	23, 24, 77	21:15	61n67	24:10-12	80, 80n18, 96
18:1	77	21:18-22	67, 68	24:13	11n12, 12, 81
18:1-3	77	21:19	45n7	24:14	74
18:3	77	21:21-22	89	24:15-16	101
18:4-6	77	21:28-31	60	24:20	101
18:6	11, 30n47	21:31	78	24:20-22	96
18:6-9	75	21:31-32	78n14	24:21	74n9, 92
18:7	74n9, 77	21:32	60	24:24	81

Index of Ancient Texts

24:29	92, 101	26:16	27n35		47n19, 50, 52,
24:32-33	82	26:20-25	86		52n30, 62, 76
24:40	45n7	26:24	59, 100	27:1-2	57, 58
24:41	45n7	26:24-25	4	27:1-10	43, 57
24:42-44	82	26:25	48n22, 86, 87	27:3-5	57
24:44	84	26:26-29	96	27:3-10	54, 57, 57n55,
24:45	81	26:29	42, 78n16, 89		103
24:45-51	81, 83, 84,	26:31	30n47, 39,	27:4	60
	96n8		43n2, 44n4, 53,	27:11	48n22
24:46	81		75	27:11-14	58
24:48	81	26:31-35	39, 99	27:14	45n7
24:48-51	56	26:33	30n47, 40, 75	27:16	86
24:49	96n8	26:33-35	42n41	27:17	86
24:51	51, 66, 70n2, 71,	26:34	22n25, 39, 40,	27:19	97
	80		47n19, 50	27:24	61
25:1	84	26:35	4, 41, 43, 44, 53	27:24-25	97
25:1-13	22, 56, 82	26:36	42, 86	27:29	87
25:2	70	26:36-46	41, 99	27:33	86
25:3	70	26:37	41	27:46	4
25:8	70	26:40	41	27:48	45n7
25:11	10, 83, 85	26:42	42	27:55-56	44
25:11-12	84	26:44	42	28:1-10	47n20
25:12	49n23, 84	26:47-50	87	28:7	55, 56, 63, 65,
25:13	82	26:48	87		67, 68, 69, 100
25:14	85	26:49	87	28:8	65
25:14-30	56, 84	26:50	79	28:10	55, 62n73
25:15	45n7	26:56	44n4	28:16	55, 60, 65, 66
25:16	85	26:57-58	43	28:16-17	100
25:18	45n7	26:57-75	43, 99	28:16-20	65, 65n12
25:24	45n7	26:57–27:10	43	28:17	12
25:26-27	85	26:58	44, 45, 73	28:19	74
25:27	85	26:59-68	45	28:19-20	59
25:29	84	26:60	47	28:20	22, 22n25, 23,
25:30	51, 66, 71, 80	26:63	16, 17n6		24, 42
25:31-46	72	26:63-64	48		
25:34	74n9	26:69	47, 48, 49n24,	**Mark**	
25:34-45	96		52	1:12-13	99
26–27	96	26:69-70	73	1:14a	91n1
26:1	24	26:69-74	35, 39	1:16	6, 7
26:1-2	96	26:69-75	9, 43, 57, 80, 85	1:16-18	6
26:3	86	26:70	45, 66	1:16-21	7
26:3-5	96	26:71	44, 46, 49, 52	1:17	29
26:13	74, 74n13	26:72	50, 55n50, 66	1:29	7
26:14-16	61, 85, 86, 87	26:73-74	49	1:29-31	7
26:15	58	26:74-75	54, 66	1:35-38	67
26:15-16	86	26:75	41, 44, 47,	3:8	102

Index of Ancient Texts

3:16	6n2, 26, 98	13:18	101	4:42-43	67
3:16-19	8, 85	13:34	84, 85n25	6:13d-16	8, 85
3:17-18	8	13:37	68	6:14	6n2, 8, 26
3:19	72, 73	14:10	86	6:16	72, 73
4:16-17	73	14:10-11	85, 86	6:17	102
4:21	83	14:11	58	6:20-49	23
5:35-43	67	14:17-21	86	6:27-28	81
5:40	67	14:21	59	6:43-46	72
5:41	5n12	14:25	78n16	6:45	79
6:45-52	10	14:27	30n47, 39	6:47	21
6:52	13n18	14:27-31	39	6:49	72
7:5	13	14:29	30n47, 39, 40	7:30	104
7:8	13	14:30	39, 40, 47n19, 50	8:13	73
7:11	5n12			8:16	83
7:13	13	14:31	40, 41	8:49-56	67
7:17	13	14:32-42	41	9:18-21	15
7:17-23	13	14:33	41	9:22	26, 27
7:18	13	14:37	41	9:28-36a	31
7:32-36	5n12	14:40	42	9:34	33
8:27-30	15	14:41	42	9:46-47	77
8:29	16	14:43	87	9:57-60	72
8:31-33	26	14:43-46	87	10:25	79
8:32	27	14:44	87	11:33	83
9:2-8	31	14:53-72	43	11:52	24
9:5	32	14:54	43	12:8-9	46n15
9:33-36	77	14:61	48	12:9	73
9:43	71	14:62	48	12:41-46	81
9:43-48	77	14:66	44	12:46	71
9:47	71	14:67	48, 49n24	13:3	46
9:49-50	70	14:68	45	13:5	46
10:15	77	14:69	47	13:23-24	80n18
10:28	37, 38n28	14:70b	49	13:23-30	9
10:28-31	37	14:71	49	13:25-27	72
10:30	38	14:72	50, 54	13:28	52, 52n30, 78n16, 80
10:31	38	15:1	57		
11:1-17	103	15:40-41	44	13:28-29	78n16
11:12-14	67	16:7	56, 63, 63n2, 64, 67, 103	13:28b-29	78n14
11:17	101			14:15-24	78
11:20-24	67	16:8	65	14:34-35	70
11:26	71			17:3	78
12:28	9, 79	**Luke**		17:3b-4	36
12:41-44	23	1:1-4	61	18:17	77
13	68	4:14a	91n1	18:28	38n28
13:3-4	68	4:38	7	18:28-30	37
13:3-5	68	4:38-39	7	19:11-27	84, 85n25
13:13	73	4:39	7	19:46	101

117

Index of Ancient Texts

21:1-4	23	**Acts**		**Philippians**	
21:7	68	1–12	103	3:2	100n1
22:3	86	1:15-20	57, 58, 59, 100, 103	**1 Timothy**	
22:3-6	85, 86	1:18	61	1:18-20	100n1
22:5	58	1:19	61	4:1-3	100n1
22:14	86	7:54	82	6:3-5	100n1
22:18	78n16	11:19-21	102	6:20-21	100n1
22:21-23	86	11:26 D	102		
22:22	59	15:7-11	103	**2 Timothy**	
22:28-30	37, 38	23:14	55n50	2:12	46
22:29-30	78n16	23:21	55n50	2:16-18	100n1
22:31-32	15n1, 52n30, 103			2:20-21	100n1
		Romans		3:1-9	100n1
22:31-34	39	9:16	104		
22:34	47n19	9:19	104	**Hebrews**	
22:39-46	41	9:22	104	3:7–4:11	57
22:47	87	9:33	29n46	6:4-6	56
22:47-48	87	16:17-18	100n1	6:4-8	70
22:54	43			7:21	59, 60
22:54-71	43	**1 Corinthians**		10:26-31	57, 70
22:57	45	1:12	103	12:15-17	70
22:62	52n30	3:22	103	12:17	56
23:1	57	9:5	103		
24:5-7	63n2	15:5	52, 62, 64, 64n5, 103	**James**	
24:12	52n30			5:12	48
24:34	52, 52n30, 62, 63n2, 64, 103	**2 Corinthians**		**1 Peter**	103
		7:8	59	2:8	29n46
John		7:8-10	59		
1:42	6n2, 26	11:3-4	100n1	**2 Peter**	103
6:16-21	10	11:12-15	100n1	1:14	100n2
13:21-30	86	11:21b-23	100n1	2:1	100n1
13:36-38	39			2:13	100n1
13:38	47n19	**Galatians**		3:9	104
18:1	41	1:6-9	100n1		
18:2	87	1:8-9	100n1	**Jude**	
18:2-5	87	1:15-17	17	4	100n1
18:13-27	43	1:18	103	12-13	100n1
18:28	57	2:4	100n1		
21	4, 104	2:7-9	103	**Revelation**	
21:1-14	15n1, 62	2:11-13	102	2:17	79n16
21:15-17	4n10	2:11-14	102	19:6-10	78n16
21:15-22	103	2:12b	102	22:17	104
21:18-19	100n2	5:7-8	100n1		

Index of Ancient Texts

OLD TESTAMENT PSEUDEPIGRAPHA

2 Apocalypse of Baruch
29:4-8   79n16

1 Enoch
62:14   79n16

Jubilees
1:25   16

Sibylline Oracles
3:763   16

Testament of Job
37:2   16

Testament of Solomon
1:13   16

DEAD SEA SCROLLS

1QSa   79n16
4QpPs 37   79n16

JOSEPHUS

Antiquities
17.320   78n15

RABBINIC LITERATURE

m. Sanhedrin
10:2   61n70

m. Yoma
8:9   36n22

b. Yoma
85b   36
87a   36

APOSTOLIC FATHERS

1 Clement
5.2-4   100n2

2 Clement
3.2   46n15

Ignatius
To the Smyrnaeans
1.1   102

CLASSICAL AND ANCIENT CHRISTIAN WRITINGS

Acts of Peter and the Twelve Apostles
9.17   55

10.30   37

Aristotle
Poetics
25.1460b.32-34   105n10

Eusebius
Historia ecclesiastica
3.4.6   102
3.5.3   101

Gregory the Great
Epistle
4.33   18n9, 108n3

Jerome
Commentary on Matthew
2.14.26   54n43

Plutarch
Moralia
870C   49n23

Tatian
Diatessaron   107

The Venerable Bede   53n36

Xenophon
Memorabilia
2.6.33   88

ADDENDUM

Responses to Reviews

First and foremost, my thanks to all reviewers of *Peter – False Disciple and Apostate according to Saint Matthew*. Their reviews have included both compliments and criticisms. The compliments have given me encouragement. The criticisms have prompted further thinking on my part. Naturally, this addendum will concentrate on those criticisms. So as not to leave a false impression of personal animus toward reviewers who have issued criticisms, the following responses will contain no bibliographical information. To my responses:

I have argued that Matthew's unique description of Peter as "first" among the Twelve in 10:2-4 may exclude him from the "last ones," who by becoming "first ones" at the end will "inherit eternal life," and may thereby include him among the "first ones," who by becoming "last ones" at the end will not inherit eternal life (so 19:29-30). But are we then safe, asks a reviewer, to conclude that since Judas Iscariot is listed last in 10:2-4 he will become first in the eschatological reversal and thus inherit eternal life? No, because Judas is not *designated* "last" as Peter *is* designated "first," whereas both "first ones" and "last ones" appear prominently and repeatedly in 19:29 – 20:16.

But does not "last ones" signify lastness *in the kingdom* rather than lostness outside it, since the parable about first and last laborers in a vineyard (20:1-16) has to do with "the kingdom of heaven"? No, because the kingdom currently includes false disciples, who in the end will be excluded according to the parables of the tares and the wheat, the good and the foul fish, and the man without a wedding garment (13:24-30,

36-43, 47-50; 22:1-14). All these parables deal with "the kingdom of heaven."

In 19:30 the "first ones," who will be "last ones," are described as "many." The text does not say that "all" the first ones will be last ones. So may Peter as "first" in 10:2 fall outside the merely "many" and thus retain salvation? No, because the text does not distinguish "many" from "all," which appears nowhere in 19:29 – 20:16. Instead, "many" simply describes the first ones, destined to be last ones, as large in number, as usually elsewhere (3:7; 4:25; 7:13, 22 et al.).

To denote false discipleship and apostasy, why does not Matthew describe Peter as the one "who also denied him [Jesus]" the way he does describe Judas Iscariot as the one "who also betrayed him [Jesus]"? But this description of Judas comes from common tradition (see the parallels in Mark 3:19; Luke 6:16). Matthew merely takes over the tradition. But "who also denied him [Jesus]" does not appear in the tradition concerning Peter. So Matt 10:2 lacks such a description, and Matthew adds "first" in anticipation of Jesus' declaration that the first ones will be last ones.

In regard to Peter's questioning whether it is Jesus whom he and the other disciples see walking on the waters (14:22-33), one reviewer has asserted that Peter's initial doubt did not relate "to Jesus' self-identification" (as I said it did) – rather, "to whether it is Jesus and not some apparition." But Jesus said, "It's me. Don't be afraid." So it is hard not to see that Peter's "Lord, if it's you" relates exactly to Jesus' self-identification. Besides, "whether it is Jesus" seems synonymous with the question of "Jesus' self-identification."

Because I have noted that in Matthew false as well as true disciples address Jesus as "Lord," more than one reviewer thinks I take Peter's addressing Jesus with "Lord" in 14:28, 30 "as a mark of false faith." But I do not take it that way. I simply note that in itself the address "Lord" indicates neither genuineness nor falsity of discipleship, so that the address in 14:28, 30 says nothing either way about the quality of Peter's discipleship.

At the close of this episode "the ones in the boat" worship Jesus and say to him, "Truly you are God's Son" (14:33). A reviewer has argued that they do so not because Jesus has walked on the waters and enabled Peter to do the same, but because Jesus has stilled the storm. So there is no need to exclude Peter (as I have done) from those who worshiped and confessed Jesus in the boat. From that standpoint, to be sure. But the standpoint itself is *un*sure, because the text says only that the wind abated, not that Jesus said or did something to still the storm (as he did in a different incident recorded in 8:23-27). And on what grounds are we to say that Jesus' walking on the waters and enabling Peter to do the same did not join the wind's abatement to prompt a worshipful confession of Jesus?

A number of reviewers have argued that by the time of the worshipful confession, Peter had gotten back into the boat and that therefore "the ones in the boat" who worshiped and confessed Jesus must have included Peter. Hence it was wrong of me to say that in his confession at 16:16 Peter merely played catch-up with the other disciples, and did so only as a result of divine revelation, whereas the other disciples, including Judas Iscariot, needed prompting only by their experience on the stormy sea. But if Matthew had meant to include Peter among "the ones in the boat" we would expect him to have written, as usual, "the disciples," because "the ones in the boat" seems to make a distinction between them and the two, Jesus and Peter, who had been out on the waters. After all, Jesus too is in the boat by the time of the confession; yet he is obviously not included among those in the boat who worship and confess him.

Later, Judas Iscariot apostatized. Yet 14:33 includes him among the worshipful confessors of Jesus' divine sonship. This inclusion, I have argued, subverts the argument that Peter's upcoming, similar confession (16:16) forestalls a Matthean portrayal of Peter as ending up an apostate like Judas. To sidestep this argument, one reviewer has even supposed that Judas may not have been in the boat with the worshipers who confessed Jesus' divine sonship. Supposition without support! For an equation of the twelve apostles and the twelve disciples, see 10:1-2.

If the confessors in 14:33 did not include Peter, argues a reviewer, why does 16:16 feature him as a confessor? One is tempted to answer that 16:16 features him thus *because* 14:33 did not include him among the confessors there. A better answer: In 16:16 Matthew is following the tradition contained also in Mark 8:29 and Luke 9:20.

Reactions to my treatment of 16:13-20 ("the pinnacle passage" according to one reviewer) have mystified me because of astounding misrepresentations of that treatment. For example, one reviewer has said, disapprovingly, that according to me "the rock on which Jesus builds his church (Matt 16:18) is Jesus himself." Nothing of the sort appears in my treatment. Other reviewers have taken my treatment of Jesus' pronouncing a blessing on Peter (16:17) as a "rebuke." Wrong! I explicitly interpreted the revelation to Peter as a blessing in the sense of a "privilege" just as in 13:16, where Jesus pronounced a similarly revelatory blessing on all the disciples, including Judas Iscariot, who turned out to be false and who as a follower of Jesus was promised (without a stated condition) to "sit ['in the regeneration'] on [one of] twelve thrones, judging the twelve tribes of Israel" (19:28). So the reception of a blessing need not imply true and lasting discipleship or ensure final salvation.

I have yet to discover a refutation of my identifying "this [foundational] rock" in 16:18 with "the [foundational] rock" consisting of "these words of mine [i.e., Jesus']" in 7:24, as supported by "these words" of Jesus in 7:28; 19:1; 26:1 with reference to his major discourses (cf. "these parables" in 13:53; also 11:1). A hypothetical subtext in Aramaic might favor Peter as the foundational rock, but not necessarily; and such a subtext would lack canonicity. What we actually have is Matthew's Greek text, which needs no Aramaic subtext for a natural interpretation.

True, 16:19 gives Peter a leading role ("I [Jesus] will give you the keys [κλεῖδας] of the kingdom of heaven"). But it seems to have escaped some reviewers that the woe-begotten, hypocritical scribes and Pharisees use keys to "lock [κλεῖτε] the kingdom of heaven" against others and do not enter it themselves (23:13). In other words, didactic authority falls short of final salvation; and Matthew adds that right after giving Peter the keys, Jesus called him "my snare" (16:23). The fact that this epithet refers to the damned elsewhere in the First Gospel (four times, three of them unparalleled, in 13:41-42; 18:7-9) undermines the attempt to build final salvation for Peter on his reception of the keys. Besides, in 18:18 Jesus extends the associated authority to bind and loose (16:19) to all the Twelve, among them the quintessential false disciple and apostate, Judas Iscariot. So nowhere in such authority does there lie a guarantee of ultimate salvation.

According to Mark 9:5; Luke 9:33 Peter says on the Mount of Transfiguration, "Let us [Peter, James, and John] make three tents." Matthew changes the first person plural subjunctive into a first person singular indicative: "I [Peter] will make here three tents" (17:4). I have described the change as turning a foolish suggestion into a ridiculously egotistical declaration. One reviewer has countered by saying, "Matthew gives Peter credit for more energy by offering to make them [the tents] himself." But Matthew's adding that God the Father negated Peter's declaration "while he [Peter] was still speaking" casts the declaration in an even worse light than the suggestion suffers in Mark and Luke.

In regard to the miracle of "Peter's Penny" (17:24-27), a reviewer has described it as done "for Peter's express benefit. Nobody else gets that treatment." Contrary to my interpretation, therefore, Jesus' treatment of Peter was not "brusque." But Jesus is said to have corrected Peter's misconception on the payment of a tax even before Peter had a chance to report his conversation with the tax-gatherers. Furthermore, the episode ends without a report that Peter followed Jesus' instruction to catch a fish with the required payment in its mouth, or that Peter then payed the tax.

Perhaps most disappointing has been the failure of some reviewers (including those of often sterling scholarship) to address the heart and soul of my argument, i.e., the way Matthew reports Peter's denials of Jesus. (Other reviewers, even of a negative bent, have also noted this failure, which violates the maxim that refutations should address above all the strongest opposing arguments.) No need exists to detail my argument here (see pp. 43-62); but I have in mind, for instance, Matthew's inserting into Peter's first denial of Jesus the unparalleled phrase "before all" in correspondence with Jesus' statement in 10:33 that he will deny before his Father in heaven anyone who denies him (Jesus) "before people." Matthew also inserts the unparalleled phrase "with an oath" into Peter's second denial (26:72). The insertion marks him as someone who according to the likewise unparalleled 5:20, 33-37 lacks the superior righteousness required for entrance into the kingdom of heaven.

A reviewer who does pay attention to Peter's using an oath in 26:72 (and again in 26:74) tries to ameliorate the violation of Jesus' prohibition in 5:33-37 by citing "the rather nuanced approach to the issue of swearing in Matt. 23:16-22." But 23:16-22 does not in the least cancel, or even qualify, Jesus' earlier prohibition of oath-taking; and galvanizing a damaging inference in regard to Peter is Matthew's distinctive report that at the very time of Peter's oath-taking Jesus withstood the high priest's attempt to make him answer under oath (26:63-64; see above, p. 48).

Some argue that Peter's having followed Jesus into Caiaphas's courtyard, even though "from afar" (26:57-58), portrays Peter as a true disciple, especially since the other disciples did not join him. But the textual contrast is not with those disciples – rather, with Peter's earlier insistence that he would die *with* Jesus, if necessary (26:35). Against this insistence, Peter is sitting "with the servants [of the high priest]"; and Matthew adds "to see the end" and a likewise unparalleled "outside" to "in the courtyard" (26:69). The added "outside" not only distances Peter farther from Jesus; it also starts a series of regressions in which Peter goes "out of" the courtyard altogether into the gateway (26:71). Finally, having gone "out of" the gateway as well, he weeps bitterly "outside" (26:75). So much for a brave following of Jesus.

I connected this stress on Peter's weeping bitterly outside with Matthew's five unparalleled statements of Jesus that false disciples will be thrown "into the darkness farther outside" or "into the furnace of fire," where there will be "weeping and gnashing of teeth" (13:41-42, 49-50; 22:13; 24:51; 25:30). Reviewers have lodged several objections to the connection:

• "Bitterly" does not make a natural interpretation of teeth-gnashing, because the latter connotes anger and rage, as in Acts 7:54, rather than remorse and despair. But in Acts 7:54 teeth-gnashing is caused by "being sawn through," a figure of speech for mental pain (cf. the association of bitterness with such mental or physical pain in Acts 8:23; Rom 3:14; Col 3:19; Heb 12:15; Jas 3:11, 14; Rev 8:11; 10:9-10).

• Peter "went" out; he was not "thrown" out. But at his hearing before the Sanhedrin Jesus had no agent, such as an angel or a servant in earlier passages, to throw Peter out; and one of those passages – viz., 24:51 – exhibits variety of expression ("put his portion with the hypocrites") in reference to weeping and gnashing of teeth (cf. 7:23; 25:12 for further variety of expression in regard to the fate of false disciples).

• A noun for weeping occurs in the earlier passages, whereas a verb occurs for Peter's weeping in 26:75. Since the noun and verb are cognate to each other, however, this objection smacks of pilpulism; and a use of the noun for Peter's weeping would have been syntactically awkward.

• Peter only wept; he did not gnash his teeth. (One reviewer has even argued that Matthew's omission of teeth-gnashing was meant to distinguish Peter from the damned.) But Matthew's "bitterly" (shared with Luke 22:62, though quite possibly through Matthean influence on Luke) may well represent Matthew's interpretation of teeth-gnashing; and Heb 12:15-17 associates bitterness with "com[ing] short of God's grace" despite seeking it "with tears."

Peter – False Disciple and Apostate according to Saint Matthew

Have I overlooked the possibility of forgiveness, including a possibility of forgiveness "for all sins except blasphemy against the Holy Spirit (6:12; 12:31-32; 18:15, 22)," asks a reviewer. But 18:15, 22 has to do with disciples' forgiving each other and therefore has nothing to do with the possibility of God's or Jesus' forgiving an apostate. The forgiveness of all sins except blasphemy against the Holy Spirit (12:31-32; cf. 6:12) is predicated on repentance. So the reviewer's argumentive point requires a refutation of my exegetical arguments *against* taking Peter's bitter weeping "outside" as repentant, and *for* taking it instead as remorseful in parallel with Judas Iscariot's awkwardly juxtaposed remorseful suicide (Matt 26:75 – 27:10; see pp. 57-62 on the chronologically and topographically awkward juxtaposition, and cf. the impossibility of restoring saltiness to salt [a figure of speech for disciples] that has lost it and is therefore "thrown outside" [5:13]).

Judas returned his thirty pieces of silver. So does he come off "better and more repentant" than Peter (as inferred by a reviewer)? The comparison is illegitimate since Peter, unlike Judas, had nothing to return.

Because of Judas Iscariot's suicide in 27:3-10, "the eleven disciples" in 28:16, who have obeyed Jesus' command to meet him in Galilee, must include Peter even though 28:7 omits the phrase "and Peter" that appears in the parallel at Mark 16:7. Agreed, but does Peter's inclusion among the Eleven rule out falsity of discipleship and (as one reviewer has asked) give Matthew's "last word" in favor of Peter? If it did, however, one would not have expected the earlier omission of "and Peter"; for Matthew has repeatedly kept as well as added "Peter" in paralleled passages. As for the "last word," does not the unparalleled statement that some of the Eleven or (depending on a translational question) all of them "doubted" (28:17) create a certain amount of doubt on our part concerning the genuineness of Peter's (and others') discipleship?

Most importantly and as already highlighted, the parable of the tares and the wheat points out explicitly that false disciples – though apparent as such prior to the end – are to remain tolerated in the kingdom right up to the end (13:24-30, 36-43; cf. 7:24-27; 22:11-14; 24:10-12, all unique to Matthew). Moreover, though already announcing Judas Iscariot as Jesus' betrayer and therefore a false disciple, Matthew includes Judas among those commissioned, empowered, and blessed by Jesus in 10:1-42; 13:16-17. So commissioning, empowerment, and blessing do not guarantee final salvation any more in Peter's case than in Judas's.

Though the falsity of some disciples becomes apparent prior to the end, Jesus prohibits expelling them judgmentally at present and assigns the expulsion to angels at the end (cf. 13:24-30, 36-43 [unparalleled] with 7:1). Hence Matthew makes Peter's falsity apparent but stops short of pronouncing on his own an explicit judgment. Jesus, however, does have judgmental authority (see 7:21-23; 25:31-46, for example). As regards the false disciple Judas Iscariot, then, Matthew follows tradition by quoting Jesus' explicit judgment against Judas (see 26:24 with Mark 14:21; Luke 22:22).

But a reviewer asks, "Is Matthew, in making Peter's falsity apparent to his readers without himself declaring him lost, not simply thereby asking his readers to judge Peter themselves?" Answer: No, Matthew is making his non-judgmental self an example of obeying Jesus' teaching on the matter, an example to be followed by others.

In view of the juxtaposition in 26:69 – 27:10 of Peter's denials and remorse and Judas Iscariot's remorse and suicide, the objection that "there is no direct comparison, no narrative juxtaposition, of Judas and Peter anywhere in Matthew" can be dismissed without comment. Requiring comment, though, is the "question . . . whether the salvation – or loss thereof – *of characters in the narrative* is a matter of interest for Matthew," i.e., whether "the unflattering characterization of narrative characters necessarily impl[ies] a verdict about their eternal salvation or otherwise." Well, the mountain of Matthew's redactional negativity toward Peter – in contrast with Matthew's usual, generally acknowledged softening of Mark's negativity toward the Twelve as a whole – calls for the provisional answer, "Yes!" (provisional because Jesus retains the last word on Judgment Day).

Ah, but does not Matthew's redactional negativity toward Peter consist in "often very small differences in [the] wording of passages shared with Mark in particular," so that I have had "to make judgements and posit things that aren't actually explicit" and only "to urge an *interpretation*, an inference, in every instance" (emphasis original)? So asks a reviewer. Ironically, the numerous publications of this reviewer are filled with interpretive inferences. More to the point: All interpreters engage in interpretation (obviously!) and thereby draw judgmental inferences. Those who see a positive portrayal of Peter in Matthew do so, too. At issue, then, is whether the negative differences in Matthew's portrayal are "very small" (or few, it might be added).

Peter – False Disciple and Apostate according to Saint Matthew

But if at the close of Matthew 26 Peter looks apostate, does not the follow-up concerning Judas Iscariot, "the iconic failed disciple," seem "a bit redundant"? To the contrary, emphatic! Otherwise, the obvious sharpening of negativity in Matthew's account of Peter's denials of Jesus makes no sense.

Then there is an often-raised question of historical plausibility: At least by the AD 50s Peter was known to have been privileged with a private appearance of the risen Jesus, to have been counted as one of the three pillar apostles, to have engaged in an itinerant ministry (see, e.g., 1 Cor 9:5; 15:5; Gal 1:18; 2:7-9, 11-14, not to mention passages in the later Book of Acts), and – after the AD 60s – known to have died as a Christian martyr. So "under what plausible circumstances would the author of Matthew have hoped to make credible a picture of Peter as a damned apostate?" A fair question, but there are comparable questions:

• Early on, for example, James the brother of Jesus was likewise known to have been privileged with a private appearance of the risen Jesus, to have attained headship over the mother church in Jerusalem (see, e.g., 1 Cor 15:7; Gal 1:19; 2:12, not to mention passages in the later Book of Acts), and – after the AD 60s – known to have died as a Christian martyr. In a similar vein, Paul alludes to an itinerant ministry carried on by Jesus' other brothers (1 Cor 9:5). So how is it historically plausible that late in the first century the Gospel of John portrayed Jesus' brothers as worldlings and rank unbelievers in him (John 7:1-9), and this without a word about later conversions? Instead, Jesus commits his mother into the care of the beloved disciple rather than any one of his brothers (John 19:25b-27). Under what plausible circumstances, then, would the author of John's Gospel have hoped to make credible a picture of James and Jesus' other brothers as unbelieving worldlings who, like all unbelievers, "will not see life" because "the wrath of God abides on them" (John 3:36)?

• Under what plausible circumstances would the author of Matthew's Gospel have hoped to make credible a picture of some or all of the eleven apostles as doubting Jesus' resurrection? Yet nobody disputes that Matthew did so (see 28:16-17).

• And the big enchilada: Under what plausible circumstances would any of the evangelists have hoped to make credible their portrayals of a Jewish peasant crucified as a blasphemer and two-bit rebel in a backwater region of the Roman Empire as God's Son and the world's Savior (cf. 1 Cor 1:18, 21)? Yet we know they did.

At least for Matthew's portrayal of Peter we have abundant evidence of an emphasis in this Gospel on persecution and its attendant danger of apostasy. Textual evidence permitting, then – or, rather, favoring – it looks reasonable to conclude that in a circumstance of persecution Matthew turned the historically rehabilitated Peter into an unhistorical example of the danger of persecution-induced apostasy (cf. the uniquely Matthean reference in 24:10 to exactly that kind of apostasy).

Furthermore, to think that nothing new, such as this interpretation of Matthew's Peter, can be accepted requires the rejection of a good deal of the progress made in modern biblical scholarship – for example, in treating the canonical Gospels as individually distinctive rather than thoroughly harmonizable – and shuts the door to further progress.

As to the date of Mark's and Matthew's writing, I need only refer to detailed discussions in my *Mark: A Commentary on His Apology for the Cross* (Grand Rapids: Eerdmans, 1993), 1026-45, and *Matthew: A Commentary on His Handbook for a Mixed Church under Persecution* (2nd ed.; Grand Rapids: Eerdmans, 1994), 599-609. Incidentally, Matthean priority would lead to the conclusion that Mark and especially Luke recognized in Matthew a disagreeably negative portrayal of Peter, eliminated as much of it as possible, and added countervailing material. Whatever the solution to synoptic interrelationships, that countervailing material distorted perceptions of Matthew's portrayal in the subsequent history of interpretation.

So let us take Matthew's portrayal of Peter as a pastoral warning and other NT portrayals of him as pastoral encouragements, and use these different portrayals in accordance with pastorally perceived needs. Which is to say that sometimes different pastoral needs supersede historical and theological consistency. How to tell when? By analysis and comparison of textual data.

See also:

Robert H. Gundry, "'Matthew's Peter a False Disciple and Apostate?' Questions and Answers," *Expository Times* 127/9 (June, 2016): 441-44

Robert H. Gundry, "On the Petering Out of Peter's Faith," *Histos* 11 (2017): XXVIIIa-b

Scot McKnight, "Bob Gundry Responds to Larry Hurtado," *Patheos*, 25 January 2016, patheos.com/blogs/jesuscreed/2016/01/25/bob-gundry-responds-to-larry-hurtado/

"The EerdCast, Episode 4: Robert Gundry," *EERDWORD: the Eerdmans blog*, 9 December 2015, eerdword.com/2015/12/09/the-eerdcast-episode-4-robert-gundry/

www.ingramcontent.com/pod-product-compliance
Lightning Source LLC
Chambersburg PA
CBHW070915160426
43193CB00011B/1464